ALBA OF THE RAVENS

ALBA OF THE RAVENS

In Search of the Celtic Kingdom of the Scots

JOHN MARSDEN

Constable · London

First published in Great Britain 1997
by Constable and Company Limited
3 The Lanchesters, 162 Fulham Palace Road
London W6 9ER
Copyright © John Marsden 1997
The right of John Marsden to be identified as the author
of this work has been asserted by him
in accordance with the Copyright, Designs and Patents Act 1988
ISBN 0 09 477430 7
Set in Monophoto Sabon 10¼ pt by
Servis Filmsetting Ltd, Manchester
Printed in Great Britain by
St Edmundsbury Press Ltd
Bury St Edmunds, Suffolk

A CIP catalogue record for this book
is available from the British Library

This book is dedicated
to my wild, winged neighbours,
the ravens of Acha Mor

CONTENTS

LIST OF MAPS

ACKNOWLEDGEMENTS

Any book such as this one owes an inevitable debt to the scholarship of very many others, from the chroniclers and annalists who set down the historical record which forms its raw material to the historians of more recent times who have cast so much light on its interpretation, and it is a debt I have tried to acknowledge if not in the main text then in the accompanying notes and references.

There are others, however, who are not so acknowledged and it is to them I would offer a note of personal gratitude here: to Derek Bryce of Llanerch Publishers for his timely assistance with *The Battle of Magh Rath*; to John Gregory for permission to draw freely once more on his fine translations from Adamnan and Bede; and to Michael Robson for his unfailing generosity with innumerable enquiries pursued from library shelves in Edinburgh to a battlefield in far Caithness.

Final words of thanks, first to Carol O'Brien at Constable for her enthusiasm and encouragement; and, once again, to my wife Jenni not only for her efforts as copy-checker, proof-reader and indexer, but also as geographer and motorist. Without her, I'm quite sure that my search for the Celtic kingdom of the Scots would have been long since lost without trace in this 'land of the mountain and the flood'.

JM

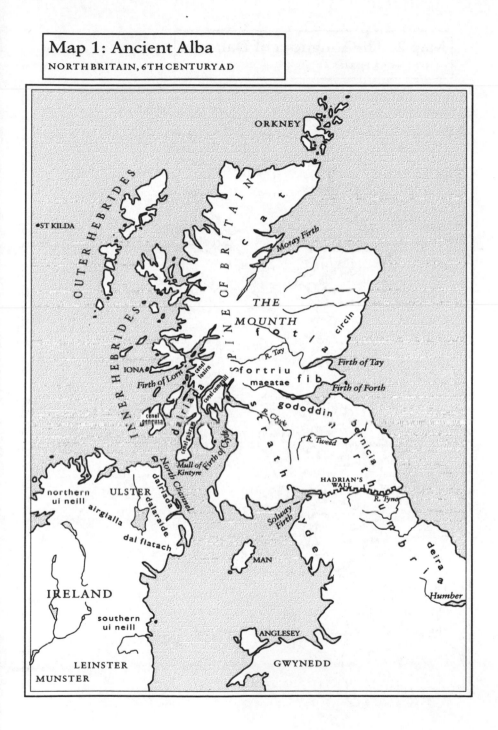

Map 1: Ancient Alba

NORTH BRITAIN, 6TH CENTURY AD

ORKNEY

ST KILDA

OUTER HEBRIDES

INNER HEBRIDES

SPINE OF BRITAIN

cat

Moray Firth

THE
MOUNTH

fotla

circin

R. Tay

fortriu

fib

Firth of Tay

IONA

Firth of Lorn

cenel loairn

maeatae

Firth of Forth

dalriada

cenel ongaill

gododdin

cenel oengusa

R. Clyde

strath

bernicia

R. Tweed

Mull of
Kintyre

Firth of Clyde

North Channel

clyde

HADRIAN'S
WALL

northumbria

northern
ui neill

ULSTER

dalriada

airgialla

dalaraide

R. Tyne

dal fiatach

Solway
Firth

MAN

deira

IRELAND

southern
ui neill

Humber

ANGLESEY

LEINSTER

GWYNEDD

MUNSTER

Map 2: The Kingdom of Dalriada
6TH–8TH CENTURIES AD

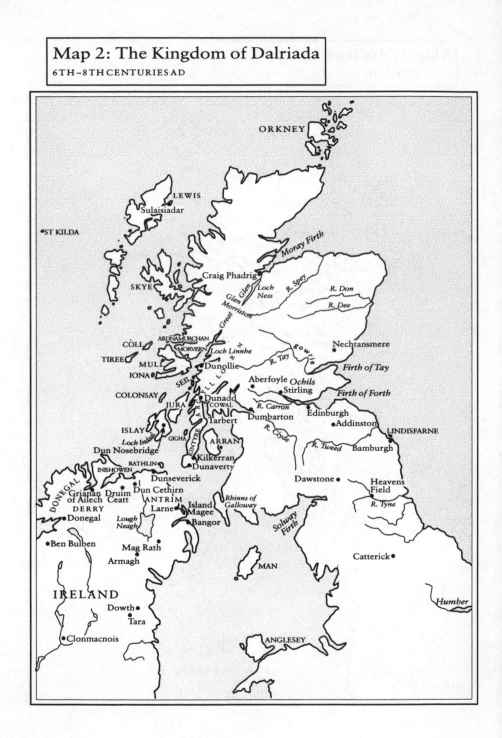

ORKNEY

LEWIS
Sulaisiadar

•ST KILDA

Moray Firth

Craig Phadrig

SKYE

Loch
Ness
Loch Morriston
Great Glen
Glen Morriston
R. Spey
R. Don
R. Dee

COLL
ARDNAMURCHAN
MORVERN
Loch Linnhe
Nechtansmere

TIREE
MULL
Dunollie
R. Tay
Gowrie
Firth of Tay

IONA
SEIL
Aberfoyle
Ochils
Stirling
Firth of Forth

COLONSAY
JURA
Dunadd
COWAL
R. Carron
Edinburgh

Tarbert
Dumbarton
Addinston

ISLAY
GIGHA
ARRAN
R. Clyde
LINDISFARNE

Loch Indaal
KINTYRE
R. Tweed
Bamburgh

Dun Nosebridge

RATHLIN
Kilkerran
Dunaverty

INISHOWEN
Dunseverick
Dawstone •
Heavens
Field

DONEGAL
Grianan
of Ailech
Druim
Ceatt
Dun Cethirn
ANTRIM
Rhinns of
Galloway
R. Tyne

DERRY
Larne
Island
Magee

•Donegal
Lough
Neagh
Bangor
Solway
Firth
Catterick •

•Ben Bulben
Mag Rath
MAN

Armagh

IRELAND
Humber

Dowth •
Tara

•Clonmacnois
ANGLESEY

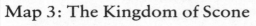

Map 3: The Kingdom of Scone
9TH–11TH CENTURIES AD

ORKNEY
Deerness
Scapa Flow

Cape Wrath

LEWIS

sutherland
Thurso
Skidamyre • • Wick
caithness

ST KILDA

INNEGALL

ross
R. Oykel
Dornoch Firth
Tarbat Ness
Moray Firth
Burghead
Forres • • Elgin
Strath
Bogie
Essie • R. Don
Lumphanan
R. Dee
THE
MEARNS
• Fettercairn

SKYE

Great Glen

angus

MULL
IONA
Oban
Monzievaird •
Dunblane •
Stirling •
Dunfermline •

atholl
R. Tay Birnam •
Scone •
Dunkeld
Dunsinnen
• Glamis
St Andrews
Abernethy
Forteviot
INCHCOLM
Loch
Leven

JURA

KINTYRE

ISLAY

ARRAN

strathclyde

lothian
LAMMERMUIRS
Carham
R. Tweed
Melrose
Wark

Dunbar

Berwick
LINDISFARNE
Bamburgh

Alnwick

galloway

Rhinns

Solway Firth

cumbria

Carlisle •
R. Tyne
Tynemouth
Jarrow
Chester-le-Street
Durham •
R. Wear
R. Tees
Stainmoor
Ripon •

Whitby •

Northallerton •

Bangor •
Moville •

MAN

Armagh •

IRELAND
Kells •
Tara
Clontarf •
Clonmacnois •
Dublin
R. Liffey
Glendalough

Carlingford Lough

ANGLESEY

York •
Humber

PREFACE

It was in the late summer of 1991 that I finally completed what was intended as a thoroughgoing, but non-academic, narrative history of the kings of Anglo-Saxon Northumbria, and wondered then whether I might attempt a similar account of the kings of Dalriada, the earliest kingdom of the Scots. The emergence of both kingdoms was, after all, closely contemporary, growing out of the 'age of migrations' which engulfed western Europe through the decline of the Roman imperium and made itself felt upon mainland Britain in the wake of the departing legions: the Northumbrian Angles emerging out of the settlement of Germanic tribes and warbands north of the Humber at much the same time as the Dalriadic Scots crossed from Antrim to establish themselves on the seaboard of Argyll.

These Scots and Angles, then, represented the two latest arriving of the four peoples who occupied the territory of what is now Scotland through the Dark Ages, and consequently their early histories – cultural and spiritual no less than military and political – were to become inevitably entangled. None the less, and for all the parallels and points of contact, I was soon to recognise that the two kingdoms presented two quite different subjects for a narrative history and that if my projected account of Dalriada was possible at all it was a possibility best attempted not yet awhile. There were, in any case, other projects directing my more immediate attention to Norse sea-raiders and Irish holy men. Yet the idea persisted and within a year or two had not only acquired for itself a book title but already overreached in scope the time-scale of the kingdom of Dalriada which was, of course, only the first incarnation of what I had come to think of as the 'Celtic kingdom of the Scots'.

While the Anglo-Saxon kingdom of Northumbria was effectively extinguished when the Danes seized York in 865, the Scots of Dalriada were to emerge from the submersion of their kingdom beneath the Norse onslaught to become the cultural and political kernel of the medieval Scottish nation. What had begun as an Irish colony on the coast of Argyll was to outlast the ascendancy of the Picts and the ambitions of the Angles, to somehow survive the viking onslaught which opened the way for Norse conquest of the western seaboard, and to re-emerge on Tayside as the kingdom of Scone dominating the passage of Scotland's history into the Middle Ages. The history of this Celtic kingdom of the Scots can be said then to extend across five and a half centuries bounded by the obituary of its founding dynast Fergus Mor, entered in the Irish annals at the year 501, and the death of Macbeth, Scotland's last Celtic high-king, at the hands of Malcolm Canmore in 1057.

A thoroughgoing narrative history of any kingdom and people through a period of more than five hundred and fifty years would represent a formidable undertaking, but such an account of the Celtic kingdom of the Scots would rely on so diverse and uneven a range of sources – from Irish annals to Scandinavian sagas, by way of English chronicles, medieval Scottish king-lists, and Gaelic tradition – as to be virtually impossible in any consistent quality of detail and, for that reason alone, what follows here cannot be offered as 'the history' of its subject. It is structured, instead, as a chronological sequence of portraits of kings, setting down as fully detailed an account of each one as the sources enable and placing it into its historical context to achieve at least a semblance of continuing narrative. The six kings have been selected for inclusion here by reason of their strategic significance for the evolution of the kingdom, but it must be admitted that each one also represents an historical figure of especial personal interest to the author who knew he would necessarily be spending a great deal of time in their company. Each one of them, none the less, remains in some measure an historical enigma – ironically, the more significant the king, the greater the enigma – and it was that thought which suggested *In Search of the Celtic Kingdom of the Scots* as a sub-title.

Which must not, however, be allowed to imply that what follows here is any kind of 'travelogue', even though I have opened each chapter by calling to mind just one location with which history or tradition has forged for me a particularly close association with its subject. This 'search' is one which has been conducted first and foremost among the 'early sources', the surviving documentary record of the distant past which provides the essential raw material of all genuinely historical writing.

The title itself is taken from a quatrain said to have been composed by the Irish holy man Columcille on voyage from Ireland to his greater destiny as 'Saint Columba of Iona' and, while that traditional ascription must be considered no better than dubious, the phrase *Alba of the Ravens* does have the resonance of at least medieval antiquity. The Irish proper noun *Alba* derives from *Albion*, which is the oldest recorded name for mainland Britain, and the earliest Irish usage of *Alba* similarly indicates the full extent of the British mainland. It was only later, and subsequent to the establishment of the kingdom of the Scots, that *Alba* came to be applied specifically to the northernmost region of Britain now known as Scotland.

It is more than probable, then, that *Alba* would have been the name by which the first Scots who crossed over from Antrim at least fifteen hundred years ago called the land in which they found themselves – and is still today the name by which Scotland is called in modern Scots Gaelic.

On 22 August in the year 1138, David I of Scotland came in arms against the English at the Battle of the Standard a few miles outside Northallerton in Yorkshire. The last of the sons of Malcolm Canmore and Anglo-Norman in his every aspect, David's battle-host on that day was made up of an extraordinary coalition of peoples. Warrior aristocrats only recently imported from France and the Low Countries, Northumbrians of Anglian descent, Islesmen descended from the Norse as often as from the Gael, Highland and Lowlandmen of Scotland's most ancient Pictish and Britonic stock, all of them charged their enemy roaring the Gaelic war-cry '*Albanaich!*', which is translated into English as 'Men of Alba!'

It might be said with some justice that the Celtic kingdom of the Scots had been consigned to antiquity for a full generation before the year 1138, but it might also be said, and with no less justice, that the battle-shout *Albanaich!* was the last full-throated echo of an extraordinary epic history . . . upon which these following pages will seek now to throw such light as they are able.

I

'From thee shall come the kings . . .'

FERGUS MOR

SEEN FROM THE WEST across the Crinan Moss in mid-Argyll, the hillfort of Dunadd has the appearance of being set into the land like the heavy domed boss set into a shield of the Celtic Iron Age.

Located to the south-west of the Kilmartin valley, where a rich concentration of stone circles, cairns and slabs carved with cupmarks, rings and spirals marks out a prehistoric landscape of ritual significance, and to the east of the river Add – hence its name from the Gaelic *Dún Att*, 'the fort on the Add' – Dunadd represented a natural place of defence in a time when war was waged with the iron sword. An isolated rocky plug more than 67 metres in diameter and rising to a height of some 48 metres above the flood plain anciently known as *Mòine Mhór*, 'the great moss', it would have been virtually impregnable to surprise attack and presented an uncompromising prospect for any but the most determined siege.

Its ramparts of natural formation were anciently raised up with stone-built walling, very much of it long since collapsed and crumbled away but still recognisable to archaeologists as having been constructed in two different periods of occupation in the later Iron Age. The natural citadel formed by its highest point may have been already occupied as a fortress more than three thousand years ago and by the same Bronze Age people whose craftsmen carved into stone the 'cup and ring' marks still to be seen at nearby Cairnbaan and Kilmichael Glassary. There is certainly good archaeological evidence for its having been fortified when the mainland to the south was a province of the Roman empire in the first centuries AD, but the substantially greater proportion of antiquities uncovered by three excavations since 1900 has been assigned to the period between the sixth and ninth centuries when Dunadd is known from the historical record to have been a stronghold of the Scots of Dalriada.

The first excavation, which was carried out in 1904 with techniques so unsophisticated as to have resulted in destruction as often as discovery, did at least reveal an unusually great number of quernstones, round-cut rocks fashioned for the grinding of cereal crops. Some fifty such stones were found at Dunadd, of which two have been re-examined in the light of more recent scholarship and shown to be cut with exceptional craftsmanship from carefully selected rock transported some distance for the purpose. The fact that one of them is decorated with a finely carved cross of similar form to those found in the gospel books of the ancient Irish church has been taken as confirmation of the quernstone having been associated at Dunadd with a ritual, even religious, significance far beyond the mere milling of grain.

Another excavation, carried out some twenty-five years later in 1930, brought to light very many examples of metalwork – axes and tools, fragments of swordblades and of spearheads, silver rings and a fine piece of decorated bronze – with moulds for making elaborately ornamented jewellery and fragments of amber, mica and jet. All of which has made it possible for archaeology to confirm the historical evidence for Dunadd as a place of great importance in the Dalriadic kingdom: the weaponry indicating a warrior aristocracy and the jewellery confirming their wealth and prestige, while the many quernstones point to its having been a centre for agrarian tribute, where subject farmers paid a proportion of their harvest to their overlord as taxation in kind. Dunadd was not, of course, the only notable fortress of Dalriada. The hillforts at Dunaverty on the Mull of Kintyre, at Tarbert in Knapdale and at Dunollie close by Oban, are mentioned no less often in the earliest sources, but it is the fortress on the Add alone which can display its own impressive claim to having been the first royal capital of the kingdom of the Scots.

Even today, when an illustrated signboard points the way for the modern visitor, the ascent of Dunadd by way of the rocky path spiralling up the hillside cannot be said to offer any gentle walk back into the past and to imagine making the same ascent under a torrent of iron and stone unleashed by defending warriors leaves no shadow of doubt as to its formidable military qualities. The path leads upwards and around to a natural cleft through the rock some three metres wide which would have been barred by stout wooden gates to serve as the port of entry into the defended enclosure, where buildings of timber and wattle – all trace of which, as of the gates, having long since disappeared – would have housed fighting men, craftworkers, probably clerics and, assuredly, warrior kings.

Above the expanse of this hillfort interior and immediately below the highest point of its natural citadel lies the flat rock surface which represents the one ancient artefact left in place at Dunadd when so much else was carried off to the display cases of museum collections. It is almost as if the very stones of the hill itself are still clinging with a jealous tenacity to one last relic of its former eminence, because into this rock is carved the most impressive testimony to the ancient significance of Dunadd in Dalriada.

There are, in fact, a number of carvings about the rock.[1] One is an unintelligible inscription in *ogham* – the earliest Irish writing formed by strokes cut along and across a perpendicular – and above it a fine portrait in outline of a boar. Both of these carvings have been attributed to the Picts and sometimes associated with their conquest of Dunadd entered in the annals at 736, even though that association is founded on no better authority than convenient coincidence. Similar, but not identical, images of a boar do appear on Pictish symbol stones and expert opinion is convinced of a Pictish origin for the sculptor of the Dunadd beast, but there might also be some relevance in the fact that it was the bones of the pig, instead of the usual sheep, which made up the overwhelming majority of animal remains excavated at Dunadd in 1930. So too, the inscrutable inscription proposed as an undeciphered 'Pictish' ogham has been otherwise and no less plausibly suggested as an inept copy of an archaic Irish ogham inscription cut into stone by an illiterate mason. The interpretation of the two most prominent features carved in the rock, however, has been generally accepted by scholars for more than a century and fortunately so, because upon it hinges the great significance of Dunadd for the kingship of the Scots.

One of these takes the form of a circular basin, 28 centimetres in diameter and some 20 centimetres deep, hollowed into the rock and polished smooth. Just some three and a half metres beyond it is carved the unmistakable impression of a footprint, less than a centimetre in depth and comfortably able to accommodate a man's right foot wearing a thick sock. A man who set his foot into that carving would be looking in a direction just to the east of north and out along the mountain chain anciently known as *Druim Alban*, the 'Ridge of Britain', from a commanding perspective which calls again to mind the impression of Dunadd as the boss set into a shield hanging from the western shoulder of north Britain.

Ritual centred on some form of sacral stone is known to have characterised Celtic kingmaking from Tara to Scone, and so too is there later evidence from Ireland and Scotland for the proclamation of a new chieftain by the ceremonial placing of his foot into the footprint of his forebears. Thus the footprint cut into rock at so prestigious a site, taken together with the close proximity of a rock-basin and all that it would imply for ritual anointing, point inevitably to Dunadd as having been the place of inauguration for Dalriadic kings.

It must be said, though, that there are footprints cut into rock elsewhere in Scotland, even as far north as Clickhimin in Shetland where no Celtic king of Scots was ever known to have set his foot, and, if such carvings are survivals from more distant prehistoric antiquity, it may have been that the Dalriadic Scots occupying Dunadd adopted an already ancient monument into their own ceremonial of kingmaking. Archaeological evidence can confirm the Dalriadic occupation of Dunadd between the sixth and ninth centuries, but such dating cannot approach the precision of the historical record and no Irish annalist makes mention of Dunadd – at least under any form of that name – before the last quarter of the seventh century. Consequently, it is not possible to positively identify this place as the capital fortress of any one of the very earliest kings of Scots and still less to know which of them might have initiated whatever inaugural ceremony around its footprint in the rock, but if there is one place in all the vast landscape of north Britain from which to start out upon a search for the Celtic kingdom of Scots, that place can be nowhere else but Dunadd.

'THE IRISH IN BRITAIN'

What is meant today by the term 'Scots' is, of course, greatly changed from the most ancient meaning of the name. The modern definition of a Scot can be reasonably taken to be a person born if not necessarily in Scotland then to parents of Scottish descent, yet the very great majority of those who now quite justifiably consider themselves Scots must be ultimately descended from Pictish, Britonic, Anglo-Saxon, Norse, and Norman forebears and it is impossible to know just how few modern Scots are the direct descendants of the people who were known by that name sixteen centuries ago. The national name 'Scotland' is of relatively modern construction, certainly by comparison with the original form of 'Scots', which is a term of such great antiquity that at the time of its first recorded appearance no more than a marginal fraction – if, indeed, any at all – of the land now known as Scotland could have been considered 'the land of the Scots'.

In the light of which, it might be useful at this point to investigate what is known of the origin and earliest usage of 'Scots' as the name of an ancient

people. The modern form of the name quite certainly derives from the Latin
Scoti which first occurs in the writings of Ammianus Marcellinus, a Roman
historian of the late fourth century. In his closely contemporary account of
the 'Barbarian Conspiracy' – an apparently concerted and evidently devastating attack by predatory peoples on the northern frontiers of Roman
Britain in the year 367 AD – Ammianus identifies the two principal aggressors
as *Scoti* and *Picti*. If these 'Scots and Picts' can be reasonably taken to have
been the same two enemies of Rome who were known as *Hiberni* and *Picti* to
the orator Eumenius writing almost a century earlier in 297, then it would
follow that the name *Scoti* had at some point in the fourth century super-
seded the older *Hiberni* as the Latin term for raiders of Irish origin.

While *Hiberni* can be taken to have been the formal Latin name for the
Irish, it is probable that *Scoti*, like *Picti*, represented a nickname applied by
the Roman military to the hostile peoples they faced on their northern frontier along Hadrian's Wall. *Picti* can be translated directly from the Latin as
'painted people', inferring its having originated as a reference to an enemy
who wore warpaint into battle, unless the many place names incorporating
the elements Pit – or Pet – can be taken as evidence for some form of 'Pict'
having been the name by which the native tribes from beyond the Forth called
themselves. *Scoti*, by contrast, is a name with no obvious Latin meaning and
has been most plausibly suggested as the Latin form of an originally Irish
term for 'plunderer'.

This original identity of the Scots as a people from Ireland is fully confirmed by later Irish authors, writing in Latin and familiar with classical
Latin sources, who use *Scoti* in just that sense. Most prominent among them
was Adamnan mac Ronan, the learned abbot of Iona at the end of the
seventh century whose *Life of Columba* not only makes regular use of *Scoti*
as a name for all Irish people and of *Scotia* for Ireland itself, but also uses the
term *Scoti Britanniae*, the 'Irish in Britain', for the Irish settled in Argyll. So
too does Adamnan's junior contemporary, the Venerable Bede, whose
Ecclesiastical History of the English People written in Northumbria in the
730s includes the earliest account of the four peoples of north Britain in the
centuries after Roman occupation. While Bede draws on Anglo-Saxon tradition for the arrival of his own people, the Angles of Northumbria, he resorts
to Irish legend for his explanation of the presence of the indigenous Britons,
the Picts north of the Forth, and the Scots from Ireland. It might even be suggested that the general application of the name 'Scots' to the Irish in
north Britain effectively began with Bede, and his account, for all its obviously mythic elements, corresponds quite precisely to modern historical
understanding of the peoples occupying what is now Scotland in the

centuries subsequent to Roman Britain. Especially significant is the fact of Bede's recognising these four peoples by their four different languages, because language is the decisive element in defining a Celtic people and, thus, a factor of crucial bearing on the Celtic kingdom of the Scots.

These peoples known as Celts – another name first deriving from the classical sources where they are called *Keltoi* in the Greek and *Celtae* in the Latin – emerged from the great prehistoric invasion by Indo-European tribes out of Asia Minor who swept across Europe to reach the western extremities of its Atlantic seaboard by the first millennium BC. Whatever might have been the precise sequence and true nature of the Celtic settlement of western Europe still awaits the resolution of a long-running scholarly debate involving archaeologists and prehistorians, but it is thought now that an Indo-European advance guard of 'proto-Celtic' peoples were already establishing themselves as far west as Ireland by the second millennium BC. If the first Celts were settled in the British Isles during what is popularly known as the Bronze Age and later waves were still arriving as refugees from the advance of Rome across continental Europe in the last century before Christ, then the Celtic settlement of the west can be said to have extended over some two thousand years. In the course of so many centuries Celtic settlers would have inevitably mingled a bloodstock already diffused by passage through the gene pools of Eurasia with those of the descendants of earlier prehistoric peoples of western Europe, thus rendering any concept of a 'Celtic race' utterly meaningless. The term 'Celtic' can, in fact, only be applied as a strictly cultural identity, and to those ancient peoples whose language represented one of two forms of descent from a prehistoric Celtic mother tongue, the *Goidelic* forebear of Scots and Irish Gaelic and the *Brythonic* from which Welsh is descended.[2]

The peoples of the British Isles can be said to have made their first real entry into the realm of recorded history at their earliest points of contact with Rome, and the Romans, while identifying their different tribes by a bewildering assortment of Latinised names, had no hesitation in recognising them all as Celts. Having marched its legions beyond the Tay in a fruitless attempt to extend its conquest north to the Grampians, despatched its warfleet as far as Orkney on a seaborne survey of the northern coastline, and looked across to Ireland in contemplation of an invasion never in the event attempted, the Roman Empire finally settled to the task of civilising, administrating and defending a *provincia Britannica* contained within the mainland territory bounded by the Channel coast and Hadrian's Wall. So it came about that, while the Celtic Britons within those bounds were citizens of a Latin-speaking empire for almost four hundred years, the peoples of north

Britain – certainly those north of the Forth and to some extent those north of the Tyne – remained, to a greater or lesser degree of independence, outwith the Roman imperium.

Beyond the Forth–Clyde line lay the formidable land-mass of the Highlands fringed on two coastlines with the archipelagos of the northern and western isles, all of which comprised the vast domain of perhaps the most ancient and certainly the most enigmatic of the peoples of north Britain, those tribes still remembered by their fourth-century Roman soldiers' nickname of 'Picts'. Virtually everything that history knows of them has been gleaned from a documentary record set down by neighbouring and most often hostile peoples, into which the Picts have a habit of making a sudden and usually dramatic appearance followed by a similarly peremptory disappearance. What very little is known of their language is principally derived from the form of names in a 'Pictish' king-list preserved only in medieval Scottish manuscript and from place names of supposedly Pictish origin significantly concentrated in those regions of Scotland which Bede identified as territory of the Picts. From this admittedly fragmentary evidence has been drawn the conclusion that the Pictish tongue was of a 'p-Celtic' character related to that of the Britonic Celts and yet perhaps also retaining non-Indo-European elements of a still more ancient prehistoric culture.

The Picts, then, might be cautiously recognised as a cultural and social fusion of a Celtic warrior aristocracy with tribal survivals from the pre-Celtic peoples of farthest north Britain, and they were, without any doubt at all, a most formidable warrior people, accomplished sea-raiders and tenacious guerilla fighters who presented the most enduring threat to Roman Britain through all four centuries of its history. Very much less intractable than the Picts were their Celtic neighbours to the south, the Britonic tribes whose territory extended from the Forth–Clyde line down to Hadrian's Wall. The *Votadini* around the Forth and the *Damnonii* on the Clyde were tribes generally well-disposed towards the Romans and encouraged by them as effectively client states who could provide an extensive 'buffer' zone immediately beyond their empire's northern frontier in Britain.

When seen through the wide-angle lens of the prehistorian, the greater impact of the Roman Empire might appear to have lain in imposing a halt on successive waves of migration and settlement which are recognised now as the landmarks in the progress of humankind through prehistoric antiquity. But that ancient momentum was a sleeping dragon awaiting the time when – in the words of Professor Stuart Piggott – 'the movements of peoples in the immemorial manner of prehistory were to begin again, for the Roman grip on northern Europe had become relaxed and ineffective.'[3] As the Roman ascendancy gave way to the decline of empire by the end of the fourth century, its frontiers could no longer hold and in the year 410 AD, when Alaric's Goths were at the gates of Rome, the Empire abdicated what remained of its military responsibility for *provincia Britannica*.

When the last of the legions were withdrawn to the continent, the Romano-British aristocracy south of the Wall found themselves suddenly burdened with their own defence and resorted – as, indeed, the Romans had done before them – to recruiting Germanic warbands as a garrison against the renewed onslaught of Pict and Scot. Largely recruited from Angles, whose continental homelands lay beyond the Elbe in the north of what is now Germany, these warrior–farmers were settled north of the Humber on land granted in return for military service when danger threatened. Instead, they were to rise in mutiny against their paymasters in the mid-fifth century and emerge a hundred and fifty years later as the massively powerful kingdom of Northumbria with its northern frontier on the Firth of Forth.

The northward advance of the Northumbrian kingdom brought these Angles into inevitable conflict with the north Britons who had, by the sixth century, cast off any trace of Romano-British veneer and reverted to their former Celtic tribal character. So it was that the Votadini of the Forth, who became the first casualties of Northumbrian expansion, were known to the contemporary author of an elegy commemorating their last great battle by their tribal name in its Britonic form of *Gododdin*. By reason of the Northumbrian advance being initially directed towards the Forth, the Damnonii Britons on the Clyde were destined to long outlast the doomed Gododdin. Their kingdom, centred on its capital fortress of *Al Cluta* on Dumbarton Rock, was to survive until the late ninth century and to play out its own strategic role – benevolent and otherwise – in the early history of Celtic Scotland.

FERGUS, SON OF ERC

The Northumbrian advance into north Britain lay more than a hundred years in the future when the royal house of Dalriada in Antrim crossed the North Channel to the land they called Alba and there established the first 'kingdom of the Scots'.

The Scots, as the 'Irish in Britain', were, of course, Celts, but Celts of a culture whose essential difference from those of the other Celtic peoples of

[26]

mainland Britain hinged upon its different form of Celtic language. While the Britonic 'p-Celtic' and Goidelic 'q-Celtic' variants were descended from the same prehistoric mother tongue, it is possible that the Irish Goidelic represented the more ancient form of linguistic descent, which in turn has been taken to indicate the Irish – and Scottish – Gaels as direct cultural descendants of the earliest wave of fully-fledged Celtic settlement in the west. What is still more demonstrably true of Celtic Ireland is the fact of its having escaped conquest by Rome and the consequent preservation intact of its ancient Celtic character, customs and cosmography. The original Scots out of Ireland, whose first region of settlement is still known as Argyll, from *Airer Goidel*, 'the seaboard of the Gael', thus brought with them to Britain the language of what was probably the most ancient and certainly the best preserved Celtic culture of the west, and the tongue from which Scots Gaelic is ultimately descended.

The sequence and chronology of the settlement of these 'Irish in Britain' is a question to which these pages will later return, but the point where that settlement makes its first appearance in the formal historical record is to be found at the entry corresponding[4] to the year AD 501 in the Irish annals compiled by an eleventh-century abbot of Clonmacnois.

> *Feargus Mor mac Earca cum gente Dalriada partem Britanniae tenuit, et ibi mortus est.*

'Fergus the Great, son of Erc, with the people of Dalriada held part of Britain; and there he died.' Within that one sentence from the *Annals of Tigernach* – effectively the first entry in the history of the kingdom of the Scots – is contained virtually all that is known from the most authoritative early sources of the founding dynast of the kingdom of Dalriada in Britain.

The Irish annals, which comprise the principal historical record of early Scotland, are all of them documents of medieval and later compilation set down between the eleventh and seventeenth centuries. While the annals were variously compiled from sources of much greater antiquity, even in some cases closely contemporary with the events they record, the Irish annalists were still transcribing a record of events many centuries distant in time and of which they themselves may have had no other knowledge. The annalist, then, was effectively a scribe attempting to synchronise the contents of various documentary sources into a chronological record of people, places and events whose names and significances need not have held any meaning for him whatsoever. Consequently, the value and reliability of the ancient

Irish annals as an historical source depends at least as much on the scribal accuracy of the annalist as it does upon the quality of his sources and his skill in selecting from them.

One of the most ancient – if not, in fact, the most ancient – of the sources used by these annalists is believed now to have been a chronicle begun in the early eighth century in the monastery on Iona. While that document itself has been long since lost, much of its content has been shown to survive in the more reliable Irish annals where it represents the most authoritative source for the history of early Scotland, and this 'Iona chronicle' would have been the obvious source from which Tigernach ua-Broein – the abbot of Clonmacnois whose own obituary is entered at 1088 and to whose scholarship is attributed the annals which bear his name – derived his record of the life and death of Fergus Mor, son of Erc and king of Dalriada.

If such was indeed Tigernach's original source of information, it still could not be considered a contemporary record when the earliest date assigned to the Iona chronicle was some two hundred years after Tigernach's date for Fergus' obituary. Neither does the same or any similar entry appear in the *Annals of Ulster*, compiled in Fermanagh in the late fourteenth century and considered to be the most reliable and complete of the Irish annals, a fact which has cast some scholarly doubt on the historical authenticity of even the little that is known of Fergus Mor. None the less, the late Professor John Bannerman, who is recognised as the outstanding modern authority on the subject, was able to confirm that 'the history of Dalriada in Scotland may be said to begin with the advent of Fergus Mor mac Erc'.[5] Neither is there any shadow of doubt in the medieval sources, Scots or Irish, of the dynastic stature of Fergus the Great, son of Erc, and it is to those later sources, even though their evidence is rooted at least as often in tradition as in history, that the search for Fergus Mor must now turn.

The *Tripartite Life* of Saint Patrick, although perhaps based on an eighth-century original, was set down at Armagh no earlier than the end of the ninth century. It was thus written at least sixty years after the transfer of the royal centre of the Scots out of Argyll to the former Pictish kingdom of *Fortriu* on Tayside, a fact of chronology clearly reflected in an anecdote from the *Tripartite Life* which tells of the saint's travels in Antrim and his visit to the court of Erc, king of Dalriada, while Fergus was still a young man.

And Patrick was welcomed in the land by Erc's twelve sons. Fergus Mor, son of Erc, said to Patrick: 'If thy venerability would sway my brother in the division of his land, I would give it to thee.' Patrick said to Fergus:

'Though not great is thy land at this day among thy brothers, it is thou who shalt be king and from thee shall come the kings of this country [Irish Dalriada] and over Fortriu for ever.'

And Patrick left many of his churches and foundations in the [Irish] territory of Dalriada.

The first importance of that story here lies in its evidence for the recognition of Fergus, a full four centuries after his death, as the forebear of the then only recently established Scots kings of Fortriu. Its account of Patrick's 'prophecy' is obviously written with benefit of hindsight, if only because even the original Pictish kingdom of Fortriu did not come into being until some two hundred and fifty years after the latest date assigned to the saint's death. There is a very much less elaborate version of the story elsewhere in the *Tripartite Life* telling of Patrick's prophesying Fergus becoming king over his brothers as his reward for being the only son of Erc who had not tried to steal the saint's horses. Both versions are very probably later reworkings of a still earlier tale, already current by the very early ninth century on the evidence of a reference to Patrick's blessing of Fergus contained in the *Book of Armagh*, and which certainly cannot be dismissed as without any plausible historical foundation. Saint Patrick's principal area of activity did lie in the north of Ireland and would have included the Irish territory of Dalriada in Antrim where, as elsewhere, he would have assuredly made contact with local kings. Few modern historians would claim certain knowledge of Patrick's true dates, but most recent scholarship places his mission to Ireland in the second half of the fifth century, corresponding to the entry of his obituary at 493 in the *Annals of Tigernach* and making his mission closely concurrent with the most likely period of Erc's kingship of Dalriada in Ireland.

Other than the isolated entry of the death of Erc at the year 474 in the *Annals of the Four Masters* – a seventeenth-century compilation not always thoroughly reliable in the historical value of its sources – all that is known of the father of Fergus Mor is the name of his own father recorded in the Irish genealogies as *Eochaid Muin-remor* and for whom the genealogists claim descent from Conaire, son-in-law of the legendary Irish king *Conn Céadchathach*, 'Conn of the Hundred Battles'. There is, however, full agreement among the Irish sources that Erc was the last king of Dalriada to rule his kingdom from Ireland and that it was in the next generation that its royal house migrated from Antrim to Kintyre. Consequently, the historical evidence contained in the medieval accounts of these 'sons of Erc', although late in date, widely at variance and greatly encrusted with legend, has significant bearing upon the foundation of the kingdom of the Scots.

The annotated list of kings of Dalriada included in the *Chronicle of the Kings* – a text dated in its present form to the later twelfth century, but ultimately deriving from sources of much greater antiquity, and most fully preserved in a fourteenth-century manuscript[6] – names just one of Erc's sons as having been in the kingship of Scots.

> Fergus, son of Erc, was the first of Conaire's race to receive the kingdom of Alba . . . He reigned for three years.

Another medieval source, this time of Irish origin, offers its own evidence in support of that same reign-length. The *Synchronisms of Fland Mainistrech* (Flann of Monasterboice who died in 1056) is another annotated list of kings, of Ireland as well as Scotland and arranged along the lines of an historical chronology.

> Twenty years after the battle of Ocha, the family of Erc, son of Eochaid Muin-remor, went to Alba; namely the six sons of Erc; two Oenguses, two Loarns and two Ferguses.

The annals offer a variety of dates for the battle of Ocha, but Flann places it in the year 478, which would make 498 his date for the migration of the princes of Dalriada from Ireland to Scotland and, when taken together with Tigernach's entry of Fergus' obituary at 501, would confirm his reign as having been of the same three-year duration recorded in the *Chronicle of the Kings*. Flann's identification of 'six sons of Erc', by contrast, would seem more characteristic of legend than history, especially when set beside the corresponding passage from the slightly later eleventh-century verse chronicle of kings of Scots known as the *Duan Albanach* ('Song of the Men of Alba').

> Three sons of Erc, son of pleasant Eochaid,
> Three men who received Patrick's blessing
> Took Alba and great were their deeds –
> Loarn, Fergus and Oengus . . .

The apparent confusion of these later sources as to the number and names of the 'sons of Erc' and how many of them migrated to Scotland grows greater with each one consulted, the few quoted here being no more than a sample of a much wider-spread inconsistency which can be taken as a clear indication of legend having long since overwhelmed whatever might have been its genuinely historical foundation. To find the earliest key to the likely origin of the tradition it is necessary to seek out the evidence of just one more document, that bearing the title *Senchus fer nAlban* ('History of the Men of Alba').

The original text of this *Senchus* has been shown to be of mid-seventh-century origin, but the form in which it has survived is of the tenth century, by which time its earlier content had been overlaid with later legendary accretions. There are, none the less, still some passages which appear to have survived from the original and one of them, containing a detailed seventh-century survey of the kindreds and fighting strengths of Dalriada in Scotland, identifies its three principal *cenéla*, or clans: the *Cenél Loairn* (clan of Loarn); the *Cenél nOengusa* (clan of Oengus) whose territory the *Senchus* confirms as being on Islay; and the *Cenél nGabráin* (clan of Gabran), who is known from the early sources to have been the ruling kindred of Dalriada until the later seventh century and while directly descended from Fergus Mor was yet named not for him but for his grandson, Gabran. The genealogical matter of the *Senchus*, which is contained in passages heavily encrusted with legend, attributes Erc with having twelve sons, of whom six – including two Ferguses and two Loarns – came out of Ireland to Scotland and it was for one of these Loarns that the Cenel Loairn was named, while the Cenel Oengusa was named for an Oengus who – according to the *Senchus* alone among all the sources – did not accompany his brothers to Scotland.

The first conclusion which can be drawn from all this complex tangle of names out of old books is that the intention of the 'sons of Erc' tradition must have been to associate the eponymous forebears of two kindreds of Dalriada in Scotland with the Dalriadic royal house. The number three had long been endowed with special, even magical, significance in Celtic tradition which would have conveniently accommodated 'three sons of Erc' and no less significant was the number twelve at a time when Celtic Ireland was still integrating Christian symbolism with its pre-Christian culture. There is, thus, every possibility of 'twelve sons of Erc' and 'three sons of Erc' representing two quite independent, but equally unhistorical, traditions in the same sea-divided kingdom and the variant configurations of those figures found in the medieval sources can be taken to represent attempts by later genealogists to reconcile those two traditions into one pseudo-history.

Out of all of which it is still possible to salvage at least one genuinely historical personality, that of Fergus Mor mac Erc, king of Dalriada and ancestor of kings of Scots, but he can only be properly recognised as such in the singular context of kingship in Celtic Ireland.

THE KINGDOM OF DALRIADA

Very much more is known of kings and kingship in ancient Ireland than is known of similar institutions in the other Celtic cultures of Britain and that knowledge derives largely from the literature of early Irish tradition underwritten by the evidence of classical geographers and historians. The sagas of the *Ulster Cycle* centred on the hero Cuchulainn, for example, are placed by their authors around the time of Christ, although they probably more closely reflect events of three centuries later, but the fact of kingship being established in Ireland by the first century AD is fully confirmed by closely contemporary classical geographers and historians. Ptolemy's *Geography*, which is certainly the oldest known account of Ireland and perhaps informed by a source as old as the first century BC, firmly identifies a number of Irish royal centres and Tacitus' biography of his father-in-law *Agricola* tells of the Roman commander meeting with an Irish king who had been driven out of his kingdom to seek sanctuary on the mainland.

There were, of course, very many kings in Celtic Ireland by reason of its social structure based on blood-kinship, where the essential social unit was the tribe – called in Irish the *túath* – acknowledging the authority of its *rí*, or king, who claimed descent from an eponymous, and probably legendary, founding forebear. Succession, thus, followed also along lines of blood-kinship, but passed so frequently to the king's brother before it passed to his son as very often to establish two or more parallel and potentially rival lines of future succession. The same custom of kingship followed the Irish to Scotland where it was to characterise, and too often bedevil, six centuries of succession to the kingship of Scots.

By the time of Ireland's entry into the clearer light of history from the second half of the fifth century, the *rí túaithe* (tribal king) can be seen to represent the least order of kingship, ranked below the *ruiri*, or over-king, who himself acknowledged the overlordship of a *rí ruirech* ('king of over-kings'). The nominally supreme authority of the *ard rí*, or 'high-king' of all Ireland, was a later development which cannot be said to have come into being until the seventh century.

Kingship in Celtic Ireland, then, pertained in the first instance to the king's tribe rather than to the land they occupied, and so Erc must be recognised, as must his successor Fergus Mor, as king of a people whose name appears variously in the early sources – as it does in the writings of modern historians – in the archaic Irish forms of *Dál Réti* and *Dál Riata* as well as the form of *Dalriada* used here. They were one of the number of tribes called in Irish tradition *Érainn* – a name linked with, if not deriving from, *Ériu*, the most archaic name for Ireland – which can be taken to indicate their descent from the most ancient pre-Celtic peoples of Ireland, and there is strong evidence from the legendary history of the Dalriada to confirm them as such when it tells of their having at one time had territory in Munster. Alwyn and Brinley Rees, eminent authorities on Celtic tradition, have shown that 'Munster is the primeval world, the place of origin' in the mythic prehistory of Ireland and while the presence of Érainn 'is recorded for many parts of the country, the *Sen Érainn*, "the Old Erainn", belonged to Munster'.[7]

If the origins of the Dalriada did lie with Ireland's aboriginal peoples, then their tradition of descent from Conaire can be recognised as an attempt by the early genealogists to provide them with a spurious lineage from the Celtic warrior nobility of Irish legend, while the reference in the early ninth-century *Book of Armagh* to both Fergus and his son Domangart as *mac Nise*, 'sons of Nes', would indicate a more ancient line of mythic descent from an early Irish river-god. None the less, a legendary history at least as old as the eighth century has no doubt that it was Conaire's son *Coirpre Riata* (Cairbre Riada) who brought the people of Dalriada out of Munster to escape a great famine in the later third century AD and led them north to establish a new homeland, called thereafter *Dál Riata* or 'Riada's share', in the north of Ireland.

Whether or not they were the same tribe known to Ptolemy as *Robodgii* and occupying much the same territory in or before the first century AD, when these people of Dalriada first enter the formal historical record they are settled in the north of Ireland, or more precisely in the north-east corner of what is now Antrim, where their capital stronghold was the steep-sided promontory fort at Dunseverick just a few miles along the coast from the famous Giant's Causeway. The situation of this original Irish kingdom of Dalriada in the political map of fifth-century Ireland was to cast a long shadow over the first centuries of the kingdom of the Scots and for that reason alone is worth a summary overview here.

The territory of Dalriada lay within what remained of the ancient province of Ulster and rendered it subject to the overkings of the *Ulaid*, who were most often drawn from the kindred of the *Dál Fiatach* in the west of what is now County Down. The neighbours of the Dalriada to the west and south were of the people known as *Cruithin* – the Goidelic form of the name 'Briton' indicating their having anciently settled in Ireland from the mainland[8] – whose ruling kindred of the *Dál nAraide* (Dalaraide) were to play their own disastrous part in the later history of Dalriada. Further to the west lay the territory of the northern branch of the *Uí Neill*, the 'race of Niall' descended from *Niall Noígiallach*, or 'Niall of the Nine Hostages', two of whose sons had earlier in the fifth century made war on the Ulaid, destroying their ancient capital fortress of *Emain Macha* near Armagh and carving out for themselves 'sword-land' extending west from the River Bann and as far south as Ben Bulben in Sligo. It was from this northern power-base centred on Derry and Donegal that the Ui Neill were to achieve their great ascendancy in the sixth century and to play out their own strategic role, for both good and ill, in the history of the Dalriadic kingdom of the Scots.

All the historical evidence for early Ireland, even as early as that of the Latin historians complaining of raiders crossing the Irish Sea to plunder Roman Britain, confirms its people as having been among the most accomplished seafarers of Dark Age Europe. It is thus almost impossible, when the Mull of Kintyre lies just some twelve miles distant from the Heads of Antrim, to imagine the people of Dalriada having not made that short sea-crossing of the North Channel to settle on mainland Britain before the last years of the fifth century. While there is no formal historical record of their so doing, there is an undeniable weight of evidence from the most ancient Irish tradition to propose Fergus Mor and his royal kindred as having been not the first, but the last, ancient settlement of the Irish in Alba.

THE EVIDENCE OF IRISH TRADITION

The peat-cutting at Sulaisiadar on the Isle of Lewis in 1982 uncovered a stone axe which has been dated by archaeologists to the Neolithic period of around 3000 BC. While a tool some five thousand years old can hardly be described as 'new', this handsomely crafted axe shows no sign of ever having been used and seems to have survived its long centuries under a blanket of peat in virtually 'mint' condition. Its haft is of hawthorn wood, but its head is crafted of porcellanite stone from Antrim and its presence on Lewis, the most northerly of the Western Isles, can only be explained by there having been some form of human contact – inevitably by sea, probably by way of trade, but still possibly as migration and settlement – between the north of Ireland and the Outer Hebrides at the time, or even before the time, when the standing stones were raised.

It would be asking too much of strictly scientific archaeology for its account of the prehistoric peoples of the west to compete with the vivid narrative of the same subject contained in the oldest Irish tradition which is preserved now in manuscript volumes compiled between the eleventh and fifteenth centuries, but was originally set down at least as early as the eighth century by monastic scribes who fashioned cycles of myth and saga out of the oral legacy passed down by uncounted generations of bards. These early

Irish myths and sagas are probably the oldest vernacular literature in Europe and, when allowance is made for the constraints of biblical chronology and the aggrandisement of dynastic ancestors, can be read as a mythic history of Ireland framed by a culture and cosmography of prehistoric antiquity.

The central source for the earliest epochs of this mythic history is the *Lebor Gabála Érenn* (the 'Book of Invasions of Erin') in which the successive cultures of Irish prehistory are presented as literal 'invasions' of Ireland, beginning before the Flood with the advent of the primeval people of Cessair – whose first arrival, incidentally, is located in Munster – and culminating in the conquest of Ireland by the 'Sons of Miledh' who can be recognised as a mythologised form of the Goidelic Celts. Whether or not it would be realistic to suggest this evidence from tradition as drawing on genuine recollection of ages past, it is remarkable how impressively the 'folk-history' contained in these early Irish myths and sagas does correspond to the modern understanding of Ireland's prehistory. Still more important here are its numerous references to Irish activity in Alba which can be taken as undeniable evidence from the oldest tradition for prehistoric settlement of the Irish in north Britain.

The first such settlement is ascribed by the 'Book of Invasions' to the 'people of Nemed' who accomplished the third 'invasion of Erin' and might be cautiously recognised as a Neolithic culture. Nemed himself is said to have died of the plague before his people were overwhelmed in battle by the predatory *Fomoire*, who can be taken to represent a mythologisation of prehistoric sea-raiders from the northern and western isles of Scotland. Thus were the people of Nemed driven out from Ireland and one third of their number, according to one version of the legend, journeyed northwards to find a new home in Alba.

After the people of Nemed, Ireland was next settled by the *Fir Bolg* – 'The Men of the Bags' indicated by the tradition as a people akin to the Fomoire and most plausibly identified as an early Bronze Age culture of Ireland – who were driven out in their turn by the next wave of invaders. The account of their expulsion preserved in the legend of 'The Migration of the sons of Umor' from the fifteenth-century *Book of Ballymote* tells how the Fir Bolg were defeated in battle with a new invader and the few of their number who survived fled from Ireland to settle 'in Arran and in Islay and in Rathlin and in Britain and in other islands besides'. There is a curious eighteenth-century footnote to this legend in Martin Martin's *Description of the Western Isles of Scotland* where the account of his visit to Hirta, the largest of the St Kilda island group lying to the west of North Uist, mentions 'an antient Fort on the South end of the bay, call'd *Dun-fir-Volg*'. If St Kilda could ever be proved to have been one of those 'other islands besides' settled by Bronze Age refugees from Ireland, then this 'fortress of the Fir Bolg' would have a strong claim to be the most ancient place-name evidence for the 'Irish in Britain', but it can, at least, be taken as evidence for the legend of the Fir Bolg, if not the people themselves, having long ago found its way to the most westerly of the Western Isles.

When the mythic history moves into the first centuries AD and the shadow-land where the evidence of tradition overlaps with that of the formal histori-cal record, it makes ever more frequent reference to the Irish in Alba, specifically indicating land-taking and settlement where it had earlier men-tioned only battles and sea-raiding. While none of these references can be taken as securely historical in themselves, they can be taken as evidence for genuine historical activity, because – as the eminent historian of early Irish kingship, Professor F. J. Byrne, has written – 'comparative studies in epic lit-erature have shown us that legends of an heroic age usually embody a kernel of historical fact'.[9]

The legend of Deirdre – found in the *Book of Ballymote* and also in the fourteenth-century *Yellow Book of Lecan* – tells of her fleeing from the fury of the first-century Ulster king Conchobar and finding her way to north Britain with the sons of Uisliu who 'were sixteen years in Alba, and they took possession of Alba from [the Isle of] Man northwards'. The later version of the legend places these *Uisneach* in Cowal and in Lorn, both of which were to lie within the territory of the historical kingdom of Dalriada, and neither might it be pure coincidence that the legendary Conn of the Hundred Battles is said to have fought one of them on Kintyre, the first heartland of the Dalriadic kingdom of the Scots.

It is when the evidence of tradition bears on people and events which the historian would place in the third and fourth centuries AD that its claims for Irish settlement in north Britain become most extensive, and best sub-stantiated by the corresponding historical evidence for Irish raiding develop-ing into colonial settlement in north and south Wales, as well as in the south-west of England, at much the same time. Just such evidence from tradi-tion is found in the accumulation of legend around the third-century 'king of Ireland' *Lugaid mac Conn*, most of it contained in the twelfth-century *Book of Leinster* which identifies him as a son of Conn mac Airt and a hostile con-temporary of Cairbre Riada. Lugaid's reign as 'king of Ireland' began around AD 250, before which date he had spent seven years as an exile in Britain where he married a daughter of an otherwise unknown and presum-ably mythical king of Britons *Béinn Briot*. His marriage to a Britonic princess bore three sons, all of them fore-named *Fothad*, which bears such similarity to *Fothudáin*, the Irish form of Gododdin, as to suggest their grandfather's kingdom having been located in the Votadini territory around the Forth. The most prominent of these 'Three Fothads' is celebrated in the tradition as *Fothad Canainn* who became the accomplished leader of a *fian*, a freelance mercenary warband of a type prominent in third-century Ireland, with which he was able to claim for himself territory in Alba. While there is every likelihood of the original tale of Fothad having become later entangled with the cycle of legend centred on the celebrated hero Finn mac Cumaill and his *fian*, there is also a growing body of evidence for Irish mercenaries having been recruited by Roman Britain and deployed against other Irish raiders and land-takers. If the north British client kingdoms had followed this Roman practice, as they emulated so many others, then there is no reason why the Votadini should not have recruited Fothad's *fian* and repaid their services with a grant of land, and especially so when it was a Votadini warlord, Cunedda, who is credited with expelling Irish colonists from north Wales around the end of the fourth century.

Another tradition from the *Book of Leinster* – and found also in the Irish manuscript collection of the eleventh and twelfth centuries known only by its Bodleian Library catalogue entry of 'Rawlinson B502' – is similarly centred on three sons of an Irish king, but of an earlier fourth-century date and known as the 'Three Collas'. Their association with north Britain is of especial interest here because of its location in the west, from whence came their mother Aileach who is identified as a daughter of a nobleman of *Hí*, the old Irish name for Iona, and for whom is named the imposing ring-fort of the Grianan of Aileach in Donegal. The legend tells how the Collas fled Ireland to escape the vengeance of the son of an Ulster king they had slain in battle and found sanctuary in Alba with their mother's kin. After three years of exile they were invited back to Ireland by their erstwhile foe who endowed them with generous land-grants and courtly privileges in return for their fighting as his allies.

Thereafter two of the Collas were happy to settle in Ireland, but their eldest brother, Colla Uais, preferred to return to his 'great lands on the mainland and in the isles' of Alba. These 'Three Collas' are suspected now as figures of mythic invention to whom have been attached the real activities of the historical sons of Niall of the Nine Hostages, and it is certainly true that the Grianan of Aileach named for their legendary mother was the great symbol of Ui Neill power in the north. It is, none the less, also true that Colla Uais has been long claimed by tradition as not only the eponymous forebear of the *Uí maic Uais* ('the race of the son of Uais') in the north of Ireland, but also as the ultimate ancestor of the Clan Donald in the west of Scotland.

[37]

One more legend, 'The Exile of Conall Corc' found incomplete in the *Book of Leinster* and also the subject of references in the tenth-century *Cormac's Glossary*, concerns a genuinely historical figure from the end of the fourth century. Corc, son of a king of Munster, was banished by his father to Alba where he married a king's daughter who bore him the usual three sons with whom he eventually returned to Munster as his father's successor in the kingship. The adventures of Corc are a clear reworking of a familiar formula from Irish tradition, but the greater significance of the story lies in references made to it by no less than four ancient Irish genealogies.[10] All of these expand the number of Corc's sons from three to seven and three genealogies identify the mother of one of them as having been a daughter of a king of *Cruithentuath* or 'Pictland'. This son is known to the genealogists as *Cairbre Cruithneachán* ('Cairbre the Pict-sprung') and claimed by them as the ancestor of an 'Oengus, king of Alba', a claim which can call upon some weight of historical evidence in its support. What would appear to have been the Pictish custom of royal succession through the female line led to very many historical kings of Picts being of non-Pictish origin. Seven, like three, is a number of magical significance in the Irish tradition, where it seems to have an especial association with the Picts whose mythic forebear *Cruithne* is said to have had seven sons for whom Pictland was partitioned into its seven territorial divisions. The region of Pictland wherein the genealogists locate the kingdom of Corc's 'Pict-sprung' son is that of *Circin*, corresponding to the district now known as the Mearns. The list of *regiones* corresponding to the seven divisions of Pictland found in the twelfth-century Scottish geographical tract *De Situ Albanie* brackets the Mearns together with its sub-division of Angus, a district long believed to have been named for an important king of Picts. In the light of which and with all due caution, it would be no less than plausible to identify the Munster-descended 'Oengus, king of Alba' of the genealogies with one of the two most prominent kings of Picts bearing that name. The 'Oengus, king of Fortriu' who died in 834 is one possible candidate, but the much greater – and darkly ironic – probability is that the intended 'Oengus, king of Alba' was the same mighty warlord whose campaign in the west is entered in the *Annals of Tigernach* at the year 736:

> Oengus mac Fergus, king of Picts, devastated the lands of Dalriada and seized Dunadd.

Pre-eminence among all the claims of tradition for Irish settlement in north Britain must be accorded to an extension of the legendary account, already mentioned here, of Cairbre Riada's leading his people out of famine-stricken Munster to settle 'Riada's share' of Ulster in the later third century. The extended form of the legend tells of Cairbre crossing over from Antrim with a number of his people to establish a further settlement of Dalriada on the mainland north of the Clyde, most probably in Cowal. The legend is preserved now in two fourteenth-century collections,[11] but must be at least six hundred years older than those manuscripts by reason of the same story having been already known to Bede in the second quarter of the eighth century. While Bede himself offers no explanation as to how he had learned of the legend, he is known to have been in contact with more than one churchman sufficiently well-informed on Irish tradition to have been his source for the account of the origin of the Irish in north Britain contained in the first chapter of his *Ecclesiastical History*.

> As time passed, Britain received a third people, the *Scoti* [Irish], in addition to the Britons and the Picts, and they settled in the territory occupied by the Picts. They left Ireland under the leadership of *Reuda* [Riada], and either by treaty or by the sword claimed lands among the Picts which are their home to the present day. It is after that leader that they are still known as the *Dalreudini* [Dalriada], because in their language *daal* means 'a part'.

'At the very least', suggested Professor W. J. Watson in his standard work on the history of Scotland's Celtic place names, 'it shows that in the opinion of Bede's informant there had been in the west a settlement of Scots from Ireland long anterior to that of the sons of Erc in the beginning of the sixth century.'[12]

FERGUS MOR IN HISTORICAL CONTEXT

In the light of such evidence as has been gleaned here from the early sources of both history and tradition, it might now be possible to reconstruct some realistic historical context in which to place this Fergus Mor, son of Erc and first king of Scots.

The period bounded by the last quarter of the third century and the first quarter of the fifth which saw the deterioration and eventual abdication of Roman authority in Britain might be recognised from an alternative perspective as the 'age of Irish expansion' in the course of which raiding across the Irish Sea evolved into a number of precarious attempts at colonisation on the western fringe of the mainland. The evidence for such settlements found in Irish tradition is supported not only by that of the *Historia Brittonum*, ascribed to the Welsh historian Nennius working in the early ninth century, but also by the concentration of Irish ogham inscriptions confirming an Irish presence in South Wales, Devon and Cornwall. The precise dating of these settlements is inevitably uncertain but they can be confidently placed around the fourth century, when those in Dyfed especially may have represented Irish warbands recruited by the Roman authorities.

The colony in north Wales, by contrast, would seem more likely to have come about by spontaneous land-taking than by invitation and so too, at much the same time, did the Irish settlements in north Britain. The legend of Corc has been taken to indicate the establishment of a princely kindred from Munster in the Pictish territory of the Mearns and there is evidence also for Cruithin out of Ulster settling in the Rhinns of Galloway where they would, in fact, have been making a return to the territory from which their ancestors had earlier migrated to Ireland. Whether by reason of their physical expulsion or cultural absorption, there is virtually no evidence for these settlements surviving long into the fifth century. Those Irish who were not expelled from Galloway, south Wales and the West Country were absorbed into the culture and community of the local Britonic tribes, much as were the Munstermen among the Picts. The Irish colony in north Wales was certainly driven out by the Gododdin warlord Cunedda who is said by Nennius to have brought his 'sons' – or, more probably, his warband – west from the Forth for that purpose and afterwards to have established himself and his line as Britonic kings of Gwynedd.

It would appear, then, that the one outstanding success among some number of these Irish settlements in Britain was that established in Argyll as an extension of the kingdom of Dalriada in Antrim. In the light of the evidence for contact between the north of Ireland and the greater extent of the western seaboard of north Britain extending back over thousands of years into remote prehistory, and in view also of the Mull of Kintyre lying little more than a dozen miles across the North Channel from the Heads of Antrim, it is impossible to imagine that there had been no northern Irish presence established in Argyll before the last years of the fifth century. Whether or not Cairbre – or in some sources 'Echoid' – Riada himself can be considered as a genuinely historical figure, the legendary account of his leading the people of Dalriada into Scotland can only confirm for the modern historian – as it did for Bede in the eighth century – that an Irish settlement was established in the west of Scotland north of the Clyde at least a hundred years before Fergus made his reliably historical crossing to

Kintyre. Bede believed the Irish in Argyll to have 'settled in the territory occupied by the Picts' and yet he placed Cairbre Riada's settlement on the north bank of the Clyde, by inference on the Cowal peninsula, which would have been Britonic rather than Pictish territory. Six hundred years before Bede, Ptolemy had identified the tribe occupying Kintyre around the first centuries AD as the *Epidii*, 'the people of the horse', who were evidently a p-Celtic culture and whose capital fortress would seem to have been Dunadd in its earlier Iron Age occupation. Whatever became of the Epidii and their descendants is nowhere indicated, but there is no reason why they should not have been gradually absorbed, through two or even three centuries, into the Irish settlements which were to be established as the dominant culture in Argyll by the end of the fifth century.

If those settlements – by people of Dalriada and probably also of neighbouring tribes – had been so long established in the west of Scotland, then it must have been that Fergus and his royal kindred were following, rather than leading, their subjects out of Ireland and the real significance of his arrival on the eve of the sixth century was the transfer of the royal centre of his kingdom from Antrim to Alba. While the legend claims that Cairbre had led some of his people to settle in north Britain, it does not say that he stayed there with them. Indeed, a tradition preserved in the *Book of Leinster* tells of Cairbre Riada meeting his death at the hands of the Dalaraide, whose territory adjoining that of the Dalriada in Ulster implies his being resident in Ireland at the time of his death, and nowhere in the sources is there any indication of any Dalriadic king before Fergus having taken up permanent residence outside Ireland.

The question of why an Irish king of an Irish kingdom, albeit with some of his subjects settled on the other side of the North Channel, should relocate himself and his court out of Ireland can only be explained in terms of the wider political situation. The Irish homeland of Dalriada, already tightly squeezed into barely 450 square miles of Antrim, had been brought under increasing territorial pressure by the relentless expansion of the Ui Neill into the north through the fifth century. The sons of Niall had waged their long and punishing war against the old kingdom of the Ulaid and destroyed its capital fortress of Emain Macha with the support of a number of vassal tribes – known collectively as the *Airgialla*[13] and including among them the Ui mac Uais – who were rewarded with grants of land in the south and west of what had been the formerly extensive territories of the province of Ulster.

The territory of Dalriada in Ireland – bounded in the north and east by the sea, its southern frontier just above what is now the town of Larne and its western boundary marked out by the River Bush – would have been threatened on both of its land-locked borders, in the south by the hostile Dalaraide and in the west by the relentless ambition of the northern Ui Neill themselves. The only possibility of territorial expansion, then, was by sea and to the north where people from Dalriada had been settling on the mainland and its island fringe for generations and such was the course which led Fergus across the North Channel into the land of Alba.

It is possible also that he may have had positive encouragement to do so from the Britons of Strathclyde, who would have thereby installed a friendly 'buffer' kingdom between their own territory and whatever threat might be posed to it by the Picts of the Hebrides and the mainland beyond the Clyde. It must be said that there is no firm historical evidence to support that suggestion, but it would have been a typically Roman stratagem on the part of Britons greatly influenced by Roman ways and there is later evidence for a 'non-aggression pact', which may have been as old as Fergus' time, holding between the kingdoms of the Strathclyde Britons and the Dalriadic Scots until the second quarter of the seventh century. What can be said with some confidence is that Fergus would have found it extremely difficult if not impossible to extend his kingdom on to the mainland of north Britain had the still-powerful Britons of the Clyde not wished him so to do.

So it would seem to have been that Fergus, son of Erc, came to Alba and brought with him – according to the *Senchus fer nAlban* – 'a hundred and fifty men', a figure which must be considered an underestimate on the part of the *Senchus* if it is intended to represent a king's company of kinsmen and nobility, who would have necessarily brought with them wives and offspring, serving-folk and fighting men. The figure of 'a hundred and fifty' is more realistically appreciated as a seventh-century recollection of the number of noble households accompanying Fergus to Alba and comprising the warrior aristocracy of his kingdom, but whether or not they included any other 'sons of Erc' remembered in the tradition as 'Oengus' and 'Loarn' raises quite another question.

Oengus, son of Erc, appears nowhere in the earliest sources as an individual in his own right. The fact that he does not occur in any king-list does not necessarily disallow his having been a sub-king under his brother, but the absence from the annals of any obituary for Oengus mac Erc casts the first doubt over his historicality. He is, none the less, recognised by the *Senchus* as having been the eponymous dynast of the Cenel Oengusa, who are the least noticed by the annalists of the three principal kindreds of Dalriada but whose territory is securely located on the Isle of Islay by the mid-seventh century. Oengus may well, of course, have still been the forebear of the clan named for him and yet not necessarily a brother or even a contemporary of Fergus mac Erc, and this would seem now most likely to have been the case, especially on the evidence of a note appended to the *Tripartite Life* of Saint Patrick.

This note, one of the 'Armagh Memoranda' and possibly the work of Patrick's eighth-century biographer Tirechan, contains a specific reference to the saint's visiting the 'household of the Cenel Oengusa' on his travels in Antrim and can thus confirm the 'clan of Oengus' having been already established as a noble kindred in the north of Ireland at some point in the second half of the fifth century. Taken together with the reference in the *Senchus* to Oengus as one of those 'sons of Erc' who stayed in Ireland but 'whose descendants are in Alba', the greater probability is that Oengus was a scion of the royal house of Dalriada, but of a much earlier date than any son of the historical Erc, and the forebear of a kindred who had crossed over some twenty miles of the North Channel to settle on Islay long before the arrival of Fergus on Kintyre.

A similar explanation might also resolve the question of the third 'son of Erc'. The name Loarn certainly occurs as that of a son of Erc in the genealogies of Dalriada and there is no good reason to doubt that Fergus did have a brother of that name. However, in the *Duan Albanach* Loarn is not only named as a son of Erc, but also accorded a reign-length as Fergus' predecessor in the kingship: 'Ten years Loarn, with great renown, was in the kingdom of *Oirir Alban* ['the coastland of Alba', presumably Argyll].' The reign-lengths in the *Duan* are notoriously unreliable and, as a work of the eleventh century, it must also be considered a late source – much later, for example, than the original material of the *Senchus* which gives the name Loarn to two sons of Erc and recognises one of them, 'Loarn Mor', as the eponymous forebear of the Cenel Loairn. This 'clan of Loarn' is identified by the *Senchus* as one of the three principal kindreds of Dalriada in Scotland, while annal entries for the seventh and eighth centuries confirm its territory as having been centred on the hillfort of *Dún Ollaigh* (now Dunollie, by Oban) and extending from the (apparently also eponymous) Firth of Lorn across Loch Linnhe and Morvern to Ardnamurchan.

Any realistic interpretation of this welter of evidence from the sources must recognise their compilers' need to reconcile the inconsistencies of their own source materials, inconsistencies deriving in this case, perhaps, from their confusion of two different Loarns. The same name very often recurs in different generations in the Irish genealogies and if there was an historical son of Erc by the name of Loarn, he was almost certainly not the Loarn for whom the Cenel Loairn and, by inference, the Firth of Lorn were named. Just

[43]

as the Cenel Oengusa can be taken as having been an earlier Dalriadic settlement on Islay, so the Cenel Loairn is most plausibly explained as an earlier settlement in the north of Argyll, one led by an earlier Loarn whose reign on the mainland is recalled by the 'ten years, with great renown . . . in the coastland of Alba' given him in the *Duan*.

To which might be added a helpful footnote from the seventeenth-century Irish historian and close contemporary of the Four Masters, Geoffrey Keating, who writes of earlier Dalriadic settlements in Scotland having been ruled by a *toíseach*, or 'chieftain', before the arrival of Fergus Mor to become their king. If it would be reasonable to propose the original Loarn of the Cenel Loairn having been just such a *toíseach* at some time prior to Fergus' arrival in Alba, then it would follow that the migration of the royal house of Dalriada from Ireland to the mainland obliged the ruling kindreds of earlier Dalriadic settlements in Argyll to accept Fergus mac Erc, by right of his royal lineage, as their over-king.

Placed into that context, the tradition of the 'three sons of Erc' can be clearly seen now as a conveniently tripartite device whereby the later sources were able to co-opt the two eponymous dynasts of the Cenel Oengusa and Cenel Loairn as 'brothers' to the historical Fergus Mor.

THE FIRST KINGDOM OF THE SCOTS

Beyond that interpretation of the evidence of tradition, the evidence of the king-lists and genealogies and the key entry of his obituary in the *Annals of Tigernach*, almost nothing else is known of the man said to have been prophesied by Saint Patrick as the forebear of the kings of Scots. His reign is given as three years by the Dalriadic king-list as it appears in all manuscripts of the *Chronicle of the Kings*, a reign-length which would correspond precisely to Fland Mainistrech's date of 498 for Fergus' arrival in Scotland and his obituary entered by Tigernach at 501. How long he might have reigned in Irish Dalriada before 498 is not known, unless the twenty-seven-year reign accorded him by the *Duan* can be taken as seriously as it appears to have been by the *Annals of the Four Masters*. The Four Masters, working in seventeenth-century Donegal and often less than meticulous in their fusion of history with tradition, would seem to have deducted just that number of years from his obituary at 501 to arrive at the year 474 for his succession, thus enabling them to enter the obituary of his father, Erc, at the same date in their annals.

The early sources all seem to leave the impression – and it is no more than an impression – of Fergus being already an old man when he left Ireland. It is an impression very reasonably reinforced by his death occurring just three years later, but it need not, of course, have necessarily been the case, especially when the note appended to his entry in the king-list found in just one manuscript of the *Chronicle of the Kings* makes the claim that 'he was killed by his followers'. Whatever might have been the authority for that statement is unknown, but the note does have the appearance of a later addition to the original king-list and may itself be no earlier than the twelfth century. It would, furthermore, seem at least unlikely that Fergus was assassinated by a rival faction when the kingship is known to have passed directly to his son Domangart, and so the note might be reasonably discounted as a later reflection of the intervening history of the kings of Scots where assassination by competitors was all too often the circumstance of a royal obituary.

A similar interpretation might be applied to the statement in the *Chronicle of the Kings* of Fergus' territory extending 'from the mountain of Druim Alban as far as the sea of Ireland, and to the *Inchegall* [the Outer Hebrides]', which must reflect territorial claims of a much later date than Fergus' time. While there is no contemporary record of Fergus' Scottish dominions – which, it must be said, most certainly did not extend to the Western Isles – there is reliable evidence of the territories of Scottish Dalriada as they were known later in the sixth and early in the seventh centuries, and from this can be deduced some realistic indication of the extent of Fergus' kingdom.

Its heartland undoubtedly lay in Kintyre and mid-Argyll and probably also included the Cowal peninsula, which comprised the territory of the *Cenél Comgaill* ('clan of Comgall'), a lesser branch of the ruling kindred named for a second grandson of Fergus. Its northerly extent can be placed at the northern frontier of the territory of the Cenel Loairn on Ardnamurchan, while its southern boundary lay just north of Larne in Ulster – because, of course, the kings of Dalriada were still to rule their Irish territories from their new power base in Alba for a hundred and fifty years. The eastern boundary – representing the frontier between the dominions of the Scots and those of the Picts – was the mountain range called in Irish *Druim Alban*, the 'Ridge of Britain', and in Latin *Dorsum Britanniae*, the 'Spine of Britain', running northwards from Ben Lomond, by way of Ben Nevis and Ben More Assynt, to Ben Hope in Sutherland. Bounded in the west by the Atlantic seaboard, the territory of Dalriada thus took in some number of islands, certainly Rathlin just off the north coast of Antrim, the Cenel Oengusa heartland of Islay, Jura and possibly also the Isle of Mull, which is known to have lain within the territory of the Cenel Loairn by the second half of the sixth century.

*

Such, then, would have been the kingdom which passed from Fergus Mor to his son and successor Domangart around the year 501. Of Domangart the sources tell little more than the length of his reign, entered in the king-lists as of just five years' duration, and the date of his obituary, entered by Tigernach around 506 and by the *Annals of Ulster* at 507.

There is another rare and curious reference to Domangart mac Fergus in a tract appended to the *Tripartite Life* of Patrick which names him as the 'king of Scots' among the Irish kings who attended the saint's deathbed. It is evidently a late source, because Domangart succeeded to the kingship of Scots only on the death of his father whose obituary is entered almost a decade after the latest possible date for the death of Patrick, but its special value might lie in its recognition of some unusually religious trait in Domangart, a quality which is reflected again in the evidence for his having retired to a monastery before his death. The entry of his obituary in the *Annals of Inisfallen*, the oldest of all the Irish annals, chooses the word *quies*, which is used customarily for the death of an ecclesiastic, and refers to him in the unusual form of 'Domangart of Kintyre', two clues to prompt the possibility of Fergus' son having died in monastic retirement.

The popular tradition of Saint Columba having introduced Christianity to Scotland in the second half of the sixth century still seems to be as indestructible as it is untenable, because there is no question of the kingdom of the Scots having been other than Christian from its very first foundation. So too, there is abundant evidence for some number of Irish holy men having found their way to Scotland decades before Columba, most of them following in the wake of the royal house of Dalriada and one of the first and most significant being Ciaran of Saigir who founded the monastery of *Kilkerran* ('Ciaran's church') at the head of what is now Campbeltown Loch in Kintyre.

If, as seems very likely, Domangart did enter Ciaran's church to die the 'straw death' of a monk who had once been a king, then he was setting a precedent which was to be followed almost a hundred years later by his grandson and successor in the kingship of Scots, the mighty warlord who was known to the annalist as 'Gabran's son, king of Alba'.

2

'Gabran's son, king of Alba'

AEDAN

THE ISLE OF IONA, some three square miles in area and lying barely a mile across the sound from the south-west coast of Mull, is known to be formed of the oldest rock of the earth's crust. It can thus be said, and quite scientifically so, to be an island made in the very beginning of the world, and it is foretold in Gaelic tradition[1] as the last place to be overwhelmed at the world's end, because this tiny island has been held in high honour for fully fourteen hundred years as the most sacred shrine of the Gael.

The investment of the landscape with the myths and legends within which he preserved the memory of his ancestral past seems to have been an especial characteristic of the Irish Celt since prehistory and one which was quite undiminished by his passage out of pagan antiquity into the Christian era. Just as the earliest Irish tradition succeeded in associating almost every mountain and river-crossing, inland lough and island of the sea with the adventuring of pre-Christian gods and heroes, so the literature of Irish hagiography took great pains to identify precise locations for the activities of the saints of Ireland and, in so doing, would seem to have endowed their sanctity upon the very forms and features of the land. That same practice was to follow in the wake of the Irish Celts who settled in north Britain and there it is clearly reflected in the name by which Iona is called in the Gaelic. *Í Chaluim Chille*, 'I(ona) of Columcille', has been shown to preserve the most ancient form of the island's name[2] linked with that of the saint from whose patronage it derives its claim to pre-eminence among the holy islands of the western sea.

What is known now of the sixth-century holy man still called by the Irish

[47]

Colm Cille ('Colum of the church'), but more widely recognised by his Latin name-form of *Columba*, has been encrusted with a great weight of spurious tradition over at least a thousand years, but there is nowhere any shadow of doubt as to the historical Columba having been a figure of signal importance to the history of the Celtic kingdom of the Scots. While neither of the two most ancient *Lives* of the saint to have survived intact – the Latin *Vita Columbae* set down by Adamnan, abbot of Iona, at the end of the seventh century and the Irish *Betha Coluim Cille* compiled at Derry some four hundred and fifty years later – can be considered an ideally historical document, together they preserve the greater substance of what history can be confident that it knows of this extraordinary holy man.

The Irish *Betha* locates his birthplace at Gartan in Donegal, while the Adamnan *Vita* confirms the year of his birth as having been AD 521 and it is Adamnan also who provides the earliest record of the saint's distinguished ancestry in the royal line of the northern Ui Neill, when he confirms Columba's father to have been a grandson of Conall Gulban, son of Niall of the Nine Hostages. This Adamnan *Life of Columba* was set down within a century of the saint's lifetime by a member of his own kindred, who followed him into the abbacy of Iona and was esteemed throughout Ireland and north Britain as a distinguished churchman and counsellor of kings. Still preserved in a manuscript written no more than a decade after its author's death, it represents the source of greatest authority for the life and times of the saint himself and, for that reason alone, it is to Adamnan that the historian must look first for the oldest and most authoritative account of Columba's decision to leave his native Ireland and spend the rest of his life in Scotland.

Indeed, it is from the evidence of Adamnan that Columba's 'pilgrimage to Britain' in the year 563 has been known to history for thirteen hundred years, but the reason for his having undertaken that pilgrimage has been subjected to a variety of interpretations, the most unhistorical of them being the tale of his banishment from Ireland for causing a battle to be fought over his illicit copying of a psalter. This is a version of events which has no foundation in the earliest reliable sources, least of all in the Adamnan *Life* which explains Columba's motive quite unequivocally as 'wishing to become a pilgrim for Christ' and indicates the saint in quest of the 'white martyrdom of exile', a practice widely pursued in the ancient Irish church and one which brought very many of its holy men, before and after Columba, out of Ireland to the Hebrides and beyond. It might, none the less, serve to complement rather than contradict Adamnan's essentially spiritual account if Columba's arrival in Scotland were to be placed into its political context and linked to the saint's blood-kinship, through his grandmother's lineage, to a noble kindred of Dalriada, but that is a question which must await some later consideration here.

From the viewpoint of the earliest sources, then, the first spiritual significance of Iona is to be recognised as that of the principal church of Columba's 'white martyrdom'. It was there that he died in the year 597, when his burial in its earth first established I-Columcille as the great centre of pilgrimage which, in very many if not all respects, it has remained through fourteen centuries. The steady stream of modern pilgrims, and other varieties of twentieth-century traveller, delivered to the island each summer by the ferry shuttling across the sound from the Ross of Mull is estimated at an annual total of more than 250,000 souls. While there is virtually nothing now to be seen on Iona which is known to be as old as Columba's time and the last of his remains were taken off the island more than eleven hundred years ago, all of those visitors have come, in whatever individual form of homage, to an island made holy by the man with a greater claim than any other to be recognised as Scotland's patron saint.

Almost every one of them has also been told by a guide or read in a guidebook that this island was the traditional place of burial for kings of Scots. So, indeed, it would seem to have been – although for rather fewer kings and over a somewhat shorter period of history than most guidebooks would have the visitor believe – by reason of a tradition first properly established by the mac Alpin dynasty in the ninth century, but the association of Iona with the kingdom of the Scots is very much more ancient than that time and can be shown, in fact, to be as old as the first entry of Columba's monastery into the historical record.

In view of the immense spiritual, cultural and political importance of the church on Iona down so many centuries, it is at least curious that there is nowhere any reliably historical record of the date of its foundation. While the Irish annals enter dates of foundation for most of the great monastic churches of Ireland, they can show no such entry for that of Columba's monastery on Iona. All that can be said with certainty of the date of its foundation, on the most reliable evidence of the early sources,[3] is that it cannot be placed any earlier than 563, the year confirmed by Adamnan to have been the year of Columba's arrival in Scotland, or later than 574, in which year he indicates Iona to have been already effectively established as the royal church of the kingdom of the Scots.

To which must be added the evidence of the two most reliable of the Irish annal collections – the *Annals of Ulster* and those of Tigernach, both of them informed by an original Iona source – when they enter at 574 the obituary of Conall mac Comgall, king of Dalriada and great-grandson of Fergus

Mor, adding that it was he 'who granted the island of Ia to Columcille'. While the date of a grant of land for a monastery is not necessarily the same as the date of its actual foundation, Adamnan is able to show Iona as having been well enough established by 574 to be chosen as the place of consecration for Conall's successor as king of Dalriada. One of the most impressive – and historically significant – chapters of his *Life of Columba* is the one containing an account of the saint's vision of 'an angel of the Lord, who had been sent to him and who held in his hand a glass book of the ordination of kings'. Into that book was inscribed the name of Aedan mac Gabran as the successor to the kingship of Dalriada, and 'the saint, in obedience to the word of the Lord, sailed across to the island of Iou [Iona] and there, as he had been bidden, ordained Aidan as king'.

In those few lines is contained the evidence for the earliest event reliably located on Iona to which can be assigned a securely historical date, and the first record also of the ceremonial induction of any king in the British Isles. Adamnan offers no indication as to whether Columba's ordination of Aedan was a public or private ceremony and, of course, the historian can do no more than wonder whether there might also have been some corresponding secular form of inauguration, even one centred around that footprint cut into the stone at Dunadd.

Columba's thirty-four years in Scotland spanned the reigns of two kings of Dalriada, but he would seem to have formed an especially close relationship with just one of them. While Conall mac Comgall is the subject of only a single passing reference in the Adamnan *Life*, his nephew and successor, Aedan mac Gabran (for whom Adamnan, like Bede, uses the Latin name-form of *Aidan*), is given prominence in no less than four chapters where he is consistently portrayed as a formidable warrior king calling on the saint for counsel and support. That portrait is probably a more accurate reflection of the political instincts of the holy man than the reverential inclination of the king, and is certainly most realistically appreciated in the light of Professor Archie Duncan's astute assessment: 'Behind Adamnan's pious Aedan consecrated by Columba's hand lies a tough opportunist, enemy of all his neighbours and master of most of them.'[4]

Professor John Bannerman took a similar view when he recognised Aedan as 'the most ambitious and certainly the most successful king of Dalriada', and looked still further into the future with his suggestion that 'it is possible that the close co-operation between church and state established in Aedan's reign was the basis of the ultimate supremacy of the Scots in Scotland'.[5] It may well, in fact, have been that Columba and Aedan had more in common than their stereotypical roles of holy man and warrior king might imply, but both of them can be recognised now as figures of the greatest significance in the early history of Scotland. Each was to play his own decisive part in achieving the first ascendancy of the kingdom of the Scots, but to appreciate the scale of that achievement it must be set against the background of the seven decades separating the succession of Aedan from the death of his grandfather, Domangart.

'THE FLIGHT OF THE MEN OF ALBA'

The eleventh-century *Duan Albanach* describes the reign of Domangart, son of Fergus Mor, as 'five always turbulent years'. It offers no more detail and whatever, if any, substance there might have been for its statement, no turbulence around the kingdom of Dalriada was to come to the notice of any Irish annalist between the death of Fergus in 501 and that of his son around 507.

One of the very few details that are known of Domangart's reign is the identity of his queen, whose name is entered in a genealogy from the *Book of Ballymote* as *Fedlim folt-choem*, 'Fedlim the fair-haired', and who was apparently an Irish princess from the south of Galway. She bore Domangart two sons, Comgall and Gabran, who were to reign over their father's kingdom, each in his turn, through the next half-century, the first to succeed being Comgall, whose name follows that of Domangart in the king-lists and whose obituary is entered by Tigernach at around 537 and by the *Annals of Ulster* at 538. Both of those annals agree on the length of his reign having been thirty-five years, which is at least curious when no more than thirty-two years separate their entries of his death from that of his father and the few years' discrepancy is, perhaps, best explained by Domangart having abdicated his kingship in favour of Comgall to enter monastic retirement just two or three years before his death.

Comgall mac Domangart is identified by the *Senchus* as the eponymous dynast of the *Cenél Comgaill* sept of the ruling kindred of Dalriada, but his reign appears to have been remarkable for nothing more than its unusual longevity. It passed without any event of sufficient importance to merit notice in the annals and the *Duan Albanach*, having described his father's brief kingship as 'turbulent', says only of Comgall that he ruled 'without strife'. This apparent tranquillity of the first four decades of the Irish kingdom in Argyll was not, however, to outlast the reign of Gabran, who succeeded to the kingship on the death of his brother. The continuing silence of the annals throughout the greater extent of Gabran's twenty years in the kingship would suggest most of his reign in Dalriada to have been as peaceful as those of his father and brother, until the suddenly dramatic appearance in the year 556 of a new and formidable power in the land of north Britain.

The man whose name is entered in the Pictish king-list as *Bridei filius Mailcon* and was known to Tigernach as *Bruidhi mac Maelchon* is recognised now as having been the first genuinely historical high-king of Picts. If, as is thought most likely, this 'Bruide, son of Maelchon' was, in fact, a son of Maelgwyn, king of the Britons of Gwynedd and direct descendant of Cunedda, then Bruide can be said also to represent the first genuinely historical example of matrilinear succession to the kingship of the Picts.[6] For a prince from north Wales ultimately descended from the royal house of the Gododdin Britons around the Forth to have become king of Picts, his claim must have rested on his descent in the female line and, in all probability, on his mother having been born a Pictish princess, but there is nowhere any doubt of the power and authority of Bruide, king of Picts. Bede, writing less than a hundred and fifty years after his death, called him *rex potentissimus* ('a most powerful king'), while Adamnan indicates his capital fortress having been Craig Phadrig by Inverness and confirms his imperium having extended as far as Orkney. The evidence of the Pictish king-list, on the other hand, suggests that it took Bruide some time to extend his authority to the southern reaches of Pictland and that he may not have achieved the overlordship of all the Pictish kingdoms until just a few years before his death in 584.

His impact on the Scots of Dalriada, however, was already being felt a full quarter-century earlier, on the evidence of the *Annals of Tigernach* at the year 559:

> The death of Gabran mac Domangart, king of Alba.
> The flight of the men of Alba from Bruide mac Maelchon, king of Picts.

The typically terse form of the annal entry is here – as it is so often in the oldest Irish annals – infuriatingly unenlightening. Even when 'men of Alba' is taken to mean 'Scots of Dalriada' – as it does elsewhere in the annals – there is no indication of where they fled to or of where they fled from, and neither is any explicit connection made between their flight and the death of their king Gabran. The placing of Gabran's obituary as the first entry under that year would imply his having died before the flight of his people from Bruide, were it not for the sequence of the same two entries being reversed in the no less reliable *Annals of Ulster* suggesting otherwise, and yet neither annalist uses any form of words to indicate Gabran's suffering a violent death.

It has been suggested that Dalriadic Scots of the Cenel Loairn had already begun to move out of the north of Argyll and up the Great Glen – as, indeed, they were known to have done three centuries later – only to be driven back when they approached Bruide's territory. There is one other body of evidence with likely bearing on these same events which indicates Gabran having led the first advance of the Scots of Dalriada east of the 'Spine of Britain' into the territory of the southern Picts and north Britons. The fact of Gabran's obituary being entered in the *Annales Cambriae* (the 'Welsh Annals' appended to Nennius' ninth-century *Historia Brittonum*) can be taken to confirm his association with the north Britons, but the most illuminating contribution has been found in two other medieval Welsh sources preserving the ancient genealogies of the north Britons,[7] both of which identify Gabran's queen, Luan, as a daughter of a king of Britons whose territory extended to Brechin in Forfarshire. The name of the neighbouring district now called Gowrie was anciently *Gouerin*, *Goverine* and *Gowrane*, and appears in a Welsh poem attributed to the sixth-century bard Taliesin as *Gafran*, which is precisely the form in which Gabran's name is entered in the Welsh genealogies.

Gowrie, then, would seem to have been named for Gabran as Cowal was named for his brother Comgall. While there is no record of his activities before his succession to the kingship of Dalriada in 538, Gabran must have been over thirty by that time and may even have been over fifty, having waited many years to succeed his brother. If he had acquired some territory from his father-in-law's lands in the east, perhaps in the form of a dowry, he would seem to have spent some years of his brother's reign in Dalriada in establishing himself as a sub-king in the district since named for him. On the political map of the early sixth century, the district of Gowrie would have lain within the region where the territory of the north Britons bordered on that of the Picts, and where an outlying settlement of Dalriadic Scots would have drawn the hostile attentions of a Pictish king out of the north who was ambitious to extend his imperium to the southern territories of Pictland.

In that context, 'the flight of the men of Alba from Bruide' may well represent an expulsion of a Scots settlement from the eastern territory where they had been established by Gabran, an interpretation supported by the use of the Irish noun *immirge* ('withdrawal' or 'evacuation') in a corresponding entry from the *Annals of Ulster*. While there is no specific reference in the annals to a battle resulting in the death of Gabran or the flight of the Scots, the consequences of whatever might have been the true nature and extent of Picto–Scottish hostilities in 559 were those of a decisive defeat of the king of Dalriada, as becomes evident throughout the reign of Gabran's successor, Conall mac Comgall, when the kingdom of the Irish in Britain was apparently rendered subject to the overlordship of the high-king of Picts.

The single most important event of Conall's kingship, which otherwise represented the lowest point in the first century of the kingdom of the Scots, was the arrival of Columba in Scotland and the political implication of his 'pilgrimage to Britain' coinciding with so great a decline in the fortunes of the 'Irish in Britain' cannot be overlooked. Adamnan makes specific reference to the battle of Culdrevny – the momentous defeat of Diarmait mac Cerbaill, king of Tara, and the southern Ui Neill by the Ui Neill of the north in alliance with the king of the *Connachta* ('men of Connaught') – having been fought in the shadow of Ben Bulben in Sligo two years before Columba left Ireland and the *Annals of Ulster* entry of the victory of the northern host concludes with the words 'through the prayers of Columcille they conquered'.

So it must have been that the arrival in Scotland of the holy man whose prayers had secured victory for his own line of Niall at Culdrevny represented an omen of new hope for the embattled kingdom of Dalriada. So too, while Columba's male forebears were of the *Cenél Conaill* kindred of the northern Ui Neill ('the clan of Conall', son of Niall), his father's mother is claimed by the genealogies to have been the daughter of Loarn, 'son of Erc'. What has already been said here of the 'sons of Erc' tradition must cast doubt on the genealogist's claim for his grandmother as the niece of Fergus Mor, but it is still possible that she was born of the ruling kindred of Dalriada and yet more probable that both she and, through her, Columba also were descended from the noble lineage of the Cenel Loairn. Not only, it must be remembered, was blood kinship the very foundation of the politics and society of Celtic Ireland, but the Isle of Iona was located within Cenel Loairn territory.

It was Conall mac Comgall, according to the Irish annals, 'who granted the island of Ia to Columcille', and yet Bede is in no doubt that it was Bruide, the 'most powerful king' of Picts, who 'gave him possession of the island'. This apparent contradiction of one eminently reliable source by another is best explained by Conall's having been subject to a Pictish overlord whose approval he would have needed to make the grant of Iona to Columba. The conclusive evidence for the diminished stature of Conall's kingship is found in his obituary as it is entered by Tigernach and other annalists at the year 574. These same annals had recognised each of his three predecessors as *ri Alban*, 'king of Alba', and yet they style Conall, son of Comgall and great-grandson of Fergus Mor mac Erc, *ríg Dálriada*, 'king of Dalriada'. In view of the fact that annal entries for that period applied the name Dalriada exclusively to the Irish territory of the kingdom, it is quite clear that the annalist was able to acknowledge Conall as a king in Ireland, but not as king in Alba where he was subject to a Pictish overlord.

There is also ominous evidence for the possibility of Conall having either lost or been threatened with the loss of his over-kingship of the other noble kindreds in Argyll. This is just what might be implied by an entry in the *Annals of Ulster* at 568 which refers to his fighting a campaign in *Iardoman* (an old Irish name for the Inner Hebrides) with the Irish king Colman Bec of the southern Ui Neill as his ally. Whatever might have brought a king of Meath on an expedition to the Hebrides is nowhere recorded, but if Conall had some claim on Colman's military alliance – as was often, for example, an obligation of a marriage treaty – he would have looked to him for assistance had he been no longer able to raise an adequate warband in Argyll. The entries of the same expedition in the *Annals of the Four Masters* and the annals in the *Book of Leinster* recognise Conall not as *rí*, but only as *toíseach* of Dalriada, and identify the targets of his campaign as the islands of Islay, which would indicate his enemy as having been the Cenel Oengusa, and Seil, which lay closer to Cenel Loairn territory. The Four Masters suggest Conall's expedition as a raid for plunder, but it is more probable that Conall's stature had been so greatly damaged by his submission to a Pictish overlord as to enable rival chieftains of his own people to bring his kingdom to the point of civil war. The kingdom of the Scots, evidently in grievous decay by the year 574, stood in need of a warrior king of outstanding qualities to succeed Conall mac Comgall and it was to find just such a successor in Aedan, son of Gabran.

THE SUCCESSION OF AEDAN

The fifth chapter of the third and last book of Adamnan's *Life of Columba*, that 'concerning visions of angels', is a document of the greatest significance for the kingdom of the Scots. Not only does it contain the evidence for the saint's ordination of Aedan mac Gabran into the kingship on Iona, but its foregoing account of Columba's encounter with the angel is an almost unique fusion of mystic vision with historical record in the early sources.

When the memorable man [Columba] was living on the island of Hinba,[8] one night in a trance he saw an angel of the Lord, who had been sent to him and held in his hand a glass book of the ordination of kings. The venerable man took it from the angel's hand, and at his bidding began to read it. In the book he was charged to ordain Aidan as king, but refused, because he had more love for Iogenan, Aidan's brother; but suddenly the angel stretched out his hand and struck the saint with a scourge, and its livid mark on his side endured for all the days of his life. And he added these words: 'You must know for certain that I have been sent to you by God with the glass book, that in accordance with the words you have read in it you should ordain Aidan to the kingship. But if you are unwilling to obey this command, I shall strike you again.'

And so, after this angel of the Lord had appeared for three nights in succession, holding the same glass book in his hand, and had charged him with the same bidding from the Lord concerning the ordination of that king, the saint, in obedience to the word of the Lord, sailed across to the island of Iou and there, as he had been bidden, ordained Aidan as king; for Aidan arrived there during these days. And as he spoke the words of ordination, he prophesied concerning the future of Aidan's sons, grandsons and great-grandsons; and laying his hand upon his head he ordained and blessed him.

If the implication of Adamnan's suggestion of Columba's preference for Aedan's brother as the new king is to throw some veil of suspicion over the legitimacy of Aedan's succession, there is other evidence from rather later tradition to cast a still darker shadow of doubt as to whether he was Gabran's son at all.

A story, of which the earliest surviving copy is included in the Rawlinson manuscript, tells of the Leinster king Eochaid mac Muredaig having been driven from his kingdom by his brother and taking refuge with his queen at the court of Gabran. During their stay there, Eochaid's wife, Feidelm, gave birth to twins. So too did Gabran's wife, Luan, and on the same day, but, while both of her twins were daughters, the Leinster queen became the mother of twin sons. Gabran was away on a foray at the time and Luan, being anxious to present him with a son, persuaded Feidelm to exchange one of her boys for one of the twin daughters. Soon afterwards, Eochaid was able to return to Ireland and there reclaim his kingdom, not knowing that he left a son behind in Scotland to be raised as Gabran's heir and to become the future king Aedan of Dalriada. The other son, Brandub, was to succeed his father into his kingship and, many years later, when Aedan invaded Leinster to bring its king Brandub to battle, his real mother, who was by that time a very old woman, confronted her twin sons and confessed with great weeping to the deceit practised at the time of their birth. Whereupon, of course, Aedan could only withdraw from his challenge and from his twin brother's kingdom.

For all its transparently fictional character and the absence of any corroborative evidence in the historical sources, the tale seems to have enjoyed a wide and enduring currency. It is included in the fourteenth-century *Yellow Book of Lecan*, appears to have been one of the lost tales of which only the titles are listed in the twelfth-century *Book of Leinster*, and formed the subject of an Irish poem written before 1100. None the less, the whole story must be considered entirely unhistorical, and fortunately so for the legitimacy of many centuries of Scottish royal succession, because nowhere in the earliest sources – namely Adamnan's *Life of Columba*, the *Senchus fer nAlban* and the Irish annals – is there any doubt of Aedan's having been the legitimate son of Gabran mac Domangart.[9] In fact, the tradition connecting Aedan with Leinster cannot be considered to be any older than the eleventh century and has been shown recently to have a more genuinely historical bearing on the eleventh-century king of Scots Malcolm II rather than on Aedan, in which later context it will once again bear consideration here.

There are, however, one or two incidental references contained within this otherwise fictional tradition which offer fragments of evidence, confirmed by the Welsh sources, for his association with the north Britons. The eleventh-century Irish poem mentioned above locates the place of Aedan's birth 'near the Forth' and refers to him as a sub-king 'of Forth'. Aedan's obituary is entered, as is that of his father and similarly confirming a Britonic interest in his activities, in the *Annales Cambriae*, while the genealogy of the royal houses of the north Britons – the *Bonedd Gwyr Gogledd* or the 'Descent of the Men of the North' – claims Aedan as the grandson, presumably through his mother, of the Strathclyde king *Dyfnwal Hen* ('Donald the Old'). There is one other possible reference to him in the *Book of Carmarthen* and certainly two more in *The Welsh Triads*, a body of Britonic tradition of great antiquity and no less historical interest, the first of them crediting him with one of the 'Three Faithful Warbands of the Island of Britain' and another blaming him for one of 'Three Unrestrained Ravagings of the Island of Britain'.

The evidence associating Aedan with the north Britons is substantial and casts its long shadow across much of his career, but it points first to his having followed his father's example through the years before his succession to the kingship of Dalriada. Aedan was over seventy at his death, a very great age by the standards of the sixth century, and would have been into his forties by the time he became king of Dalriada, but some reign-lengths ascribed to him by the king-lists and annals indicate his having reigned elsewhere for some five years before succeeding his cousin Conall in 574. The obvious explanation must be that he had established himself as king of some territory of the north Britons, claimed through his mother, and located in the region of the Forth. The medieval Irish *Life* of Saint Berach, which is thought to derive from a very early original, tells of Berach visiting Aedan's fortress in search of a site for his 'monastery in Alba' and of Aedan granting the fort to him for that purpose. The location of this fortress, according to the *Life*, was far outwith the borders of Dalriada at *Eperpuill*, now Aberfoyle to the west of Stirling on the upper reaches of the Forth where there have been found the remains of a hillfort and the local autumn market was traditionally known as 'Berach's Fair'.

Against that background, it might now be possible to reconstruct the historical event which Adamnan represented in terms of angelic visitation and a book of glass. Columba's obedience to divine command in his choice of Aedan for the kingship of Dalriada does bear a quite distinct resemblance to the ritual kingmaking of pre-Christian Ireland, where the druid emerged from a three-day trance to proclaim the decision of the otherworld as to who should succeed as the new king. The succession on the death of Conall was apparently due to pass from the line of Comgall to that of Gabran – of whose five sons only two, Aedan and Eogan, are named by Adamnan (who uses the Latin name-form of Iogenan) or noticed by the annalists. Of these two claimants to the kingship, Columba is said to have 'had greater love for Iogenan', whose death is entered in the annals at 597 and in the same year, curiously, as Columba's own obituary, a preference which might have amounted, in fact, to nothing more than the saint's being better acquainted with Eogan than with his brother. If Aedan had been away in the east for at least five years, and possibly much longer at a time when the custom of fostering out princes to noble or royal kindreds elsewhere was widespread, he need have had no occasion to meet with Columba before 574.

While that suggestion might be considered largely speculation, there is sufficient historical evidence to suggest a very great likelihood of challenge and contention to whichever son of Gabran had claimed the kingship. The best that a holy man, even one of Columba's personal charisma and political acumen, could do for the stability of the kingdom, having doubtlessly reached his decision through days of prayer in retreat, would be to present the new king as one chosen at the command of an awe-inspiring angelic visitation. Whatever political instinct or divine inspiration did, in fact, prompt Columba's choice of Aedan – and he cannot have been unimpressed by the return of the king's son from the east, already a king in his own right and with a formidable warband at his back – everything that is known of the history of Dalriada through the following quarter-century bears out its wisdom and foresight.

There is, however, an item of evidence from the annals to indicate the succession having been attended, on at least one occasion, by bloodshed. The *Annals of Tigernach* enter 'the battle of Delgu in Kintyre' at 574, 'in which fell Dunchad, son of Conall mac Comgall, and many others of the allies of the Cenel Gabrain'. The whereabouts of *Delgu* on Kintyre are no longer known and neither is there any indication of the identity of the enemy who slew the son of Conall mac Comgall and 'others of the allies of the Cenel Gabrain', but the absence of Aedan's name indicates the battle having been fought before his ordination into the kingship, or at least before his succession had been fully established. While its date, location and casualties initially suggest the battle as one fought between rivals for the kingship, it need not necessarily have been so. The same annal entry might be just as plausibly interpreted as indicating the ruling kindred of Dalriada in contention with a new and ambitious Ulster over-king seeking to exploit a disruption of the kingship in the aftermath of the death of Conall as an opportunity to extend his overlordship. If such was the nature of the blood-fray on Kintyre, it was fought over the same question which would be brought to resolution in the following year by a conference of kings at Druim Ceatt in Derry.

DRUIM CEATT

Two years before Aedan succeeded to the kingship of Dalriada, Baetan mac Cairell of the *Dal Fiatach* established himself as over-king of the province of Ulster. While Baetan was undeniably one of the most impressive Ulster kings of historical times, the later medieval account of his reign preserved in the fifteenth-century *Great Book of Lecan* and elsewhere was assuredly reflecting his ambition rather than his achievement when it acclaimed him as *ri Erenn ocus Alba*, 'king of Ireland and Scotland'.

What remained of the anciently mighty Ulster kingship in the wake of its devastation by the sons of Niall in the early fifth century is known to have passed on occasion to kings of the Dalaraide, but very much more often to the royal kindred of the Dal Fiatach. Into the second half of the sixth century, their own internal dynastic conflicts had brought the Cruithin peoples of the Dalaraide into decline and rendered them, in consequence, subject to the overlordship of the Dal Fiatach. So too, in the normal way of things, would the people of Dalriada in Ireland also have been subject to the Ulster over-king, had not the direction of their allegiances been complicated by the migration of their royal house to Scotland at the end of the fifth century.

The power and wealth of an over-king hung, in essence, upon the number of lesser kings who acknowledged him as their overlord and delivered to him hostages as their guarantee of submission. From those subject kings and peoples, he was able to claim *cain* and *cobach* ('taxation' and 'tribute'), and to call on them for military support, because the subject king was obliged to supply specified numbers of fighting-men when the over-king mustered his forces for a *slógad*, or 'hosting'.

Such ambitions as Baetan might have nurtured for the expansion of his dominions were drastically restricted by the ascendancy of the northern Ui Neill, by their heartlands of Derry and Donegal in the west and by the territories of their client kingdoms of the Airgialla in the south. Yet, even in the later sixth century, an Ulster over-king could still demand submission from the lands and peoples east of Lough Neagh, including those of Dalriada in Ireland and it would be his claim to overlordship of Dalriada which offered Baetan his most realistic prospect of expansion. To compel the submission of the king of Dalriada by right of that king's territory in Antrim would imply and, when any risk of conflict with the Picts had receded, eventually secure for him dominion over the territories of Dalriada in Scotland.

Seen in that context, the battle fought on Kintyre in 574 might very well represent evidence for an inaugural strike on the part of Baetan in a time of weakness of the kings of Scots. So too, the claim made by the tract in the *Great Book of Lecan* for Aedan mac Gabran having submitted to Baetan 'at *Ros na Ríg* in *Semne*' would appear too historically plausible to be discounted as mere aggrandisement, especially when it is couched in such specific terms and so much like an annal entry as to represent a genuine historical record. Aedan's submission to Baetan must have been extracted late in 574 or early in 575 – taking place, obviously, after Aedan's succession to the kingship and, inevitably for reasons which will become clear, before the events at Druim Ceatt later in the same year – and no less significant than its date is its location on the peninsula now known as Island Magee, curving out from the coast of Antrim just south of Larne, which lay just outwith the southern frontier of Dalriada.

Whatever significance Aedan attached to his acknowledgement of Baetan as overlord, which would have been made only with the greatest reluctance and all the more so if it involved the giving over of hostages, as a newly inaugurated king still consolidating his hold on a sea-divided kingdom, he would have had very little choice in the matter. What can be said of his submission to the Ulster over-king is that it would have brought to the surface all the tensions surrounding the politically anomalous situation of Irish Dalriada, and that what befell on Island Magee can be seen as the prelude to what befell not long afterwards at Druim Ceatt.

As is so often the case with the contemporary documentary record of events recognised now as having been of supreme historical importance, the evidence of the earliest sources for the conference of kings at Druim Ceatt is infuriatingly fragmentary. It is nowhere noticed in the *Annals of Tigernach* and its entry in the *Annals of Ulster* at the year 575 is thought to be a later insertion. The earliest references to it occur in the Adamnan *Life of Columba*, but while they confirm the saint's having been present at the assembly they say virtually nothing of his part in its proceedings, dealing only with his prophecies and other activities assigned to that time and place but unrelated to the substance of the assembly itself. As has been fully demonstrated by Professor Bannerman,[10] the unfortunate by-product of the saint's crucially important role in the proceedings at Druim Ceatt has been to allow their true nature to be encrusted and obscured by largely unrelated Columban tradition and yet, by happier accident, the one surviving cogent account of those proceedings has been preserved in a preface to the praise-poem attributed to the bard Dallan mac Forgall and known as the *Amra Coluimcille* ('Eulogy of Columcille').

This preface to the *Amra* is preserved in several manuscript collections, none of them older than the eleventh century, and while the text itself is older than any of its manuscripts it cannot have been set down in the form in which it now survives any earlier than the ninth century. None the less, James Kenney has suggested in his standard work on the early Irish sources that 'it may be that all our copies depend on a re-editing, perhaps in the eighth century, of an original text of the sixth'.[11] It is from this *Amra* preface then, and before any other source, that history can be said to know of the *mór dail*, or 'great convention', at Druim Ceatt, of its whereabouts, of the identities of the four principals in attendance, of the question at issue there and of the terms of its resolution.

Druim Ceatt – of which the spelling appears as variously in modern works as it does in the early sources, but which is invariably translated as 'The Ridge of Cett' – is the hill now called The Mullagh or Daisy Hill near Limavady in Derry. It was to this place, then, in the year 575 that Aedan mac Gabran came from Scotland with Columba to meet Aed mac Ainmure of the northern Ui Neill 'and to make peace between the men of Erin and of Alba concerning Dalriada'. The earliest sources apply the name Dalriada exclusively to the Irish territory and refer to the Scottish territory of Dalriada as 'Alba'. The question under consideration at Druim Ceatt, then, was the political position of Dalriada in Ireland, and clearly one in which Aedan, as its newly ordained king, was a figure of central importance, while the official reason for Columba's accompanying Aedan lay in his capacity as the king's *anmchara*, literally 'soul friend' but better translated as 'spiritual counsellor'. The other of the two kings in attendance, *Áed mac Ainmurech* (Aed, son of Ainmure), had yet to achieve the pinnacle of Ui Neill ambition in the kingship of Tara, but had already emerged since 570 as the figure of supreme power among the Ui Neill of the north and thus the great rival to the Ulster over-king, Baetan mac Cairell. Baetan, whose designs on Dalriada had brought about the assembly in the first place and whose interests were to be so very much affected by its outcome, is conspicuous by his absence from Druim Ceatt, when the only other principal named by the *Amra* preface as having taken part was Colman mac Comgellan 'of Dalriada'.

This Colman had evidently been invited to represent the people of Irish Dalriada at the conference of kings, and it is in his voice that the *Amra* preface announces the judgement at its conclusion.

> And this is the judgement that he gave: that their expedition and their hosting [of Irish Dalriada] belong to the men of Erin, because the hosting goes always with the land, but their taxation and their tribute belong to the men of Alba, otherwise their ship-service alone belongs to the men of Alba; all else, however, belongs to the men of Erin.

As is still so often the way of the political pronouncement and manifesto, the great significance of the judgement at Druim Ceatt lies in its implication rather than in its substance. The exclusion of Baetan mac Cairell from its proceedings must mean that the first purpose of the conference was to extricate Aedan and his sea-divided kingdom from subjection to the over-king of Ulster and in that objective, shared for their own reasons by all participants in the assembly, lies the significance of the judgement: that the taxes and tribute of Irish Dalriada should belong to 'the men of Alba', by which must be meant the kings of Dalriada in Scotland, thus assuring the independence of what becomes thereafter the kingdom of the Scots; that military service goes with land and thus belongs to the 'men of Erin', without specifying whether those men of Erin meant the kings of Ulster or, more probably, of the northern Ui Neill; and that *muir-coblach*, or 'ship-service' – by which is meant the military obligation of the Dalriadic war-fleet – should pertain exclusively to the king of the Scots.

In that last item of the judgement might lie the key to the true nature of the outcome of Druim Ceatt because the war-fleet of Dalriada was clearly of the greatest strategic importance to Aedan as the warrior-king of a sea-divided realm. It would have been an especial object of Baetan's ambition, when it could have availed him of a potentially decisive naval weapon in any future conflict, be it with the Picts or, more probably, with the Ui Neill. The denial of such naval power to his most dangerous enemy would, thus, have been a valuable achievement of Druim Ceatt for Aed mac Ainmure, and so too must have been his implied new role as 'lord protector' of Irish Dalriada, providing the Ui Neill with their first foothold in the east of Ulster.

The sum of what was brought about at Druim Ceatt, then, was an alliance of the Cenel Gabrain with the northern Ui Neill, and the key figure in its negotiation can have been none other than the holy man Columcille. Whether or not there is any truth in the claims of bardic tradition for his arrival there wearing a blindfold so that he should not set eyes on the land of Ireland and with Scottish turfs bound beneath his sandals so that he should not set his foot on its soil, Columba's presence at Druim Ceatt did represent his return to his native land after twelve years of exile in Alba.

The true reason for his having come there must have been one of quite extraordinary moment, because it represented an immense spiritual sacrifice in terms of its being a step back from his avowed pursuit of the white martyr-dom of exile. That reason was, without any doubt at all, a political crisis of overwhelming urgency and one which he – as counsellor and, indeed, sponsor to Aedan mac Gabran and as blood kin, in fact first cousin, to Aed mac Ainmure – was in a unique position to resolve. Columba, then, represented the key figure at Druim Ceatt as the holy man of extraordinary political acumen who had devised and put into place an alliance which was to assure not only the survival, but the first ascendancy, of the kingdom of the Scots.

'AEDAN OF THE WARRIORS'

A later account of Druim Ceatt from the fifteenth-century *Lebor Brecc* styles 'Aedan of the warriors' as 'sovereign of Alba, full of arms' and with every justice, because nowhere in the early sources is there any reference to Aedan after 575 which does not associate him in some way or other with warfare or contention. When he is next noticed by the annalist, he is engaged on the long-range sea-raid entered in the *Annals of Ulster* at the year 580:

An expedition to Orkney by Aedan mac Gabran.

The annalist, here as so often, is less than generously informative, but there is, perhaps, just enough evidence available from other sources to reconstruct something of the nature and purpose of Aedan's venture into the northern isles.

There is no specific reference to Orkney to be found anywhere in the formal historical record through the five centuries between the Roman naval expedition sent by Agricola around the northern coasts of Scotland in AD 84

[63]

and Columba's visit to Bruide mac Maelchon's fortress in the year 564, when Adamnan mentions the presence of a 'vassal-king of the Orcades' at Bruide's court. Adamnan also indicates this 'vassal-king' having given over hostages to Bruide and can thus confirm the islands of the Orkney archipelago, lying some ten miles across the Pentland Firth from the northern tip of Caithness, having been subject to the overlordship of the high-king of Picts fully fifteen years before the time of Aedan's expedition.

These peoples of Orkney, like those of Shetland and the Outer Hebrides, were descended from ancestors of the prehistoric Iron Age who raised the circular stone-built towers known now as *brochs*, an ancient architectural form unique to north Britain and most densely concentrated in the northern mainland and the northern and western isles. The name *broch* derives from the Norse *borg*, meaning 'fortress', and these towers must have represented the most formidable fortifications at the time of their construction and occupation, a period extending through the last few centuries BC to no later than the third century AD, when they would have been impregnable to any lesser force than a Roman legion.

Professor W. J. Watson's work on place names led him to 'suspect that many, if not all, of the island brochs were pirate holds' and to suggest that 'it is not unlikely that it was the depredations of the Picts of the Isles which gave rise to the legends of the Fomorians' or *Fomóire* of Irish tradition.[12] The sixth-century descendants of those proto-Pictish pirates were evidently recognised by Columba as being similarly hostile and he is said by Adamnan to have specifically requested safe conduct from Bruide for seafaring monks venturing into northern waters in search of island hermitages.

> 'Some of our community have lately sailed out in the hope of finding a desert place in the endless sea. If by chance after their long wanderings they come to the islands of the Orcades, give strict charge to this vassal-king, whose hostages are in your power, that no harm should be done to them within his borders.'

Columba is known to have been accompanied on his visit to the high-king of Picts by two other Irish abbots with island monasteries in the Hebrides. One of them was Saint Comgall of Bangor in Down and the medieval *Life of Comgall* contains an account of a Pictish raid on his monastery on Tiree which can be precisely dated to the year 564. It is unlikely to have been an isolated incident, especially in the years following the Pictish onslaught of 559, and any number of similar attacks on other Irish monastic foundations and secular settlements in the Scottish highlands and islands may have passed unrecorded. If outbreaks of sea-raiding from the Picts of the northern and western isles continued throughout the later sixth century – and there is no reason why they should not have done – then Aedan's 'expedition to Orkney' can be explained as a retaliation for any such resurgence of pirate activity. If it was so, then he was certainly not the first Irish king to have undertaken such action, on the evidence of a very old poem, ascribed to a court poet of the first century AD and preserved in the Rawlinson manuscript, telling of 'ventures on the numerous isles of the Orcs' by the semi-historical king Labraid Loingsech as early as 200 BC.

While there is no surviving record of the events, still less of the outcome, of Aedan's expedition, they would seem to have been of sufficient interest to inspire the bardic storytellers if they were, in fact, the subject of *Eachtra Áedáin mac Gabráin* ('The Expedition of Aedan, son of Gabran'), which is one of the lost tales whose titles alone are listed in the *Book of Leinster*. It is inevitable that plunder would have been the principal object of even a retaliatory expedition, but there might also have been an underlying strategic purpose to test out the response of the Pictish high-king to an attack on the periphery of the territory of which he was overlord. What can be said with full confidence of the expedition of 580 is that it supplies an impressive demonstration of the naval power of Dalriada which had been the subject of its own special provision in the judgement at Druim Ceatt.

When its territories extended from Antrim to Ardnamurchan and overland routes were always dangerous and often inaccessible, the principal thoroughfare of the kingdom of Dalriada was the sea. Its ruler was, thus and of necessity, a sea-king crucially dependent on naval capability, and his warship was the same craft which, in every essential of design, had served the maritime peoples of the west for thousands of years and is still to be found today in parts of the west of Ireland.

The oceangoing *curragh* – or more often in the early sources, *curach* – of some eleven metres or more in length, formed of oxhides stretched over a wicker frame built around a keel, and driven by oar and by sail, was a craft designed over uncounted generations for Atlantic seafaring in both peace and war. It was fast, manoeuvrable, and resilient, light enough to be carried on the shoulders of its crew, virtually unsinkable and able to make landfall running up a shingle beach and hauled ashore above the tideline in a creek or sheltered cove.

Great fleets of such craft had enabled the raiding of Roman Britain by *Picti* and *Scoti*, some number of them would have transported the noble households of Dalriada to their new territory in Argyll, and one of them assuredly brought Columba and his monks to the Isle of Iona. It is from the voyages of holy men rather than from those of warriors that history knows of the oceangoing range of the curragh, and most especially from evidence for the travels of the sixth-century Saint Brendan of Clonfert, who is more popularly remembered as 'Brendan the Navigator'. One of the texts of the *Life of Brendan* preserves the earliest account of the construction and equipment of a curragh, and there is an abundance of fully reliable evidence to show Brendan and other like-minded holy men voyaging to the Faeroes, Iceland and Greenland, if not still further out into the north Atlantic. These seafaring saints were clearly the heirs to an ancient and excellent tradition of navigation and seamanship, and so too must have been the crewmen and craftmasters of Aedan's war-fleet.

Apart from the obvious implication of references by the annalists to campaigns which can only have been accomplished by sea, there is no other record of the Dalriadic war-fleet in Aedan's time, but the survey of military obligations in the *Senchus fer nAlban* was set down within fifty years of Aedan's death and its precise details of ship-service in Dalriada cannot be so greatly changed from those of the later sixth century. They set out the requirement that every twenty households should provide the fighting crew for a *secht-sess*, or 'seven-bench' curragh, which – allowing two men to each oar and seven oars on each side – would indicate a total complement of twenty-eight men for each craft. Taking account of the numbers of households assigned by the *Senchus* to each of the three principal *cenéla*, the survey has been taken to indicate[13] Dalriada's total naval forces at some two thousand men aboard some seventy warships.

Such then is the most realistic assessment of 'the warband of Gafran's son, Aedan, who went to sea for their lord' as it is called in the Welsh Triad honouring the 'Three Faithful Warbands of the Island of Britain'. It has been suggested that the Triad is a specific reference to the Orkney expedition and it may well be so, but it might otherwise apply to Aedan's next military venture, most convincingly dated to 583 or 584 and entered by Tigernach as 'the battle of Man, in which the victor was Aedan mac Gabran'.

The true location of Aedan's victory has been the subject of some confusion, and for good reason, because the Irish name *Mano* was applied in just the same form to both the Isle of Man and to the district of Manau forming part of the Gododdin territory on the Firth of Forth. The frequent association of Aedan with the north Britons found in the early sources has led some historians to wonder whether he might have been more likely to have won his 'battle of Man' around the Forth than in the Irish Sea, but the Irish historical context and, still more conclusively, the entry of the same conflict in the *Annales Cambriae*[14] have led to the rejection of the north British option as misled. Now that the *Mano* of the sources can be recognised as having been the island of that name, Aedan's battle there shows him to have been once again in contention with the *Ulaid*.

The Isle of Man is a place of ancient significance in the earliest Irish tradition, where it is believed to have been the wave-bound stronghold from which the sea-god Manannan mac Lir ventured out to make his frequent appearances in the myths and sagas. So too the interest of the men of Ulster in this island at the centre of the Irish Sea and some forty miles off the coast of Down was already of long standing even in the last quarter of the sixth century when it attracted the interest of Baetan mac Cairell. When his plans to offset the expansion of the Ui Neill in the north of Ireland by extending his own dominion to include the Scottish territories of Dalriada were thwarted in his absence at Druim Ceatt, it would seem that Baetan redirected his attention to the annexation and occupation of Man. The evidence is at least as skeletal as that usually offered by the annalist, but two entries in the *Annals of Ulster* correspond so well to the evidence of the tract on Baetan in the *Great Book of Lecan* as to allow for only one plausible interpretation.

The entry in the annals of two Ulster expeditions to Man, the first at 577 and the second in the following year, must relate to the claim made for Baetan in the *Great Book of Lecan* that 'Man was cleared by him of *gaill* so that dominion over it belonged to the men of Ulster from that time forward'. The Irish term *gaill* translates as 'foreigners' or 'aliens' and was generally applied to the Norse and Danish invaders of the ninth century, but to whom it might have been applied at least a hundred years before the first viking longship reached Ireland is less than certain. While it would seem unlikely that Britons should be called *gaill*, they would have been the most likely occupants of Man in the sixth century. The term would much better describe the Northumbrian Angles and they are known to have taken possession of both Man and Anglesey but not until around 622, so, unless there had been an earlier and otherwise unrecorded Anglian occupation of Man, it can only have been Britons who were driven out of the island by the Ulster over-king still seeking to enlarge his dominions.

Baetan's annexation of Man was not destined long to outlast his demise entered in the annals at 581, because it was 'in the second year after his death', according to the tract from the *Great Book of Lecan*, that 'the *Goidels* [Irish] abandoned Man'. 'The second year after his death' would correspond to 583–4, when the annals enter Aedan's battle victory on Man, from which can be inferred his expulsion of the Ulstermen from the island. There is, however, no further reference to the Isle of Man in the subsequent history of Dalriada, so the motive of Aedan's campaign would seem not to have been conquest of territory. It was more probably a deployment of his war-fleet on behalf of his Ui Neill allies with the prospect of plunder as the fruit of victory for the Scots. It would seem now that the principal purpose of all Aedan's warfaring was, in fact, raiding for plunder, as is convincingly suggested by Professor Duncan's assessment of him as 'an aggressive warrior king, whose aims are more likely to have been booty and tribute than the conquest of territory'.[15] If the same interpretation will hold for Aedan's wars in Pictland, then it might better illuminate an area of his activities where the early sources are even more unhelpful than usual.

The *Prophecy of Berchan*[16] was set down in the later eleventh century and so would not at first appear to be a genuinely 'early' source for the history of five hundred years before, but it is informed by Gaelic tradition of very great antiquity preserving otherwise unrecorded fragments of valuable historical insight. Its one passage bearing on any king of Scots before the ninth century has always been recognised as an account of Aedan and does make some very dramatic claims for his activities east of the Spine of Britain.

> Alas for the Picts to whom he will go in the east,
> if they knew the one who comes upon them.
> He will not be content that an Irishman should have
> been subject to the Picts . . .
> Thirteen years, one after another, [will he make war]
> against the Pictish host.

If the poet of the *Prophecy* was not confusing the impact of Kenneth mac Alpin with that of Aedan, who is asserted by the same source as Kenneth's ancestor, then the sources in Gaelic tradition must preserve recollections of extended warfare against the Picts which have largely escaped the notice of the annalists.

Such firm evidence as the annals do provide for Aedan in contention with the Picts amounts to the notice of just one battle specifically located east of the Spine of Britain, which is entered in the *Annals of Ulster*, but in greater detail by Tigernach at around the year 597.

> The slaughter of the sons of Aedan, that is Bran & Domangart & Eochaid Find & Artur, at the battle of Chirchind where Aedan was vanquished.

Chirchind can be securely identified as the Pictish province of *Circin* in the Mearns, where the Howe of Mearns, known anciently as *Mag-Circin*, the

'Plain of Circin', has been suggested as the location of the blood-fray of 597. The entry of Aedan's defeat in the battle of Circin can be accepted as genuinely historical and having originated as a notice in the Iona chronicle, but the prefixed note of the slaughter of his sons indicates the annalist having supplemented his original source with information taken from the Adamnan *Life of Columba*. Not only does he replicate apparent errors of genealogy made in the Adamnan text,[17] but manages also to confuse evidence for two quite different hostile encounters between Aedan and the Picts.

The other of these two conflicts was fought earlier than Circin, having taken place during Columba's lifetime while Circin was fought in the year after his death, in a different region of Pictland, and – according to Adamnan's account 'Of the battle of the Miathi' – resulted not in Aedan's defeat but in his victory, albeit one won at great cost.

> The holy man was on the island of Iou when he said suddenly to his attendant Diormit, 'Ring the bell.' Summoned by its sound, the brothers ran quickly to the church, led by their holy superior himself. Kneeling down there he said to them, 'Let us now pray earnestly to the Lord for this people and for King Aidan. For at this hour they go into battle.' After a little while he left the oratory and looking into the sky, said, 'Now the barbarians are put to flight; and to Aidan has been granted victory indeed, but an unhappy victory.' Moreover, the blessed man told prophetically of the number of those killed from Aidan's army, three hundred and three men.

To which is added further detail in Adamnan's next chapter which is entitled 'A prophecy . . . concerning the sons of King Aidan'.

> At another time before the above-mentioned battle the saint asked King Aidan about the succession to the throne. When he replied that he did not know which of his three sons, Artuir, Echoid Find, or Domingart, would be king, the saint then spoke as follows: 'None of these three will be king, for they will fall in battle, slain by their enemies . . .'
>
> All these things came to pass afterwards in their own time, in complete fulfilment of his words. For Artuir and Echoid Find not long after were slain in the battle of the Miathi mentioned above. Domingart was routed in battle and killed in the land of the Saxons.

The evidence of Adamnan, being so much earlier than that of the annals, must take precedence as the more accurate record of events, and especially so in the light of another entry in the *Annals of Ulster* which refers to events of the year 599 and records with no further detail 'the slaughter of the sons of Aedan, that is Bran and Domangart'.

The annalist who compiled the entry of the battle of Circin, then, would seem to have confused and conflated the record of not two but three quite separate conflicts, of which two were fought against the Picts and the other 'in the land of the Saxons', by which must be meant the Angles of Northumbria against whom Aedan was to wage his last recorded campaign. The evident confusion on the part of the annalist – who, it must be remembered, was working eight hundred years after the events described – derives from his use of Adamnan to supplement the information provided by his usual early sources and from which it is reasonable to infer that he knew those sources to offer an incomplete record of events. Consequently, the paucity of annal evidence for Aedan's warfare with the Picts cannot preclude the possibility of his having engaged them in battle on many more occasions than those recorded and might even allow for such warfare having extended over the 'thirteen years' claimed by the Berchan 'prophecy'. To indicate anything of the possible nature of such warfare it is necessary first to re-examine such evidence as can be distilled from Adamnan and the annals.

Unlike that of his predecessor, there is nowhere in all the evidence for Aedan's reign any indication of Dalriada having been subject to a high-king of Picts. It is possible that Columba's negotiations with Bruide in 564 restored some measure of their former independence to the Scots of Dalriada and Aedan's expedition to Orkney in 580 most certainly does not imply his having been restrained by subjection to a Pictish overlord, but the crucial event bearing on Aedan's relations with the Picts must have been the death of Bruide mac Maelchon in 584. Whatever vestiges might have remained of the Scots' subjection would have effectively expired with the demise of this 'most powerful king' of Picts, which event would also have left Aedan, at least temporarily, unchallenged as the great power in the land of north Britain.

The 'battle of the Miathi' is the earliest recorded instance of Aedan at war with the Picts, because the 'barbarian' enemy called by Adamnan 'the Miathi' were assuredly the same Pictish tribe known to the Roman historian Dio Cassius as the *Maeatae*, and whose name is preserved in the hill names of Dumyat (*Dun-myat* or 'fort of the Maeatae') in the Ochils and Myothill south of Stirling. The territory of these Miathi has been located around the upper reaches of the Forth and close by Aedan's own former sub-kingdom around Aberfoyle, which proximity implies his having returned in force to his old territory, if not to impose his overlordship on his erstwhile Pictish neighbours then to demand tribute of them. Other than confirming its having been fought before Columba's death in 597, Adamnan gives no indication of the date of the battle of the Miathi, but it may well have been the same 'battle of Leithri gained by Aedan mac Gabran' which is entered by Tigernach at around the year 590. The location of *Leithri* is unknown and Tigernach gives no clue as to who was the defeated enemy, but there is no good reason to deny the possibility of it being the 'battle of the Miathi', which might thus be tentatively dated to 590.

The battle of Circin, then, would have been fought and lost by Aedan some eight years later, having probably come about in very similar circumstances, when its location lay within much the same region as the kingdom in the east once ruled by Gabran and from which the Scots had fled 'before Bruide mac Maelchon' in 559. Bruide would have been long dead by 597 when Aedan came in force to the Mearns intending to claim tribute, if not overlordship, of his father's former kingdom, but his defeat in the battle of Circin can only indicate his having failed in the attempt. The unusual occurrence of Aedan's being defeated, perhaps for the first time, would have been good reason for the entry of the battle of Circin in the original Iona chronicle, from which it came to the attention of Tigernach and the Ulster annalist.

If Aedan had launched very many similar expeditions in quest of plunder in the guise of tribute, they would have been events so unremarkable as to be unnoticed by the earliest and most closely contemporary sources unless they merited attention for some especially important aspect or association. It may thus have been that the battle of Circin was noticed by the annalist for its importance not just as an unexpected defeat for Aedan, but also as marking the end of his predatory campaigns against the Picts. If, indeed, it had been so, then those wars, which probably began following the death of Bruide in 584 and ceased in 597 after the defeat at Circin, would have spanned the same period of thirteen years claimed for them by the *Prophecy of Berchan*.

Adamnan makes no mention of Circin, which was fought in the year following Columba's death, and had the battle of the Miathi not been the subject of a remarkable prophecy by his saint, there would have been no reason for him to include any mention of it in his *Life of Columba*. Similarly, the death of at least one potential heir to Aedan's kingship in the battle of the Miathi would have been the only reason for its having attracted the attention of the original annalist – if, indeed, it was the same battle 'of Leithri' entered by Tigernach's source. So too, the 'slaughter' of his son Bran and Domangart – who was probably, like Artur, one of Aedan's grandsons – would have been noticed by the annalist for that same reason, but apparently without any need on that occasion to note either the location of the battle or the identity of the enemy and it is only from Adamnan that they are known to have been slain 'in the land of the Saxons'. From which it is reasonable to infer Bran and

Domangart as casualties of an otherwise unrecorded conflict in the war with Northumbria which was to end in the cataclysmic defeat of the Scots 'at a famous place called Degsastan'.

DEFEAT AT DEGSASTAN

Fragments of evidence among the Britonic sources show Aedan mac Gabran to have been known to the Welsh and north Britons as *Aeddan vradawc*, 'Aedan the Wily'. The origin of what can be taken to be a disparaging nickname might possibly have lain in some contention between him and *Rhydderch Hael*, or 'Riderch the Generous', king of Strathclyde, as would be implied by its use in the Welsh Triad of 'The Three Unrestrained Ravagings of the Island of Britain':

> And the third Unrestrained Ravaging – when Aedan the Wily came to the court of Riderch the Generous at *Alclud* [Dumbarton Rock] and he left neither food nor drink nor beast alive.

Riderch, son of Tutagual, was the best remembered of the kings of Strathclyde and a close contemporary of Aedan, which has led to the suggestion that the Triad might be evidence for Aedan having on some occasion attacked and plundered Riderch's capital fortress on Dumbarton Rock. Other than the possible implication of a single phrase from an old Welsh poem which refers to a 'contention of Riderch with Aedan', there is no evidence elsewhere in the sources for his having attempted such a raid and no record, in fact, of any attack on Dumbarton, other than the siege by a Picto-Northumbrian coalition which ended on peace terms in 756, until it finally fell to an alliance of Norse and Danes in 871. If Aedan had successfully assailed this most impregnable stronghold of north Britain, it would have been too remarkable a conquest to have escaped the notice of the annals, and it is more likely that the 'third Unrestrained Ravaging' described by the Triad is a reference, couched in terms of typically ironic exaggeration, to some outrageous abuse of Riderch's generous hospitality than to any real act of war by Gabran's son.

Riderch's reign of more than thirty years passes just occasionally from the shadows of obscurity into the brighter light of historical record, and one such occasion is the account in Nennius' *Historia Brittonum* of Riderch's leading an alliance of north British kings against the Angles of Northumbria. The last decades of the sixth century saw the first real expansion of the northern English and their ambitions on the territory of the north

Britons beyond the Tweed led inevitably to conflict. So it was that the advance of the northern English towards the Forth prompted the Gododdin to a pre-emptive strike which met with a savage defeat at the battle of *Catraeth*, fought near Catterick in what is now North Yorkshire, at some point in the 590s. While the battle of Catraeth is nowhere mentioned by name in the formal historical record, it is described in vivid detail as the subject of the monumental elegaic poem *The Gododdin* set down by the sixth-century Britonic bard Aneirin who claims to have been one of the very few survivors of a massacre of the north British warrior aristocracy.

It must have been this decisive blood-fray at Catraeth, with all that it implied for his own interests around the Forth, which prompted Aedan to intervene on behalf of the Britons and, consequently, brought him to his most devastating defeat in battle at the hands of Aethelfrith of Northumbria in 603. Unlike the eccentric documentary record of Catraeth, the battle of Degsastan is entered by the full range of the most trustworthy early sources, by the *Annals of Tigernach*, the *Annals of Ulster*, the *Anglo-Saxon Chronicle* and, most fully of all, in the *Historia Ecclesiastica* of Bede, for whom it serves to illustrate the ferocity of the Northumbrian warlord he describes as 'a most mighty king and most ambitious for glory . . .'

> Aethelfrith ravaged the nation of the Britons more than any other English ruler . . . No ealdorman and no king made tributary to the English, or peopled with English settlers, more territory of the Britons, after extermi-nating or subjugating the natives. These successes of his provoked Aidan, king of the Irish inhabitants of Britain, to march against him with an immense and mighty army; but he was defeated and took to flight with a few survivors, while almost his entire army was cut down at a famous place called Degsastan, meaning Degsa's stone. Also in this battle Theobald, Aethelfrith's brother, was killed with all the army that he commanded. Aethelfrith put an end to this war in the year of our Lord 603 . . . And from that time to the present day, no Irish king in Britain has dared to do battle with the English.

The entry of the battle in the *Anglo-Saxon Chronicle* is derived almost entirely from Bede, but it does add a supplementary note of its own, and of curious interest, in its statement that 'Hering, son of Hussa, led the host thither'. The Old English word *here*, for 'host', was invariably applied to an enemy warband and would thus, in this context, mean the Scots army. Yet *Hering* is an obviously English name and his father Hussa, moreover, had been an earlier Northumbrian king, but of a different royal line to

Aethelfrith. When the Old English verb *laedde* is most accurately translated as 'led' in the sense of 'guided', the *Chronicle* would seem to indicate the prince of a rival Northumbrian dynasty acting as the guide to an enemy army on campaign in unfamiliar terrain, probably in the hope of himself succeeding to the kingship of Northumbria, albeit as a client of the Scots following their defeat of Aethelfrith.

If such was the treasonable ambition of Hering, son of Hussa, it was not in the event to be realised. Aethelfrith was recognised by Bede as the most formidable warlord of the northern English and the king who brought together the Anglian territory of Deira north of the Humber with his own heartland of Bernicia north of the Tyne into the vast and massively powerful Northumbrian kingdom which was to extend even beyond the Forth in the reigns of his sons and successors, Oswald and Oswy. It was his victory over the Scots at Degsastan which finally confirmed Aethelfrith in his ascendancy, but it was a victory won at evidently great cost when his brother, and with him his entire warband, were numbered among the slain. To which the entry of the battle in the *Annals of Tigernach* is able to add its own further detail when it names the warrior who slew Aethelfrith's brother as Maelumai mac Baetan.

Maelumai's obituary is entered in the *Annals of Ulster* at 610, confirming that he survived Degsastan and identifying him as a direct descendant of Eogan, son of Niall. *Maelumai Garg*, 'Maelumai the Fierce', was thus of the northern Ui Neill and he is styled in Irish sources *ríg féinnid*, which suggests him as the leader of a *fian*. Fighting at the head of such a roving warband at Degsastan, Maelumai would have been the representative of Aedan's Ui Neill allies, and yet would seem to have been just one component of a much larger Irish contingent in the Dalriadic host. A very old Irish tale appended to the famous *Voyage of Bran* legend makes specific reference to Fiachna Lurgan, king of the Dalaraide, fighting with his *fian* as Aedan's ally 'in warfare against the Saxons' and taking the part of his champion in a battle of two armies which bears a distinct resemblance to Degsastan.

It would appear, then, that Aedan mac Gabran led a great host of Scots and Irish warriors to his war against Northumbria – and it should certainly be recognised as an extended campaign rather than a single decisive conflict. The title of a lost tale, together with a cryptic and obviously misplaced annal entry, claims an attack by the same Fiachna Lurgan on the Northumbrian capital fortress at Bamburgh which apparently escaped the notice of the surviving English sources, but Bede does refer to Degsastan as the battle which 'put an end to this war'. So too, the violent deaths of Aedan's son Bran and grandson Domangart 'in the land of the Saxons' in 598 offer evidence for

Angle and Scot having been in military contention fully five years before the blood-fray at 'Degsa's stone'.

Whatever might have been the true extent and duration of their war on Northumbria, it was brought to an end by the destruction of Aedan's forces in a defeat for which only the fourteenth-century Scottish historian, John of Fordun, is able to offer any military explanation. Fordun is accused of being wildly imaginative almost as often as his work is dismissed as fictitious, but there is good evidence for his having had access to manuscript materials for the history of Dalriada long since lost, from which he very probably derived his account of how 'the army of King Aydanus was vanquished while he was himself present'. While Fordun's claim for there having been an agreed strategic plan whereby the Scots would invade Northumbria from the north as the Britons attacked from the south is best recognised as an imaginative construction from the warfare between Northumbria and the Welsh Britons a generation after Aethelfrith and Aedan, his description of Aedan's invasion force being 'daily engaged in burning and despoiling' while Aethelfrith gathered his forces to attack and defeat the Scots 'who were dispersed through the towns and fields plundering in this way' strikes a very resonant note of credibility.

It does seem curious now that there is nowhere among the abundance of evidence supplied by the sources for this very important conflict any recognisable indication of the precise whereabouts of its field of battle. Fordun tells of Aedan having 'marched into the territory of Northumbria' and Bede says he was defeated 'at a famous place' which must have been located in north Northumbria or what are now the Scottish Borders. While 'Degsastan, meaning Degsa's stone' has long allowed the great weight of opinion to favour Dawstone in Liddesdale as the battle site, those few words are thought now to have been an addition to Bede's original. The late Dr Ian Smith has argued that 'the linguistic and strategic evidence for this association [of Degsastan with Dawstone] is no longer tenable'[18] and proposed another location for the battlefield at Addinston – a corruption of 'at Aedan's stone' – in Berwickshire. Dr Smith pointed to Addinston as not only the site of an impressive ancient burial mound but also as the junction of two ancient routeways at the head of Lauderdale offering a natural point of collision for advancing Scots and Northumbrian forces.

This eminently convincing location for the place of battle might also throw some light on the question of Aedan's doubtful reputation in Britonic tradition. If, as is thought, Aethelfrith's victory enabled the expansion of Anglian settlement beyond the Tweed, then Lauderdale and thereabouts, however threatened by Northumbrian pressure, would still have been territory of the north Britons before the battle of Degsastan. The lands torched and ravaged by Aedan's advancing host, then, would have been those of the Britons and the epithet *Aeddan vradawc* – or 'Aedan the wily' in the sense of 'the untrustworthy' – would represent fully justified disapproval of a warlord whose supposed intervention on behalf of an ally enabled his warriors to plunder that same ally's lands before coming to battle with their mutual enemy.

'AT THE TIME OF HIS DEATH, HE WILL NOT BE KING'

While Bede suggests so many men of Alba and Erin left dead on the field of Degsastan, Aedan himself was not among them. He was a very old man, already into his seventies at the time of the battle, so it is unlikely that he took any personal part in the fighting, but it is still less likely that his hold on the kingship could have long endured such a terrible defeat.

There is good evidence for the annal entries of Aedan's obituary at around 608 having placed it in the year before its true date, so he can be said to have survived Degsastan by some six years. In the course of which, it would seem, he had abdicated his kingship to enter monastic retirement and die the 'straw death' at Kilkerran on Kintyre, as, indeed, his grandfather Domangart had done before him. Fordun, who is the only source to identify Aedan's place of burial, tells of his being buried at 'Kilcheran' and he is supported in that by the *Prophecy of Berchan*.

> At the time of his death, he will not be king,
> On a Thursday, in Kintyre.

The evidence of the *Prophecy* has also been taken to point with greater accuracy than any obituary entered in the annals to the true date of Aedan's death. While its Gaelic *dia dardaoin* is most meaningfully interpreted now as 'a Thursday', the more literal translation as 'the day between two fasts' quite surely intends the Thursday before Easter known in more recent centuries as 'Maundy Thursday'. By reason of his having died in religion, the death of Aedan is entered in the *Martyrology of Tallaght*, an Irish church calendar compiled in the early tenth century, under the date of 17 April, which would have been the date of Maundy Thursday in the year 609.

By which time the kingship of Dalriada had already passed – perhaps, even as early as 606 – to his son Eochaid Buide in fulfilment of the prophecy made decades before by Columba and recorded in the Adamnan *Life*. Having foretold the early deaths in battle of Aedan's son Eochaid Find and grandsons

Artur and Domangart, Columba asks that Aedan's younger sons be brought into his presence 'and the one whom the Lord has chosen from them to be king will at once rush upon my lap . . .'

> When they were called, Eochaid Buide, in accordance with the saint's word, came and rested on his lap. At once the saint blessed and kissed him, and he said to his father, 'This is the one who will survive and reign as king after you, and his sons will reign after him.'

According to the genealogy in the *Senchus fer nAlban*, Aedan 'had seven sons: – two Eochaids, Eochaid Buide and Eochaid Find, Tuathal, Bran, Baithin, Conaing, Gartnait'. Of these seven, Adamnan can be taken to show Eochaid Find having been slain in the 'battle of the Miathi' and Bran 'in the land of the Saxons', while Baithin and Tuathal are nowhere else noticed in the sources and Conaing only by the annals at the year 622 where they enter his death by drowning at sea. For all the sparse notice of him by the sources, there is a point of further interest in the form of Conaing's name, because where the name of a son occurs in a different language to that of his father, it can sometimes offer a clue to the identity of the mother. *Conaing* would appear to be a German name-form, thus indicating his mother as of Anglo-Saxon origin and suggesting that one of Aedan's queens might have been a Northumbrian Angle.

Another of Aedan's wives is known to have been a Briton,[19] and a third – by reason of *Gartnait* being a Pictish name – was almost certainly a Pict. If the Gartnait named as a son of Aedan in the *Senchus* was the same Gartnait entered in the Pictish king-list after Bruide mac Maelchon, then it would mean that a son of Aedan had succeeded to the kingship of some territory in Pictland by reason, of course, of the Pictish custom of matrilinear succession. The Pictish king-list, on the other hand, does not identify Gartnait as Aedan's son, calling him instead 'son of Domelch', which might be reasonably interpreted as the name of his mother and, thus, of Aedan's Pictish queen.

All of which would have a most important political implication if it can be taken as evidence for Aedan having established, by right of marriage as much as by the sword, a dynastic claim to a Pictish kingdom. So too, the entry of Eochaid Buide as 'king of Picts' in the *Annals of Ulster* can be taken as further evidence for Aedan having not only reclaimed his father's earlier initiative but passed on to his own son and successor a firm foothold somewhere east of the Spine. If such was, in fact, the case then it can be taken as an index of Aedan's extraordinary achievement as the son of Gabran who succeeded to a kingdom in subjection to over-kings of Ulster and of Picts and restored to that kingdom independence in Scotland and security in Ireland. He had secured for it a crucial alliance, and on impressively equal terms, with the all-powerful northern Ui Neill and also – on the evidence of his allies at Degsastan – a second Irish alliance with the formerly hostile Cruithin of the Dalaraide. He was, without any doubt at all, a most ruthless and predatory warlord, but had he been otherwise in the same world and time his kingdom would not have survived.

The measure of Aedan's achievement is, perhaps, most succinctly confirmed by the style of his obituary as it is entered in the *Annals of Ulster*, where the son of Gabran who thirty-five years earlier had succeeded a kinsman acknowledged only as king in Irish Dalriada is himself recognised at the last as *righ Alban*, 'king of Alba'.

To which must be added the great significance of Aedan's having been so especially fortunate in the incomparable qualities of the principal churchman of his kingdom. His indebtedness to the holy man Columcille – as Aedan himself would have known Columba – was, without question, very great indeed and the covenant into which Columba entered with Aedan at the time of his ordination on Iona was the guarantee of his own ascendancy and of his legacy to the successors of his royal line. When that covenant was breached in the second generation after Aedan the royal house of the Cenel Gabrain entered upon its long decline – and 'ravens gnawed the head' of Domnall Brecc.

3

'And ravens gnawed the head of Dyfnwal Frych'

———

DOMNALL BRECC

SOME THREE AND A HALF MILES to the east of Bowmore, the 'island capital' of the Isle of Islay, there stands an impressive hillfort known now by the unlikely name of Dun Nosebridge. That modern name represents a clumsy anglicisation of an earlier Gaelic-Norse hybrid name-form conjoining the Gaelic *dún* with the Norse *knaus borg*, 'fort on the crag', or, perhaps, *hnaus borg*, 'turf fort'.

Either one of those originally Norse names would still well describe this very ancient defended site. Its citadel is indeed mounted upon a craggy ridge of metamorphic rock and its distinctive tiered profile formed by ramparts long since overgrown is now dressed overall in green to give every appearance of a fortress built of turfs. The citadel of its summit, commanding a wide view to the south and south-east over the River Laggan, is enclosed by a wall originally built of rubble and forming the shape of the letter D. While the steep cliff face of this land-locked promontory provides a natural defence for its south-eastern flank, it is defended on its north-west side by two outer ramparts, the one separated from the other below by some three metres of natural rock. The upper of these is formed of earthwork and stone with a broad, flat ditch dug out behind it, while the lower rampart is best preserved at its south-west end and reduced to a narrow terrace along its greater extent.

If Dun Nosebridge is a survival from the early Iron Age, as it would certainly appear to be, then it has represented a massive prominence on the landscape through three millennia and is justly described in the most recent published account of the island as 'Islay's most spectacular prehistoric monument'.[1] For all that, it seems never to have been selected for thorough scientific excavation in modern times and, consequently, the archaeologists have surprisingly little to say about it. The standard reference work on the archaeology of Islay is able to offer a detailed survey of its structure and dimensions, but no more substantial account of its early history than the cautious suggestion that 'medieval use of prehistoric fortifications may have occurred at Dun Nosebridge'.[2]

Such right and proper official caution does, at least, permit scope for speculation which might reasonably suggest the Norse-derived name as evidence for this 'turf fort on the crag' having been in use, very possibly as a stronghold, at some point between the first arrival of vikings on Islay around 800 AD and the mid-twelfth century when Somerled was at last able to reclaim the island from the Norse kingdom of Man. Dun Nosebridge, then, can be proposed as a major fortress of the prehistoric Iron Age which was still a centre of importance in the Norse period. In the light of which it would seem at least unlikely that it had been a place of no significance through the intervening centuries when Islay formed a part of the first kingdom of the Scots, yet there is no appearance of any recognisable form of the name 'Dun Nosebridge' in the early sources for the history of Dalriada.

It is, of course, hardly possible that there could have been, by reason of the massive impact of Norse language and culture on the place names of the Hebrides. The Scandinavian settlement following so closely in the wake of the viking raids left its most enduring legacy in the profusion of Norse-derived place names which inevitably obliterated so much of the more ancient Celtic and pre-Celtic nomenclature along the greater extent of Scotland's western seaboard. One of the most celebrated examples of that process lies across the sound from Islay on the Isle of Jura – a name deriving from the Norse *Dyr ey* or 'Deer Island' – which is believed now to have been the island known to Adamnan as *Hinba* and where he placed Columba's vision of the angel who commanded him to ordain Aedan into the kingship of Scots.

Hinba can also serve as a good example of the characteristic tendency of Irish Celtic names – and names given to people as well as places – to form summary descriptions of the physical appearance of their subject. Thus Adamnan's *Hinba* represents his Latin form of the Old Irish *Inbe*, literally 'an incision', and a name clearly describing the great cleft formed by Loch Tarbert which still very nearly cuts the Isle of Jura in half. So too, Islay is also a Norse name-form, but one which does at least preserve the old Irish name-form of *Ile*, which has been interpreted as meaning 'of the big flanks'. It is a name which would perfectly describe the prospect of Islay on approach from Ireland with the twin promontories of The Rhinns and The Oa resembling great haunches lying along either side of Loch Indaal. It might be possible to use this Celtic Irish formula of naming by description of appearance to seek out the pre-Norse name of Dun Nosebridge among the list of Islay place names from the mid-seventh century preserved in the *Senchus fer nAlban*. Of the seven settlements on Islay named by the *Senchus*, only one – that called *Oidech* and generally recognised as what is now the Oa peninsula – has been identified with any degree of certainty, but which locations might have been called by the other six names remains very largely within the realm of speculation. One of those other settlements is known to the *Senchus* as *Cladrois* and assessed by the same source at sixty *tech*, or 'households', which would have made it the second largest community on Islay at some time not long before the year 650.

It would have been likely for so comparatively large a settlement to have grown up, for obvious reasons of security, around a major defensive site and this *Cladrois* does appear to have been a place of military significance if – as A. O. Anderson's edition of the early sources suggests[3] – it was the same place as the *Calathros* identified as a battlefield by the *Annals of Tigernach* at 635 and again at 736. For two conflicts to have been fought in the same place on occasions more than a century apart would suggest that battle site as having been of a significance beyond that of the merely accidental point of collision of opposing forces. It must surely have represented a focus of strategic or symbolic significance, in all probability a fortified site, and quite possibly a capital stronghold and centre of power. Such, then, would have been the likely character of the *Calathros* of the annals and of the *Cladrois* of the *Senchus*, if they do represent two forms of the same place name recognised by Professor Bannerman[4] as a compound of *cladh*, for 'dyke' or 'ditch', and *rois*, meaning 'promontory'.

At which point I feel myself stepping on to the very thinnest ice of speculation, but I can think of nowhere on Islay which would so well fit that descriptive place name as does the land-locked promontory girded by ditch-backed ramparts and known now as Dun Nosebridge. It must be said that there has been at least one learned proposal of a quite different location for Cladrois,[5] but it is certainly less than conclusive and might still leave open at least the possibility that it was upon the ramparts of Dun Nosebridge in the year 635 that Domnall Brecc met with the first of the crushing defeats which mark out the disastrous course of his reign over the kingdom of the Scots.

'SPECKLED DONALD'

When he makes his first appearance in the historical record, Domnall, son of Eochaid and grandson of Aedan mac Gabran, has yet to succeed his father as king of Scots, but he has become embroiled in a blood-fray fought out between rival factions of the southern Ui Neill in Meath and entered in the *Annals of Tigernach* at the year 622.

> The battle of Cenn Delgthen . . . Conall mac Suibne was the victor, and Domnall Brecc with him.

While the annalist offers no explanation of what might have brought a prince of Dalriada so far from home as the midlands of Ireland and there to involve himself in a conflict arising out of internal power struggles of the southern line of Niall, it is a question which will bear some later consideration here. Of more immediate interest is the incidental evidence contained in the annal entry for what is known of this Domnall Brecc himself, and it is evidence which hinges on the naming of names.

The mighty Aedan mac Gabran, 'king of Alba', had been dead for at least thirteen years by 622, but his son and successor Eochaid Buide, of whose reign the sources have very much less to tell, still had seven years left to live. Even upon the death of Eochaid, the kingship did not pass immediately to his son Domnall, who was a figure of no great significance in 622 and yet was already known to the annalist by the nickname which provides some evidence – arguably the first such for any king of Scots – for his physical appearance.

The name-styling of *Fergus Mor*, 'Fergus the Great', is more probably a reference by the sources to the dynastic stature of the first king of Scots rather than to the physical size of the man himself. The cognomen *Buide* – 'Golden' or 'Yellow' and surely a reference to hair-colouring – which is invariably applied to Aedan's son and successor would seem less likely to have been an indication of unusual appearance than simply a means to distinguish him from his namesake brother, who is called by the sources *Eochaid Find*. *Find* is usually translated as 'White' or 'Fair', so 'Eochaid Find' might also be taken to refer to hair-colouring were there not examples of the same word used elsewhere in the Irish sources to indicate seniority in age. Eochaid Find, then, might be just as plausibly taken to mean 'Eochaid the Elder', especially when Adamnan's reference to the sons of Aedan points distinctly to Eochaid Buide as having been the younger brother.

The nickname which is applied by all the sources to Eochaid's son Domnall, by contrast, is an obvious reference to his unfortunate physical appearance, when the literal translation of the Irish *Domnall Breacc* is 'Speckled Donald'. The adjective *breac* still means 'speckled' in modern Gaelic and yet the meaning of the same Gaelic word when it occurs as a noun is 'smallpox', so the name Domnall Brecc must be most realistically trans-lated as 'Domnall the Pock-marked'.

If the name under which he makes his first appearance in the annals can be taken to confirm him as having been the victim of smallpox in his childhood or early youth and to have reached manhood disfigured by its scars, it was only the first in a series of misfortunes by which history marks out the career of this son of Eochaid Buide, because whatever else might be said of Domnall Brecc he could never be described as the luckiest of men.

Domnall's first entry in the annals might, in fact, be most remarkable as the record of the one and only occasion he found himself on the winning side in battle. Scots kings and princes were to be involved – to no apparent advan-tage and often at fatal cost – in a number of early seventh-century battles fought between contending Irish dynasties on Irish soil, and Cenn Delgthen was one such. It was rooted in a long-running power struggle between rival factions of the southern Ui Neill and it represented the victory which was to establish the ascendancy of Conall mac Suibne, who is elsewhere called *Conall Guthbind*, 'Conall of the Melodious Voice'.

What might have brought Domnall Brecc to the support of Conall Guthbind at Cenn Delgthen is nowhere explained by the sources, but the implication of the annal entry is that his involvement in the battle was rather more than that of a freelance mercenary who happened to be at large with his warband in Ireland at the time. The true nature of Domnall's alliance with the victorious Conall Guthbind might well hark back to the events of some forty years earlier when another Conall, the son of Cumgall and king of Dalriada, was able to call upon the southern Ui Neill king Colman Bec as his ally in an attack on an expedition to the Inner Hebrides. Colman Bec had, in fact, been the brother of Conall Guthbind's grandfather and the presence of Domnall Brecc in Conall's battle-host at Cenn Delgthen might well represent the rendering of a military obliga-tion owed by the royal house of Dalriada for two generations. Irish alliances leading to entanglement in Irish wars with ultimately disastrous consequences do seem to have been an especially unfortunate inclination of Dalriadic kings and princes through the first half of the seventh century, and it was one fatal casualty of such a conflict which opened the way for Domnall's succession to the kingship of Scots some seven years after Cenn Delgthen.

KINGSHIP IN CONTENTION

The principal of primogeniture, whereby the firstborn son succeeded his father in the kingship, was never the usual custom of royal succession in

Celtic Ireland, where it was more often the case for the kingship to pass first to the king's brother. The succession of a king's son would, thus, most usually await the death of his uncle whose own son would then reasonably expect to be the next in line for the kingship.

So it was that the immediate succession of Eochaid Buide as king of Dalriada on the abdication of his father Aedan represented an exception to the rule, and Columba's prophecy – set down in the Adamnan *Life* – of Eochaid as his father's successor might be recognised as an attempt to endow legitimacy on an irregular succession. It might also represent a reflection of Columba's own undoubted preference for the line of Gabran over that of his brother Comgall, because any claim by the Cenel Comgaill on the kingship was evidently and entirely overlooked when it passed to Eochaid Buide. The same claim would assuredly have been reasserted in the event of Eochaid's death, and so it was, at least on the evidence of the Dalriadic regnal list preserved in the *Chronicle of Kings*, which identifies the successor as 'Connad Cerr, Conall's son'.[6]

The entry in the king-list clearly identifies Connad as having been a son of Conall mac Comgall, following Eochaid Buide in the kingship and himself reigning for just three months. All of which corresponds well enough to the entry of Eochaid's obituary in the annals at around 629 being followed in the same year by the notice of the battle of Fid Eoin in which 'Connad Cerr, king of Dalriada, fell'. Connad's first appearance in the annals had, however, already been entered by Tigernach at 627.

> The battle of Ard Corann in which the [men of] Dalriada were the victors and in which Fiachna mac Deman fell [slain] by Connad Cerr, king of Dalriada.

Fiachna, son of Deman and nephew of Baetan mac Cairell, had seized back the over-kingship of Ulster for the Dal Fiatach in the previous year when he slew another Fiachna, the Fiachna Lurgan of the Dalaraide who had been Aedan's ally against Northumbria a quarter of a century before. Thus the battle of Ard Corann – which was certainly fought in the north of Ireland and probably in Antrim – can be recognised as an act of revenge inflicted on the Dal Fiatach by the forces of Dalriada, but on behalf of their Cruithin allies of the Dalaraide.

It would appear, then, to have been another example of the involvement of Dalriadic Scots in Irish wars, akin to Domnall Brecc's alliance with Conall Guthbind at Cenn Delgthen, were it not for the annalist's curious reference to Connad Cerr as 'king of Dalriada', when Eochaid Buide was still king of Dalriada in 627 and had two years yet to live. The apparent anomaly would be best explained by the early sources' invariable applica-tion of the name Dalriada to the Irish territory of the kingdom ruled from Scotland, indicating Connad Cerr as a sub-king over Irish Dalriada before his succession to the sovereignty of the whole kingdom on the death of Eochaid Buide.

Whether or not such was the case, Connad had become deeply and dangerously involved with the dynastic contentions of northern Ireland by the time of his succession. His slaying of Fiachna mac Deman at Ard Corann in 627 had passed back the over-kingship of Ulster from the Dal Fiatach to the Dalaraide and enabled the advancement of the two sons of Scannal of the Broad Shield, son of Fiachna Lurgan. The first of these two brothers, *Congal Cláen* (Congal of the Squint-Eye), claimed the over-kingship of Ulster and his brother Maelcaich succeeded him in the kingship of the Dalaraide, but not, it would seem, without contention, when the succession of Maelcaich was challenged by Dicuil of a rival Dalaraide sept (the *Cenél Cruithen*) – with substantial support from Connad Cerr of Dalriada – in the savage blood-fray entered in the *Annals of Tigernach* at the year 629:

The battle of Fid Eoin in which Maelcaich mac Scannal, king of the Cruithin, was the victor. Connad Cerr, king of Dalriada, fell and Dicuil mac Eochaid, king of the Cenel Cruithin, fell; and Aedan's grandsons fell, Rigullan mac Conaing, and Failbe mac Eochaid [Buide]; and Osric mac Albruit, royal prince of the Saxons, with great slaughter of his people.

The battle of Fid Eoin, undoubtedly fought in Antrim, was a contest of fac-tions within the Cruithin of Dalaraide and one in which Dalriada would seem to have had no crucial interest, yet it was to cast a dark shadow over the history of the kingdom of the Scots throughout most of what remained of the eighth century and, indeed, beyond.

The most plausible explanation of Connad Cerr's interest in the internal power struggle of the Cruithin is that it derived from some form of alliance whereby the Dalaraide acted as protectors of Irish Dalriada, but whatever might have been his reason for fighting on what was to be the losing side he evidently joined the battle with all the forces available to him. The list of the slain entered in the annals can be taken to indicate each of them having fallen at the head of his own warband, so the two grandsons of Aedan would have led contingents of the Cenel Gabrain under the overall command of Connad leading his own muster of the Cenel Comgaill. Together their forces would have made up the war-host of Dalriada and, when the chieftain defended by his warriors was usually one of the last to fall in battle, the blood-fray at Fid Eoin must have been fought at the most terrible cost in casualties.

The most unexpected name found in the annal's list of the fallen must be that of *Osric mac Albruit* and the presence of a 'royal prince of the Saxons' with his warband among the Dalriadic host at Fid Eoin needs to be explained against the background of Northumbrian history since the battle of Degsastan more than a quarter of a century before. The Northumbrian king Aethelfrith who had inflicted that devastating defeat on Aedan mac Gabran was himself slain in battle in 616, when the kingship of Northumbria passed to a rival dynasty. Following the death of their father, the seven sons of Aethelfrith fled into exile – according to Bede – 'among the Scots and the Picts'. Aethelfrith's eldest son, Eanfrith, found his way into Pictland, where he married a Pictish princess and thus became the father of Talorcan, king of Picts, while his six half-brothers, Aethelfrith's sons by his second queen, apparently took refuge among the Scots of Dalriada. While Bede has the fullest account of Oswald and Oswy, who returned from exile to reclaim their father's kingdom – and will yet have their own part to play in the history of the kingdom of the Scots – he has nothing to say of the other four. Their names, however, are known from other Northumbrian sources and they all shared the initial 'O', so it would seem almost certain that one of them must have been the slain 'royal prince of the Saxons', whose name has been distorted almost beyond recognition by the annalist.[7] The most important casualty of the battle was, of course, Connad Cerr himself, whose death left the kingship of Dalriada vacant once again and with the choice of successors still further reduced by the slaughter at Fid Eoin. The succession should now have legitimately passed back to the Cenel Gabrain and so it did – in the person of Domnall Brecc, son of Eochaid Buide, son of Aedan, son of Gabran – but not, it would seem, without challenge from the Cenel Comgaill.

Domnall succeeded Connad Cerr, if not in 629 then certainly by the following year, but does not appear again in the annals for his reign until the entry of 'a battle in Calathros, in which Domnall Brecc was vanquished'. The evidence of the annalist is here at its most unhelpful, not only failing to identify Domnall's enemy at Calathros but misplacing its entry of the battle at 679, fully thirty-seven years after Domnall's death. The flawed annal record has been attributed to a loss of interest in Scottish affairs of the period by one of the annalists' earlier sources, so it is fortunate that the eminent scholarship of A. O. Anderson[8] has been able to restore the battle of Calathros to its more historically realistic date of around the year 635 and to infer from that date the most convincing proposal of the true nature of events.

The evidence of the king-lists shows Domnall Brecc having been forced to concede some portion of his kingship around the year 636 and to reign jointly thereafter with Ferchar, son of Connad Cerr, of the Cenel Comgaill. Such a concession of overlordship between kindreds would have been almost inevitably attended by bloodshed, so the entry of Ferchar into the king-list little more than a year after the battle of Calathros must suggest the defeat of Domnall Brecc having led to the division of the kingship. However accurate might have been my speculative location of 'in Calathros' around the hillfort of Dun Nosebridge, the battle was assuredly fought somewhere on Islay. It would thus be reasonable to suggest the conflict arising out of disputed overlordship of the Cenel Oengusa – by reason of Islay being the territory of the Cenel Oengusa – which would have consequently passed from Domnall's Cenel Gabrain to the victorious Cenel Comgaill.

Loss of any portion of his dominions deprived a king of its taxation and tribute, but meant also the loss of its fighting strength to his hosting, and Domnall's battle-host would have thus been deprived of the six hundred warriors entered in the *Senchus* as the military obligation of the Cenel Oengusa. The fighting strength of the Cenel Comgaill on Cowal would, presumably, have also been lost to him, thus slicing the strength of his available war-host by at least a third, and a king finding himself in such reduced military circumstances would need to seek out a new and powerful ally. Domnall, under threat from rival kindreds within Dalriada if not yet from the Picts east of the Spine, would need to look no further afield than Ulster to find such an ally in the Congal once called *Cláen* and now called *Cáech*, 'the half-blind'.

Congal, son of Scannal and grandson of Fiachna Lurgan, was a formidable power in the north of Ireland and, as Domnall's sister's son, was already close kin to the Cenel Gabrain. He was, none the less, to prove himself the most dangerous of allies, a man consumed by the fierce ambitions and bitter enmities which were to lead him, and Domnall Brecc with him, to disaster south-east of Lough Neagh on the battlefield of Mag Rath.

'MAG RATH OF THE RED POOLS'

The blood-fray fought out in 637 at the place anciently called *Mag Rath* and known now as Moira on the Lurgan-to-Belfast road has been long recognised by historians as the most disastrous of all the reverses suffered by the kingdom of Dalriada in the reign of Domnall Brecc – and yet the Scots' involvement passes entirely unnoticed by the entry of the battle in the *Annals of Tigernach*:

> The battle of Mag Rath won by Domnall mac Aed and by the sons of Aed Slaine – Domnall reigned at Tara[9] at that time – and in it fell Congal Caech, king of Ulster, and Faelchu, with many nobles; and in it fell Suibne, son of Colman Cuar.

The account of the battle set down by Tigernach – or, more properly, by the author of Tigernach's original source – is by far the most detailed found in any Irish annal. It clearly identifies the victors as an Ui Neill alliance, led by Domnall mac Aed of the Cenel Conaill supported by the 'sons of Aed Slaine' of the southern line of Niall, and its casualty list naming Congal Caech, his son Faelchu and Suibne, king of the Dalaraide, among the fallen indicates the vanquished forces as the Cruithin of Ulster.

The annalist quite properly recognises the great importance of the conflict in its Irish context where it represents the finally decisive confrontation of the Ui Neill with the Ulster kings, but his omission, for whatever reason, of any reference to Domnall Brecc and the men of Alba means that the significance of the battle for the kingdom of the Scots must be sought out elsewhere among the sources, because it is Irish tradition which most vividly remembers 'Mag Rath of the Red Pools' for the ferocity of its slaughter.

The principal sources of the traditional evidence for Mag Rath are two linked 'historical tales', *Fleadh Duin na nGedh* ('The Banquet of Dun na nGedh') and *Cath Muighe Rath* ('The Battle of Mag Rath'), both of them preserved in the fourteenth-century *Yellow Book of Lecan* and neither of them set down, at least in the form in which they survive now, before the eleventh century. While there is some reason to think *The Banquet of Dun na nGedh* to be elder of the two, there is also good intrinsic evidence to indicate *The Battle of Mag Rath* – of which two different versions are found in the *Yellow Book* – draws upon lost sources of much greater antiquity.

Effectively an explanatory prelude to the story of the battle itself, *The Banquet of Dun na nGedh* is a substantially fictional account of the source of antagonism between Domnall mac Aed and his foster-son Congal Caech. It begins with an ominous dream in which Domnall is warned of his favourite greyhound whelp gathering 'the dogs of Erin, Alba, Saxonland and Britain' to 'give the king and the men of Erin seven battles during the seven days of the week'. The story continues with an account of the high-king's preparation of a lavish banquet for all the lesser kings of Ireland, including among its bill of fare a clutch of goose eggs procured out of season as an especially rare delicacy. The eggs were actually purloined from Bishop Erc of Slane, who takes his revenge by placing a curse on the banquet and to lift the curse from his feast Domnall calls upon the twelve Apostles of Ireland to bless the eggs. So indeed they do, but not before his foster-son Congal has secretly sampled just half of one goose egg, thus bringing down the bishop's curse upon himself alone. When the eggs are placed on silver dishes and set before the assembled company of kings, Congal's goose egg is magically transformed into a red-feathered hen's egg with its silver dish reduced to a wooden plate, and thinking this a personal insult directed at him by the high-king, he explodes into a fury.

Giving voice to long-nurtured grievances against his foster-father, Congal blames Domnall for leaving him unattended in a garden as a child when he was attacked by bees 'and one of them put its venom into one of my eyes, so that my eye became awry, from which I have been named Congal Claen'. He claims that Domnall's reason for adopting him as a foster-son was to secure the alliance of the Ulster kings against his own Ui Neill rivals of the Cenel Eogain[10] and years later, after Congal had grown to manhood, Domnall had promised him the restoration of his patrimony were he to destroy Suibne Menn of the Cenel Eogain who at that time held the kingship of Tara.

> 'I went on the enterprise, O king, for the promise that my patrimony should be wholly restored to me . . . The king came out surrounded by a great concourse of the men of Erin, and he was playing chess amidst the hosts. And I came into the assembly, and made a thrust of my spear at the breast of the king and his heart's blood was on the head of the spear, so that he fell dead. But as the king was tasting death, he flung a chessman which was in his hand at me, so that he broke the crooked eye in my head. I was squint-eyed [*Cláen*] before, I have been blind-eyed [*Cáech*] since.'

Having slain the king of Tara to enable Domnall to achieve that pinnacle of Ui Neill ambition in his place, and in so doing sacrificed the sight of an eye, Congal is still denied the promised restoration of the vast dominions which had anciently lain under the kingship of Ulster, so to have set before him a common hen's egg on a wooden platter in place of that of a goose on a silver dish was for Congal the last unsufferable insult: 'And I will give battle to thee and the men of Erin in consequence . . .'

Congal Caech rushes from Dun na nGedh in his fury, and the men of Ulster with him, to go in search of allies for his war on the high-king. He goes first to his mother's father, Eochaid Buide, who will not himself aid any war against the Ui Neill, but sends in his place four sons, including among them Domnall Brecc, 'who have the command of the warriors and heroes of Alba, and they shall go with thee to give battle to Domnall [mac Aed]'. He goes next to his mother's grandfather 'the king of Britain, Eochaid Aingces', who similarly provides warriors under the command of his son 'Conan Rod' for Congal's cause . . .

> After this Congal assembled the forces of Saxonland, with their king Garb, son of Rogarb, and the forces of Britain under Conan Rod . . . and the men of Alba under the four sons of Eochaid Buide, namely Aed of the Green Dress, Congal Menn, Suibne, and the eldest Domnall Brecc. And he brought all these forces with him and gave battle to Domnall and the men of Erin around him on Mag Rath where there was a slaughter of heads between them, and where Congal Caech was slain.

Thus, with the prophetic dream of the greyhound whelp bringing the dogs of Erin, Alba, Saxonland and Britain to make war on the king and men of Erin fulfilled, concludes the tale of *The Banquet of Dun na nGedh*.

The story is clearly shot through with obvious anachronism and mythic allusion. Saint Erc of Slane, for example, was a contemporary of Saint Patrick and had been dead for a century and a quarter before the battle of Mag Rath was fought. So too, had every one of the twelve saints honoured as the 'Apostles of Ireland' been dead for decades before Domnall mac Aed became king of Tara. The dream of the greyhound whelp recalls the very many canine episodes found in the cycles of Irish myth and saga, just as Congal's sudden fury is a distinct echo of the battle-rage of Cuchulainn, and the banquet itself is a device occuring on more than one occasion in the historical traditions of both Ireland and Scotland.

None the less, there is a closely corresponding account of Congal's eye being injured by bees found in an Irish legal tract of the eighth century and the annals confirm that he did indeed kill Suibne Menn of the Cenel Eogain on the shore of Lough Swilly beneath the Grianan of Ailech in 628, thus opening the succession to the kingship of Tara for his foster-father Domnall. The same legal tract claims Congal himself reigned for a time as king of Tara until disqualified from the kingship by his injured eye,[11] a claim of admittedly doubtful historicality but one which nevertheless prompted the inclusion of his name in an early Tara king-list. It is, in fact, almost unimaginable that any claimant of other than Ui Neill lineage could have been recognised as king of Tara as early as the seventh century, but it is just possible that Domnall mac

Aed might have promised, or even been believed to have promised, his Cruithin foster-son that he would be his successor in the kingship. Any such promise of succession would have been automatically invalidated by the blinding of Congal's eye, which inevitability might well have given rise to the antagonism between the two which had arisen very soon after Domnall became high-king and had already come to battle at the hillfort of Dun Cethirn (now the Giant's Sconce, near Coleraine) eight years before Mag Rath on the evidence of the *Annals of Tigernach* at the year 629:

> The battle of Dun Cethirn, in which Congal Caech fled and Domnall mac Aed was the victor:
> > 'The battle of Dun Cethirn
> > which had red blood over grey eyes,
> > On the track of Congal the Bent
> > were thick-necked, handsome bodies.'

The battles of Dun Cethirn and Fid Eoin are both entered in the annals at the same year as the obituary of Eochaid Buide, but the precise sequence of the three events is left uncertain by the annalist. Eochaid is known to have died and been succeeded by Connad Cerr some three months before Fid Eoin, but he might for all that have still been alive at the time of Dun Cethirn. There can, of course, be no doubt of Eochaid having been long dead by the time of Mag Rath, thus making it impossible for him to have been responsible for sending his sons to fight there as the allies of Congal Caech, and neither did Eochaid have any sons, other than Domnall, bearing the names given them in *The Banquet of Dun na nGedh*.

There is, for all that, reliable historical evidence for sons of Eochaid Buide and other Dalriadic princes having taken part in more than one Irish battle of the early seventh century, the substance of which would have been known to the storyteller even if his ignorance of their names forced him to invent some of his own. The same must also be true of Congal's Saxon ally 'Garb, son of Rogarb', a name translating as 'Rough, son of Very Rough' and attached to a transparently fictional personality, but one assuredly inspired by those Northumbrian princes who are known from other sources to have fought in Ireland at around that time.

Neither was there any historical king of Britons called 'Eochaid Aingces', so his son called by the common Britonic name of 'Conan Rod' is to be discounted as another invented character, but one quite probably based on a genuinely historical model. Professor Alfred Smyth[12] has made out a most convincing case for north British warbands driven out of Cumbria by the

Northumbrian conquest finding their way to Ireland where they appear in the Irish sources engaged as mercenaries in the early 680s, and there is no good reason why earlier waves of north Britons – perhaps of the Gododdin from the Forth, who had been the first victims of Anglian expansion – should not have followed the same course to become allies of the Ulster king at Mag Rath. Such potential allies would together plausibly represent 'the dogs of Erin, Alba, Saxonland and Britain' and suggest a good measure of historical foundation for the substance of Congal's alliance as it is given in *The Banquet of Dun na nGedh*. The same cannot be said for more than one of the personal names given them by the storyteller, but the very fact of that being so must attach greater significance to the one ally of Congal Caech named in the story and also identifiable as a genuinely historical personality being Domnall Brecc, Eochaid's son.

The second of the stories from the *Yellow Book of Lecan* is of a quite different character to the first. *The Battle of Mag Rath* is evidently intended as propaganda on behalf of the Ui Neill – very much as the *Cogadh Gaedhel re Gallaibh*, a history of the wars of the Irish with their Scandinavian invaders written around the same time, is a propagandist epic for Brian Boru's Munster dynasty of Cashel. Despite its insistent focus on individual heroic combats and such absurd anachronisms as the addition of Frankish and Norse warbands to Congal's alliance, it does preserve material from more ancient sources in its account of the conflict at the place it calls 'Mag Rath of the Red Pools where they remained for six full days of the week striking and wounding during which their wounds were equal . . . until the Tuesday on which Congal Claen, the son of Scannal of the Broad Shield, was slain'.

Whenever the claims of history and tradition are at odds, *The Battle of Mag Rath* invariably sides with tradition, as it does, for example, in its account of the fate of the Cruithin king Suibne, son of Colman Cuar. The annals confidently record Suibne being killed in battle at Mag Rath and the annalist must always take precedence as an historical source, but the folk tradition of *Suibne Gelt* ('Wild Suibne') claims he fled in panic from the field, driven insane by the slaughter to live out his days as a wild man in the trees – and it is that version of events which is preferred by the authors of both *The Banquet of Dun na nGedh* and *The Battle of Mag Rath*. The death of Congal Caech in the battle entered in the annals is never disputed by the storyteller, but neither does he offer any specific account of it, referring instead to Congal's 'disappearance' and going into greatest detail when he describes the Munster champion Maelduin slicing off Congal's sword-hand in single combat.

There is no conflict of history with tradition regarding the fate of Domnall Brecc, because there is nowhere any suggestion of his having been killed at Mag Rath and, indeed, there is reasonable doubt as to whether he was there at all. The earlier version of *The Battle of Mag Rath* story in the *Yellow Book of Lecan* implies that he sent the men of Alba to fight for Congal Caech but did not himself go with them. The second version of the story, however, does include Domnall Brecc among the princes of Alba who fought in the battle. It tells of each son of Eochaid Buide engaging in single combat with a son of the high-king, excepting Domnall Brecc who is confronted by two sons of Domnall mac Aed and, being thus outnumbered, surrenders himself as a prisoner of the victorious Ui Neill. If Domnall Brecc did take a personal part in the conflict, then his capture and subsequent release after ransom probably offer the most plausible explanation of how he was able to survive a conflict from which, at least according to the stories, only one of the men of Alba escaped the field alive. If Domnall Brecc was not himself present at the battle – and it is certainly possible that he was not – he is still nowhere absolved from responsibility for the involvement of the Scots in the battle itself and in what would seem to have been the more extensive warfare surrounding it.

The entry in the *Annals of Ulster* at 637 states 'the battle of Mag Rath and the battle of Sailtire were fought on the same day', and a separate entry by Tigernach at the same year confirms the same battle of Sailtire to have been a defeat inflicted upon the rival Cenel Eogain by Domnall mac Aed's nephew Conall Cael. *Sailtire* can be safely identified – from its occurrence in *Magnus Bareleg's Saga* – as one of the ancient names for Kintyre, which would most probably suggest a battle between two Irish factions having been fought at sea in the waters off the Mull of Kintyre. This 'battle of Sailtire' has been realistically interpreted as the outcome of an attack on the coast of Cenel Conaill territory in Donegal or Derry made by the Cenel Eogain with the Dalriadic war-fleet and in support of Congal Caech. The attackers having withdrawn towards Kintyre, they would appear to have been pursued and defeated at sea by Conall Cael with the fleet of the Cenel Conaill on the same day as Domnall mac Aed and his allies won their momentous victory on the field of Mag Rath.

The last item of evidence from the sources for Domnall Brecc and Mag Rath is the most ancient of all, having been set down within living memory of the battle, and thus also represents the most decisive confirmation of Domnall's involvement in the war. It is a passage interpolated into the oldest manuscript of Adamnan's *Life of Columba*, by reason of its testimony for Domnall Brecc's breach of the covenant formed between his grandfather and

Columba and the dark shadow cast in consequence over the royal house of Dalriada.

> Cummene the White, in a book that he wrote about Saint Columba's miraculous powers, said that Saint Columba began to prophesy concerning Aidan and his posterity and their kingdom, saying, 'Believe without doubt, Aidan, that none of your enemies will be able to resist you, until first you act deceitfully against me and my posterity. On that account, therefore, give this charge to your sons, that they themselves charge their sons and grandsons and their posterity not to lose from their hands the sceptre of this kingdom through their wicked counsels. For at whatever time they do wrong to me or to my kinsmen in Ireland, the scourge that I have suffered because of you at the hand of an angel will be turned by the hand of God upon them, to their great disgrace; and their men will lose heart, and their enemies will be mightily strengthened against them.'
>
> Now this prophecy has been fulfilled in our own times in the battle of Roth [Mag Rath], when Domnall Brecc, Aidan's grandson, laid waste without cause the province of Domnall [mac Aed], Ainmure's grandson. And from that day to this they have continued in subjection to foreigners, which moves my heart to sighs of sorrow.

THE CURSE OF COLUMCILLE

The first *Life* of Columba[13] has been long since lost but is known to have been set down by *Cumméne Find*, the seventh abbot of Iona whom Adamnan called by the Latin name-form of *Cummene Albus* or 'Cummene the White'. Cummene, who was of Columba's own kindred, succeeded to the abbacy in 657 and continued in office until his death in 669, although he may have spent some of his later years in retirement on Rathlin Island. There is, however, no reason to assume his having been abbot at the time of writing his 'book about Saint Columba's miraculous powers', which must have been completed by 669 but might, in fact, have been written at any time in the preceding three decades. Cummene's uncle Segene, who had been abbot of Iona from 623 to 652, is believed to have collected together recollections of its founding saint while still within the living memory of the monastic community. These first-hand accounts assuredly provided Cummene with the source material for the book on which he may well have already been at work during or soon after Segene's abbacy.

This Cummene *Life* was evidently available to Adamnan and must have served him as the principal documentary source for his own *Vita Columbae*, on the evidence of its only surviving passage being preserved as an insertion into the earliest manuscript of Adamnan's book. That passage, which must have been composed within thirty years of the battle, represents the one closely contemporary source for Domnall Brecc and Mag Rath, so the evidence contained in its two paragraphs can be recognised as being of pre-eminent authority and manifold significance.

Its reference to the battle of Mag Rath certainly implies involvement of Dalriadic forces on the losing side, and yet Domnall Brecc himself is only accused specifically of having 'laid waste without cause the province of Domnall' (mac Aed). 'The province of Domnall' means the Cenel Conaill heartland in Donegal, which lies at so great a distance from the battlefield of Mag Rath at the southern extremity of Antrim as to suggest that Cummene was holding Domnall Brecc responsible for the attack by the Dalriadic warfleet which was repulsed at the battle of Sailtire. It is clear, however, from the context of his remarks that Cummene's principal concern centred on Domnall's breach of the covenant with Columba entered into by his grandfather Aedan mac Gabran at the time of his succession to the kingship more than fifty years earlier.

Domnall Brecc's alliance against Domnall mac Aed and his attack on the territory of the Cenel Conaill would have been recognised by Cummene as offering two-fold offence to the saint. Domnall was, of course, the son of Columba's cousin Aed mac Ainmuie, who had played so important a part in the conference of kings at Druim Ceatt, and Adamnan tells how the future king of Tara had been brought as a child for Columba's blessing 'on the Ridge of Cete . . .'

> The saint blessed him, and at once said, 'He will outlive all his brothers, and become a most famous king. And he will never be delivered into the hands of his enemies, but will die a peaceful death in old age . . .'

Domnall Brecc, then, had not only made war on a king who had enjoyed the personal blessing of Columba, but also on his people who were the saint's own 'kinsmen in Ireland' and in so doing had broken faith with the covenant upon which was founded the ascendancy of his dynasty, who would, in consequence, 'lose from their hands the sceptre of this kingdom'.

Cummene's grim confirmation that 'this prophecy has been fulfilled in our times in the battle of Roth' has been variously interpreted by historians. If the prophecy is understood to apply exclusively to the descendants of

Aedan, then Cummene may well have been referring to Domnall's successors being of other lines of descent, as indeed they were during Cummene's
lifetime. Domnall himself was already sharing the kingship with Ferchar of
the Cenel Comgaill by 637 and, while his son was eventually to reclaim the
kingship for the Cenel Gabrain, Domangart mac Domnall was not to
succeed his father until four years after Cummene's death. The passing of
the succession from Aedan's line would have been recognised by Cummene
as a part of the prophecy fulfilled, but the loss of 'the sceptre of this
kingdom' is more probably a reference to the kings of Dalriada having forfeited their territories in Ireland[14] by their alliance with the enemies of
Columba's royal kindred.

It must be said, despite Cummene's claim to the contrary, that Domnall
did not necessarily act entirely without reason. There would seem to have
been some form of military obligation between Dalriada and the Dalaraide
since at least the time of Degsastan and it may well have reflected a co-operative arrangement bearing on the neighbouring location of their Irish territories. If he had felt the need of a new alliance after his defeat at Calathros,
Domnall would have found a natural ally in Congal Caech who was his
sister's son and, thus, bound to him in alliance, if not under the terms of a
marriage treaty then certainly under the obligation of blood-kinship. 'The
sons of Aed Slaine', on the other hand, who were Domnall mac Aed's principal supporters in the southern line of Niall, were also old enemies of
Domnall Brecc, being of the same southern Ui Neill faction against whom
he had fought as an ally of Conall Guthbind at Cenn Delgthen some fifteen
years before, and in 636 – just the year before Mag Rath – Conall himself
had been killed by one of these sons of Aed Slaine. However reasonable his
motives, Domnall's involvement with Congal Caech proved to have been, in
the event, ill-advised and, in its aftermath, little short of disastrous. He had
effectively thrown into reverse the alliance of the Cenel Gabrain with the
Cenel Conaill which had underwritten the ascendancy of Dalriada for
more than half a century and, as a direct result, lost to his successor kings
of Dalriada their most ancient Irish heartland with its taxes and its tributes.

Perhaps most ominous of all for Domnall himself, and especially when the
testimony of Cummene is read in the spirit of his own time, is its implication
of the king having brought down upon himself the malediction of the saint
he had so grievously offended. Cummene's sorrowful interpretation of
events can be taken to reflect a widely held recognition of Domnall Brecc as
suffering the curse of Columcille and for such a belief to have entered
popular currency would have irreparably damaged whatever remained of

Domnall's hold on the kingship and seriously threatened his ability to raise a warband when the need arose. It is certainly possible to imagine such a difficulty bearing upon the situation in the year following Mag Rath when Domnall Brecc's name next occurs in the *Annals of Tigernach*:

> The battle of Glen Mairison in which the people of Domnall Brecc were put to flight.

The same event is also recorded by the *Annals of Ulster* at the year 638 where it is entered without Tigernach's supplementary detail and as simply 'the battle of Glen Mureson'. Neither of those annal entries offers any identification of the enemy who put to flight 'the people of Domnall Brecc', still less any explanation of the cause of the battle, but each of them does provide just one clue in its form of the place name *Glen Mairison* or *Glen Mureson*, which is most convincingly located by A. O. Anderson[15] in the Glen Morriston to the west of Loch Ness.

This Glen Morriston lies to the east of the Spine of Britain and, in terms of the political geography of seventh-century Scotland, fully thirty miles within the frontiers of Pictland, leaving the very least doubt of the victorious enemy having been Picts. There is also such a distinct similarity between the form of Tigernach's entry at 638 and that earlier 'flight of the men of Alba' entered in the annals with the death of Gabran at the year 558, as to indicate the cause of the battle of Glen Mureson having been another expulsion of Scots overlords from Pictish lands. The extension of Dalriadic kingship to Pictish territory east of the Spine had already begun in the reign of Gabran and been well enough established by the second half of the sixth century to attract the hostile attentions of Bruide mac Maelchon. Gabran's initiative having fallen victim to Bruide's ascendancy, the expansion into Pictland was renewed by Gabran's son Aedan and, despite his defeat by the Picts at Circin, sustained in the time of his sons. The likelihood of Aedan's Pictish queen having borne him two sons thus endowed with claims on Pictish kingship would explain both the entry of Gartnait mac Aedan in the Pictish king-list and the obituary of Eochaid Buide in the *Annals of Ulster* which called him *rex Pictorum*, 'king of Picts'.

Almost nothing is known of Eochaid's queens, unless the late reference in *The Banquet of Dun na nGedh* to one of them having been a Briton has any genuine authority, but there is no reason why his son Domnall Brecc should not have inherited some claim on kingship east of the Spine by right of his mother or, perhaps more probably, his grandmother having been a Pictish princess. If Domnall's claim pertained to a more northerly district of

[97]

Pictland than those of any of his forebears, then it would well correspond to the location of Glen Mureson north of the Grampians – the range anciently known as 'the Mounth' from the Irish *Monaidh* or the Gaelic *Monadliath*, 'the Grey Mountains' – which represented the natural frontier between the Picts of the north and those of the south. Such a genuinely historical association of Domnall Brecc with Pictland north of the Mounth might very well be reflected in the reference to his generosity made in *The Banquet of Dun na nGedh* claiming 'though Sliabh [Hill of] Monaidh were of gold, he would lavish it as gifts all at one time'.

The battle of Glen Mureson signalled a resurgence of hostilities between Pict and Scot which was to continue in the conflicts entered in the annals at 649 and 654. Of still greater significance is the sudden absence from the sources of any references to rule by kings of Dalriada in Pictland after 639. The 'flight of the people of Domnall Brecc' had called a halt to almost a century of Dalriadic expansion east of the Spine and no king of Scots would be able to claim kingship of the Picts for two centuries thereafter. Whether or not Domnall might be thought now to have incurred the curse of Columcille, he had achieved – in the words of Professor Bannerman – 'the loss of almost all the gains made by his predecessors in terms of territory, power and prestige'.[16] As he entered upon the second decade of his disastrous reign, it would seem that Domnall Brecc had only one thing left to lose.

DEATH AT STRATHCARRON

The last notice of Domnall Brecc in the annals is placed most reliably by the *Annals of Ulster* at the year 642, but entered in greatest detail by the *Annals of Tigernach*:

> Domnall Brecc was slain in the battle of Strathcarron, at the end of the year, in December, by Owen, king of the Britons.

Strathcarron – or *sraith Caruin* in the annalist's Irish form – is the valley of the river Carron which enters the Forth north of Falkirk, and the site of the battle may very well have been around the modern town of Falkirk. The name Owen is given in the Irish forms of *Hoan* in the *Annals of Ulster* and *Ohan* in Tigernach, but would have been *Eugein* in Old Welsh and identifies the 'king of Britons' who slew Domnall as the Strathclyde king Owen, son of Beli, whose name appears as *Eugein map Beli* in the Welsh sources.

In the light of his singularly unfortunate way of the warrior, it was only to be expected that Domnall Brecc should have met his death in battle. More surprising, perhaps, is the location of the battle, when Domnall had no earlier association with the region of the Forth, and the identity of the enemy, when there had never before been hostile contact of the Scots of Dalriada with the Britons of Strathclyde. I have long suspected that one explanation might resolve both of those apparent enigmas, and it lies south of the Forth in the orbit of the seventh-century ascendancy of Northumbria.

The evidence of the early sources for relations between the Scots of Dalriada and the Angles of Northumbria through the greater extent of the seventh century is at best uneven, but the one conclusion that can be drawn from it is that such relations veered in widely different directions in the course of the eight decades between the battles of Degsastan in 603 and Nechtansmere in 685. The defeat of Aedan mac Gabran by Aethelfrith of Northumbria at Degsastan can be seen now to mark the beginning of the Northumbrian ascendancy and the end of Aedan's way of the warrior. It must have been recognised at the time, as it was recalled by Bede more than a century later, as the focus of greatest hostility between Scot and Angle, and yet, when Aethelfrith was killed in another battle with another enemy thirteen years after Degsastan, his sons were able to find refuge in exile with the Scots and Picts.

Relations between the two peoples had evidently greatly improved when the sons and daughter of Aethelfrith arrived at the court of Aedan's son Eochaid Buide. The reason was probably the recognition by the Celtic peoples of north Britain of Aethelfrith's conqueror and successor, Edwin of Deira, as a still greater threat, especially if they saw him as Bede describes him, riding in procession with a ceremonial standard before him in apparently deliberate emulation of the Roman imperial style. Whatever was the reason for the generosity of their welcome, it is fully attested by the sources and reflected in the great enthusiasm with which the sons of Aethelfrith took to the ways of their Celtic hosts, in the light of the evidence of the Irish sources for Northumbrian princes fighting in Irish wars during the early decades of the seventh century.[17]

Eanfrith, the eldest of Aethelfrith's sons, is known to have married a Pictish princess whose royal lineage enabled his son, Talorcan, to become a king of Picts. His half-brother Oswy was to form a relationship with an Irish princess of the northern Ui Neill and their son was eventually to succeed to the kingship of Northumbria. Oswy and his elder brother Oswald would have offered their sister, the future Saint Aebba, in marriage to Domnall Brecc – at least, according to a late *Life* of the saint – had she not instead chosen to enter the church. Aebba and her brothers, all of them born and raised in the old Germanic pagan tradition, would have made their first contact with Christianity during their years of exile. The evidence of both Bede and Adamnan confirms Aethelfrith's sons and their companions having been baptised into the Christian faith during their years in Dalriada. They would also, of necessity, have become fluent in the language of their hosts and, indeed, Bede confirms Oswald's 'having acquired a perfect knowledge of Irish during his exile'. The sons of Aethelfrith, then, were greatly influenced through their long years of exile by the culture of their hosts and that influence was to play a significant part in shaping the subsequent history of Northumbria when they were restored to their father's kingdom. So too, the web of relationships formed by the Northumbrian princes in exile with the church, state and society of Celtic north Britain was to cast a long shadow over the subsequent history of seventh-century Scotland, a shadow which was to lie darkest across the last years of the reign of Domnall Brecc.

In 632, the Northumbrian king who had brought down Aethelfrith was himself defeated and slain at Hatfield – in what is now south Yorkshire – by an alliance of Penda, Anglo-Saxon king of Mercia, and Cadwallon, king of the Britons of Gwynedd. In the wake of their victory, Cadwallon's Britons advanced into Northumbria to ravage the lands between the Humber and the Tweed. A desperate attempt at resistance led by Edwin's nephew was doomed when he was slain by Cadwallon and the vast territories of Northumbria collapsed into anarchy, presenting the sons of Aethelfrith with the long-awaited opportunity to win back their father's kingdom.

Eanfrith, the eldest son, came south first, presumably from Pictland, only to be summarily slaughtered when he tried to negotiate terms with Cadwallon. The return from Dalriada of his half-brother Oswald, who was now himself the eldest heir to the kingship, met with very much greater success when he brought the Britons to battle along the line of the Roman wall and won his famous victory at the place called by Bede *Hefenfelth*, 'the Field of Heaven'. Bede's account of events attributes this impressive military triumph to divine intervention on behalf of a Christian king and recognises Oswald's summoning a bishop from Iona to found the royal church of his kingdom on Lindisfarne as the same king's act of thanksgiving for heavenly favour. The modern historian, who must explain the same events without benefit of Bede's recourse to the miraculous, might look first to Oswald's background among the Scots.

John of Fordun's fourteenth-century *Chronicle of the Scottish Nation* has already been suggested as having had access to at least one source unknown to Bede and long since lost, but with valuable bearing on the Anglo-Scottish relations of the seventh century. Fordun's unique perspective on the battle of

Degsastan would seem to have been informed by this source of probable north British origin, and so too would have been his account of what befell at the court of Domnall Brecc immediately before the return of the sons of Aethelfrith.

> Oswald and the other nobles who had sojourned seventeen years in exile in Scotland, being certified of his [Edwin's] death from trustworthy information, came into the king's presence, and begged him to grant them their liberty, and graciously deign to vouchsafe them some help whereby to win back their father's kingdom. The king, accordingly, freely gave them full leave to go away or come back – and even promised them help against Penda or any of the Saxons; but he altogether refused it against Cadwallon and the Britons, who had long been bound to the Scots by the friendship of a faithful alliance.
>
> Moreover, though less moved thereto by a liking for the Saxon race than by zeal for the Christian religion, he sent them a strong body of warriors, to the end that they might safely cross the marches of his kingdom. Being therefore supported by so large a host, they entered their father's kingdom, and were gladly welcomed by the inhabitants.

The first implication of Fordun's account lies in its indication of Oswald and his companions seeking the permission of Domnall Brecc to return to Northumbria, and would clearly indicate their owing some form of, inevitably military, allegiance to the king of Scots. If such was the case, then the reciprocal nature of such an obligation in what was still a warband society will have substantial bearing on future events, but of more immediate significance here is Domnall's warning to Oswald with regard to his own alliance with the Britons.

The absence of any evidence of conflict between the Scots of Dalriada and the north Britons before the battle of Strathcarron in 642 would point to there having been some co-operative agreement formed with the Britons of the Clyde at the time of Fergus Mor's transferring the royal centre of Dalriada from Antrim to Argyll and the substance of Domnall's statement – even as it is constructed by Fordun – suggests the same agreement having held firm from the end of the fifth century to the second quarter of the seventh. Not even the disparagement of Aedan mac Gabran reflected in Welsh tradition would seem to have been translated into real hostility between Briton and Scot, but something had quite surely ruptured that pact by 642 and it would seem, if only from the evidence of Fordun, to have been connected with the restoration of the kingship of Northumbria.

I have elsewhere[18] argued that close examination of the sources for

Oswald's victory at Heaven's Field in 633 suggests that the Dalriadic warband which had accompanied him to Northumbria formed at least a part and perhaps, even, the hard core of the war-host he assembled in the valley of the North Tyne for his battle with Cadwallon. Dalriadic warriors fighting as Oswald's allies in Northumbria would have been serving him as he and his brothers had served the kings of Dalriada fighting in Ireland, but their part in an apparent massacre of the Welsh Britons of Gwynedd which numbered Cadwallon among the dead would have been recognised by their Britonic kindred of the north as a breach of long-standing alliance and inevitably blamed on Domnall Brecc himself.

At the time of the battle in the year 633, Domnall was still unchallenged and secure in his kingship, having not yet suffered defeat at Calathros and disaster in the Mag Rath war, but five years later that situation had been entirely transformed by the concession of part of his kingship to the Cenel Comgaill and the loss of his territories in Ireland and Pictland. While Domnall's reign went into its terminal decline, Oswald had swiftly restored the fortunes of Northumbria, as is reflected by the annalist's notice of 'the flight of the people of Domnall Brecc' being followed at the same year by the entry of 'the siege of Dun Etin', from which it would appear that while the Scots were being driven back across the Spine of Britain, the Northumbrian Angles were advancing on the Forth to capture the north British stronghold of Dun Etin at Edinburgh.

Neither was Northumbrian ambition to stop there because Oswald would have annexed most of the Gododdin territory around the Forth by 642, in which year his attention was turned towards his southern frontiers where Penda of Mercia was on the march again. With the greater strength of Northumbrian forces committed south of the Humber, Oswald would have need of an ally north of the Forth–Clyde line, where his brother Oswy[19] seems to have been assigned command of the northern advance, and Domnall Brecc, precarious in his kingship and dangerously isolated in Argyll, could hardly refuse his support to the newly ascendant power in the land of north Britain. The battle of Strathcarron, then, would appear to have been a battle between Domnall's Scots, fighting as allies of Northumbria, and the Strathclyde Britons, coming to the aid of their fellow Britons of the Manau. Such a scenario amounts to nothing more than my own largely speculative construction of fragmentary references hopefully held with some glue of plausibility, but it would serve to explain how Domnall Brecc came to meet his death in battle with a king of Strathclyde in the valley of the Carron Water in the year 642.

Owen, king of Strathclyde, was the son of Beli, son of Neithon – or

Nwython in its Old Welsh form – but while the Irish sources preserve an impressive record of his brother Bruide mac Beli, who is remembered as the outstanding king of Picts of the seventh century, virtually nothing else is known of Owen other than his victory at Strathcarron. It was, none the less, a battle victory greatly honoured in Britonic tradition and commemorated by one of the later interpolations into the text of *The Gododdin*:

> I saw an array that came from *Pentir* [Kintyre],
> And splendidly they attacked around the conflagration.
> I saw a second array, rushing down from the town,
> And the men of the grandson of *Nwython* had risen.
> I saw men in array who came with the battle-shout,
> And ravens gnawed the head of *Dyfnwal Frych* . . .

The verse elegies for the heroes of the north Britons slain at Catraeth and attributed to Aneirin are thought to have entered the oral tradition – if not actually been written down – soon after the battle. *The Gododdin*, then, would have been originally composed in the last decade of the sixth century and very probably in the Gododdin territory around the Forth. When the aristocracy of the Gododdin fled the Northumbrian conquest of their ancient heartland, some of them evidently found their way to the last bastion of the north Britons on the Clyde and took with them their bardic tradition. Thus, it would seem, was *The Gododdin* brought to Strathclyde.

The poem was preserved, possibly first in oral tradition and afterwards in manuscript, in Strathclyde for more than two hundred years before it found its way to Wales with the last of the north British nobility in the early tenth century. At some point in those two centuries, probably in the capital fortress on Dumbarton Rock, the fragment in celebration of Owen's victory at Strathcarron was added to the original poem in celebration of the fallen heroes of a battle fought a hundred and fifty years earlier; and so it came about that the bitter epitaph of Domnall Brecc enters his name, in the Britonic tongue of his last enemy, as *Dyfnwal Frych*.

'IN SUBJECTION TO FOREIGNERS'

The abbot Cummene outlived Domnall Brecc by some twenty-seven years, so his reference to the kingdom being 'in subjection to foreigners' must apply to Dalriada at some period between 637 and 669, and historians long wondered as to who these 'foreigners' might have been. If Cummene's use of the noun *extranei* was intended in the sense of 'strangers' rather than 'foreigners', then he might be understood as referring to the kingship passing from Domnall's Cenel Gabrain to rival kindreds, as indeed it was to do during much of what remained of Cummene's lifetime and after. His use of the term 'subjection', however, must be decisive in its unmistakable implication of overlordship from outwith the kingdom.

The fact of Domnall's having been slain and his forces, presumably, defeated by the Strathclyde Britons at Strathcarron would reasonably suggest the king at Dumbarton having rendered Dalriada tributary as the fruit of his victory, were it not for the total absence from the sources of any suggestion of his having done so. There are, however, references from two other closely contemporary and eminently reliable authorities which have led the great weight of scholarly opinion to identify the kings of Northumbria as the over-lords intended by Cummene's 'foreigners'.

Adamnan, writing just twenty years after Cummene's death, describes Oswald as having been 'the supreme ruler over all of Britain', and Bede claims that 'he brought under his control all the peoples and kingdoms of Britain, speaking between them four different languages, British, Pictish, Irish and English'. Bede goes on to make an even more specific claim for Oswald's brother and successor, Oswy, having 'made tributary most of the Picts and the Scots in the north of Britain'. Northumbrian overlord-ship 'of the Picts', or at least those Pictish tribes south of the Mounth, was apparently first established in the reign of Talorcan, the son of Eanfrith and thus Oswy's nephew, whose kingship of Picts coincided pre-cisely with the high peak of Oswy's power. Talorcan's claim on the king-ship derived from his mother's Pictish royal blood, but his reign must be recognised as that of an effectively client king, ruling on behalf of a Northumbrian overlord.

The Northumbrian subjection of the Scots, however, emerged over a somewhat longer period and out of an alliance of Northumbria with Dalriada, rooted in mutual military obligations established by the sons of Aethelfrith during their years of exile and formalised during Oswald's reign. The decline of Dalriada after the death of Domnall running parallel to the ascendancy of Northumbria in the second decade of Oswy's reign would seem to have transformed what had been formerly an alliance of equals into one of subject and overlord whereby Dalriada was rendered tributary to Oswy in exchange for Northumbrian protection.

It is also significant that the survey which formed the original core of the *Senchus fer nAlban* was compiled at around this time, and it is ironic that had Dalriada not been placed 'in subjection to foreigners' history would have probably been deprived of its very earliest account of the kingdom of the Scots. Professor Bannerman's comparison of the contents of the *Senchus* with the terms of the resolution at Druim Ceatt led him to the very convincing conclusion[20] that the *Senchus* was originally intended as a survey of the kindreds of Dalriada in terms of their liabilities for taxation, tribute and hosting, information obviously required by a new overlord. This Northumbrian imperium over very much of north Britain had its beginnings in the expansion accomplished by Oswald before his death in battle with Penda in 642, but was largely the achievement of Oswy's reign and passed by him to his son Egfrith who succeeded his father in 671. A Pictish revolt following the expulsion of their client king soon after Egfrith's succession was savagely suppressed, but the emergence at around that time of Bruide mac Beli – a prince of Strathclyde and a brother of the Owen who had slain Domnall Brecc – as high-king of Picts was to entirely transform the political map of north Britain by the end of the eighth century. It took almost fifteen years before Bruide was ready to bring Egfrith to battle, but when he did so he inflicted a decisive defeat on the Northumbrian forces and slew their king with them at Nechtansmere near Forfar in May of the year 685.

'From this time', wrote Bede around 731, 'the hopes and strengths of the English kingdom began to ebb and slide backwards . . .'

> For the Picts recovered possession of their own land which the English had held, and the Scots in Britain and also some of the Britons regained their liberty, which they have preserved to this day.

The timing of the battle of Nechtansmere and its dramatic impact on the state of the kingdoms of north Britain, more than fifteen years after the death of Cummene but some three years before Adamnan began work on his *Life of Columba*, would explain why Adamnan might have chosen to omit Cummene's reference to Dalriada 'in subjection to foreigners' as a consequence of Mag Rath. Cummene's observations had, quite simply, been overtaken by events and were thus edited out of his source by Adamnan as no longer bearing on the situation of the later 680s. History would, thus, have been not only unaware of Cummene's crucial evidence but would have had no sure knowledge of his work at all had not the scribe Dorbbene, for whatever reason of his own, restored the passage to its proper context while setting down the earliest surviving manuscript of the Adamnan *Life*.

The successors of Domnall Brecc, then, would have been subject to a

Northumbrian overlord until the last quarter of the seventh century and even after the liberation won for the northern Celts by the Picts at Nechtansmere the decline of the kingdom of Scots was to continue through most of the next hundred years. It is possible to interpret the sequence of names, lineages, and reign-lengths as they appear in the king-lists of Dalriada as a record of succession passed between claimants from the principal lineages and on occasion shared between two kings of different kindreds. Just such an interpretation would seem to have been drawn from, if not imposed upon, the evidence of their own sources by the later medieval scribes who compiled or reworked those king-lists into the forms in which they survive today, but there is no real assurance of such an interpretation accurately reflecting the state of the kingdom of the Scots through the second half of the seventh century, and still less through most of the eighth.

It is true, of course, that the evidence of the Irish annal record continues through the same period, but it continues in a form at least as fragmentary and no less cryptic as through the centuries preceding. It is also true that the decline of the kingdom is reflected in the confusion and uncertainty of its historical record, so there is no good reason to recognise any king of Dalriada being possessed of anything like the same extent of authority as, for example, had been Aedan mac Gabran in his ascendancy. The decades of 'subjection to foreigners' would have inevitably left the kingship of Dalriada as greatly depleted in wealth as in civil authority and military command, and probably diminished, in fact, entirely beyond restoration.

The immediate successor to Domnall Brecc would appear to have been the same Ferchar of the Cenel Comgaill who had shared the kingship after the battle of Calathros and whose obituary is entered around the year 650. After him the succession passed to claimants from various branches of the Cenel Gabrain: Domnall's brother and cousin, apparently sharing the kingship, followed by Domnall's son who might possibly have reclaimed some of the Irish territories lost after Mag Rath, after him Domnall's nephew, and finally Domnall's grandson, Eochaid, who was slain in 697. At which year, the kingdom had been released from subjection to Northumbria for more than a decade, but during that time the Cenel Loairn would seem to have emerged as the newly ascendant ruling kindred.

The Cenel Loairn chieftain Ferchar Fota can be recognised as the first significant figure of this new ascendancy and the names of his sons are those next entered into the king-list. The first of them, Ainbcellach, very probably slew Domnall Brecc's grandson, Eochaid, to claim the kingship in 697, but was himself expelled and supplanted by his brother, Selbach, in the following year. Selbach is accredited by one king-list with a reign of twenty-four years which would correspond well enough to the entry in the *Annals of Ulster* at 723 which styles him 'king of Dalriada' at the time of his retirement to a monastery.

After Selbach, the kingship was splintered beyond recognition with at least five contending kindreds in place of the three principal *cenéla* recognised by the *Senchus* less than a century before. A kingdom so divided offered an irresistible temptation to a predatory neighbour and through the five years after 736 the Scots suffered a ferocious onslaught by the Pictish war-host of Oengus mac Fergus. Oengus – whose name is entered in the king-list in its Pictish form of *Onuist* son of *Urguist* – was the most formidable warrior king of Picts of the eighth century and yet is claimed by Irish tradition to have been descended from a fourth-century prince of Munster. Recognised by historians as the outstanding Pictish warlord of the eighth century, Oengus emerged out of a sequence of battles with rival claimants to claim effective high-kingship of Picts in the year 729, and next turned his ambitions to conquest of the kingdom of the Scots. The Irish annals at 736 enter his wasting of Dalriada, storming its capital fortress at Dunadd and putting into chains two kings of the Cenel Loairn, while his brother slew another in battle. The annal record of the next five years follows Oengus and his Picts rampaging through Dalriada and destroying its warlords one after another, until the decisive entry of 'the overthrow of Dalriada by Oengus mac Fergus' at the year 741 confirms his having rendered the kingdom of the Scots once again tributary to a Pictish king. Within ten years, however, the Picts had suffered a massive defeat by the Britons of Strathclyde and the *Annals of Ulster* enter 'the ebbing of the sovereignty of Oengus' at the year 750. He was able to regain his kingship of Fortriu and to reign until his death in 761, but his ascendancy was lost to him and with it his overlordship of Dalriada.

The apparently systematic slaughter of the kings and chieftains of Dalriada by Oengus's Pictish warbands would best explain the emergence of Aed Find in the wake of the 'ebbing of the sovereignty of Oengus'. His kindred seem not to have been brought to battle by the Picts, probably because their territory in Kintyre[21] lay far enough to the south to escape the full fury of the onslaught unleashed on the Cenel Loairn.

Aed Find presents a curiously impressive figure whose prominence would seem to be better reflected in the stature accorded him in retrospect by later medieval sources than it is by the sparse notices of his thirty-year reign in the annals. He is, none the less, everywhere accredited with reclaiming the kingship of Dalriada from its decline into chaos through the earlier eighth century and restoring that kingship to the principal royal line of the Cenel Gabrain. While the king-lists are at variance on the precise detail of his genealogy – being unable to agree whether his father was a grandson or, more plausibly, a great-grandson of Domnall Brecc – they admit no doubt as to Aed Find's ultimately direct descent from Fergus Mor mac Erc.

Neither could they do so, because upon the legitimacy of the lineage of Aed Find hangs the legitimacy of the dynasty founded by the son of Alpin who is everywhere acknowledged by history and tradition as having brought the kingdom of the Scots 'into the land of the Picts'.

4

'Into the land of the Picts'

KENNETH

THE CATHEDRAL KIRK of Saint Columba at Dunkeld stands on the north bank of the Tay where the course of the river has sliced its way through the southern rampart of the Grampian range but has yet to enter upon the rich fertility of the Perthshire lowland plain. This country lay within the territory of the ancient Pictish kingdom of Fortriu and Dunkeld would seem – if only on the evidence of its name deriving from the Gaelic *Dún Chailleann* or 'fort of the Caledones'[1] – to have been a place of importance long before its first appearance in the historical record.

The imposing presence of the medieval cathedral has dominated the town for centuries, but the riverside tranquillity of its setting among lawns, paths and trees, a legacy of the restoration of the town in the eighteenth and nineteenth centuries, is less than evocative of its turbulent past. So prestigious a building located in such close proximity to the Highlands was dangerously vulnerable to depredation by the wilder clans to the north through much of its history. The late fifteenth-century bishop of Dunkeld who commissioned the construction of the great tower at the western extremity of the nave was forced to take refuge in the loft above the choir on the Whit Sunday Clan Donnachie chose to attack his cathedral. The tomb still to be seen behind the altar surmounted by a carved stone effigy of an armoured man is believed to enclose the remains of that bishop's close contemporary, Alexander Stewart, Earl of Buchan and a son of the first Scots king of the house of Stewart, still notorious as 'The Wolf of Badenoch' for his burning of Elgin Cathedral and wider involvement in the lawlessness which engulfed the Highlands in the later fourteenth century.

Some two hundred and fifty years in the building, the cathedral was finally completed by the last quarter of the fifteenth century and had less than a hundred years to enjoy the high peak of its splendour before suffering the destruction wreaked upon so many great churches at the time of the Reformation. In the August of 1560, an official commission ordered the cathedral to be stripped of its lavish furnishings and, despite official instructions to the contrary, the roof of the nave was torn down. The roof of the eastern limb, the choir of the pre-Reformation cathedral, is thought to have suffered similar damage at much the same time, because it was re-roofed in 1600 and restored to serve as the town's parish church.

It was also to serve the people of Dunkeld as a refuge when the town was almost entirely destroyed by the battle which raged in its streets through some fifteen hours of an August day and evening in the year 1689. The battle of Dunkeld, fought between the government's Cameronians and rebel Highlanders, marked the end of the first Jacobite rising in Scotland and came just three weeks after the Highland army raised by John Graham of Claverhouse, the Viscount Dundee, in support of the recently exiled Stuart king James, had won their famous victory at nearby Killiecrankie. Claverhouse – who was celebrated by Sir Walter Scott as 'Bonnie Dundee', but is more realistically remembered in the Highlands as 'Black John of the Battles' – had been slain at Killiecrankie and his forces, left leaderless and unable to follow up their victory, were to suffer a crushing defeat when brought again to battle in the town of Dunkeld. The Highlanders had fortified themselves into houses which were put to the torch by besieging Cameronians who brought benches from the kirk to use as battering rams and barricades, stripped lead from its roof to mould their shot, and left every building in the town which they had not utterly destroyed damaged beyond repair. Dunkeld today, like the parkland setting of its cathedral, is very largely the result of rebuilding during the more subdued decades which followed the decisive defeat of the last Jacobite rebellion in 1746.

The tower which was raised at the western extremity of the pre-Reformation cathedral still stands, and the walls and columns of the great fifteenth-century nave remain roofless today as they have done since the 1570s, but the eastern limb, formerly the cathedral choir, is still an active place of worship as the parish kirk of Dunkeld. Its walls are of thirteenth-century construction and thus represent the oldest part of the medieval cathedral, but even when their foundations were first laid there had been a church, and a church of great importance for the kingdom of the Scots, in that place for at least four hundred years.

The obituary of the abbot of Dunkeld entered in the annals at 865 knows him by a Gaelic name and styles him 'bishop of Fortriu', an eminence which was not to be accorded his successors for another three centuries, but which bears its own testimony to the mid-ninth century stature of Dunkeld as the first royal church of the mac Alpin dynasty of kings of Scots. That same stature is reflected also in the cathedral's association with the saint to whom it is dedicated and whose relics were brought here from Iona at the mid-point of the ninth century.

No one can say with any confidence whether some part of the dust of the historical Columba might still lie interred beneath the chancel floor at Dunkeld, but calling to mind Professor Bannerman's suggestion that 'the close co-operation between church and state established in Aedan's reign was the basis of the ultimate supremacy of the Scots in Scotland',[2] I can think of no other place, not even on Iona, where the long shadow of the holy man Columcille can be sensed to touch so palpably upon the destiny of the kingdom of the Scots as in this ancient church. Even such an admittedly personal impression needs its supporting evidence from the early sources, and such is to be found in the closely contemporary account of Kenneth mac Alpin preserved in the *Chronicle of the Kings* which states that 'in the seventh year of his reign, he brought the relics of Saint Columba to a church that he had built', a church which can only have been Dunkeld.

The seventh year of the reign of this Kenneth, son of Alpin, in the kingship of Fortriu would have been 849, and thus the same year at which the *Annals of Ulster* enter 'Indrechtach, abbot of Iona, came to Ireland with the relics of Columcille'. In that year of 849, then, it would seem that a decision had finally been taken to remove from Iona the shrine of its founding saint in order to bring his relics to a place of greater safety and, at the same time, apparently dividing them between two claimants. The first claim on the relics of a holy man lay with the principal church of his monastic *paruchia*,[3] and by that right Indrechtach removed Columba's relics to the monastery of Kells in Meath to which the abbot and community of Iona had been transferred some forty years past. It would appear, though, that Kells claimed only a part of the saint's relics and allowed the remainder to pass to the new royal church of a king of Scots claiming descent from the same Aedan mac Gabran whose succession to the kingship had been founded on a covenant with Columba two hundred and seventy-five years before.

While there is no doubt of a political purpose underlying Kenneth mac Alpin's claim to relics of the patron saint of his kingdom, the essential reason for the removal of Columba's shrine from his holy island was the same as that which had brought about the evacuation of the abbot and community of Iona to Ireland – the descent of the northmen upon the western sea.

THE NORTHMEN IN ALBA

At the time of writing his *Historia*, Bede knew of just four peoples in Britain – his own English, the Scots from Ireland, the Picts north of the Forth, and the indigenous Britons, all of them occupying territory within what is now Scotland – and yet within sixty years of his death in 735 a fifth people were to make their first entry into the historical record of the Celtic west. They were, of course, the Norse who formed the first wave of Scandinavian migration west over the sea.

The northmen first appear in north Britain, as elsewhere in Europe, in the role of 'vikings', a name deriving from the Old Norse *vikingr*, or 'sea-raider', which has come to be indiscriminately, and quite improperly, applied to almost every aspect of Scandinavian activity at home and abroad in early medieval times.[4] These sea-raiders formed the cutting edge of Scandinavian expansion, but they are nowhere called 'vikings' when they are first noticed in the early sources, being identified instead as 'heathens' or 'pagans', presumably by reason of their raids being invariably targeted on monasteries. Only later, when seasonal raiding had developed into effective invasion and partial conquest of Ireland, do the Irish sources begin to call the Norse, and later the Danes, the *gaill* – a term usually translated as 'foreigners' but more emphatically rendered as 'aliens'.

It is not known when the first viking expedition from the west coast of Norway made landfall on the island periphery of north Britain, but the most recent alignment of archaeological evidence with historical probability has suggested Norse pirate adventurers having already established forward bases in Shetland and in Orkney within the last quarter of the eighth century. From these first footholds in the northern isles, initially pirate nests occupied through the summer raiding season, the full extent of the north British coastline lay within striking range of their oceangoing longships, the ultimate warship of the Dark Age seaways. The first recorded viking raid on the British Isles, which fell upon the Northumbrian monastery of Lindisfarne and is entered in the *Anglo-Saxon Chronicle* for 793, was assuredly inflicted by a Norse war-fleet operating out of Orkney or Shetland. The same, or similar, raiders returned to the Northumbrian coast again in the following year to strike as far south as the Tyne, while another fleet rounded Cape Wrath in the same raiding season to break out into the Hebrides – on the evidence of the *Annals of Ulster* at 794:

The devastation of all the islands of Britain by the heathens.

The annalist's original source for that entry would have been an immediately contemporary Iona chronicle, and its reference to *insularum Britanniae*, 'the islands of Britain', can be taken to indicate the 'devastation' having been inflicted upon the Outer Hebrides lying to the north of Skye.[5]

Suddenly, then, pagan pirates of an utterly alien culture were unleashed upon the western seaboard of north Britain, and in just those waters where the island monasteries so characteristic of the ancient Irish church presented them with richly endowed and entirely undefended sources of slaves and silver. By the following year of 795, the annals notice more than one viking war-fleet striking at monasteries off the northern and western coasts of Ireland and, most ominous of all, the entry at the same year in the eleventh-century *Annals of Inisfallen* records 'the devastation of Ia-Columcille'.

Iona was to suffer the 'fury of the northmen' again and again through the ninth century. Its monastery was burned by them in 802 and sixty-eight of its monks slain in a third raid in 806, before the abbot and his principal community evacuated this most holy island of the western sea for a newly built monastery more safely located in the Irish midlands at Kells in Meath. The transfer of the principal church of the Columban *paruchia* to Ireland would seem to have been first considered a temporary measure and Iona was certainly not completely abandoned. The abbot Cellach who made the transfer to Kells chose to return to Iona as his death approached and to be buried there, thus ensuring it as his 'place of resurrection' beside the enshrined relics of its founding saint which were evidently allowed to remain on Iona. It would seem also that some form of at least semi-permanent monastic community chose to remain there with them and, inevitably, to endure the continuing viking raids, the most infamous occurring in 825 when the principal of the residual community suffered gruesome martyrdom in defence of Columba's shrine.

There are entries in the annals also of the saint's relics having been brought back to Ireland, for whatever reason, on a number of occasions after 807 only to be returned each time to their shrine on Iona. There is, however, a reference in the *Cogadh Gaedhel re Gallaibh* – a narrative history of 'the wars of the Irish with the Scandinavians' set down no earlier than the eleventh century – to a very large Norse fleet having 'ravaged Ia-Columcille' at some time in the 840s and it may well have been that attack, or one very like it in the same period, which finally prompted Indrechtach, the 'abbot of Iona' at Kells, to decide upon the permanent removal of Columba's relics from Iona in 849.[6]

While it was still greatly revered as a holy place at that mid-point of the ninth century – a reverence reflected in its being chosen by the mac Alpin dynasty, according to some versions of the *Chronicle of the Kings*, for their traditional royal burial ground – Iona had long since ceased to be the prestigious centre of culture and scholarship of earlier centuries. Even if anything of its great library and scriptorium had somehow survived the burning of the monastery by the northmen in 802, the evacuation to Ireland five years later finally drew to a close the Iona chronicle which was to provide the medieval Irish annalists – and, through them, all the later generations of historians – with their central source of record for the first centuries of the kingdom of the Scots. Although never totally extinguished as a source of Scottish history, the Irish annal evidence is too greatly impoverished by the arrival of the northmen in the western sea to provide any detailed account of the first half-century of Scandinavian impact on Celtic Scotland. It does, however, preserve a grim catalogue of the descent of the northmen on Ireland itself.

The viking fleets who inflicted the first raids on the monasteries of the Hebrides and the Irish coast need not have comprised more than a few longships, but in their wake came much larger war-fleets to penetrate Ireland's rivers and to moor on its loughs as 'floating fortresses' from which raiding warbands were able more extensively, even systematically, to plunder the great and wealthy monasteries of the Irish mainland. Bangor was raided in 823 and again in 824, Armagh twice in one month in 832, Glendalough and Clonmacnois in 834, and Clonmacnois burned in 835. Extended seasonal raiding was followed by over-wintering as ever larger fleets became involved in operations at so great a distance from their Scandinavian homelands. Ships were brought ashore for repair and maintenance and defensive earthworks built around them while shipwrights and weaponsmiths set up their workshops nearby, thus creating coastal ship-ports which attracted new fleets arriving through the year and provided focal points for the effectively permanent settlement by the northmen in Ireland.

The seizure of a river crossing on the Liffey – called by the Irish *Ath Cliath*, 'the ford of the hurdles' – in 837 marked a new and decisive stage in what by now amounted to the invasion of Ireland by the *gaill*. The establishment there of a combined ship-port, fortress and trading-post formed the hub of Ireland's first and principal Norse kingdom which was to become known – as it is today – by the name of its ship-haven called 'the black pool' or, in the Irish, *Dubh linn*. The Norse-derived names of so many other Irish coastal towns, such as Waterford, Wexford and Limerick, attest their beginnings as viking ship-ports and it is largely true that urban centres were a Scandinavian introduction into an Ireland where the largest forms of settlement had formerly been the monasteries. These coastal townships and their environs – of which certainly Dublin and probably Limerick could be considered 'king-doms' by the mid-ninth century – can be said to represent the sum total of Scandinavian Irish territorial conquest. So too, their function, as centres for shipping, plunder, trade and tribute-taking, can be taken as a realistic index of the character of Scandinavian settlement in Ireland and contrasted quite dramatically with the presence, as it developed through the same period, of the northmen in Scotland.

In the island archipelagos around the northern and western coastline of Scotland, the vikings represented only the initial wave of the Scandinavian expansion west over sea, the sea-raider being followed almost immediately by the land-seeker in pursuit of more abundant territory for settlement than was to be found in the unpromising terrain of western Norway. It is, in fact, more than likely that viking and settler were in many cases one and the same man, who had first seen the northern and western isles on a raiding voyage and been attracted to return as a farmer to the green fertility of Orkney or as a fisherman to the not unfamiliar landscape of Shetland and the Outer Hebrides. Thus it was that such men and others of like purpose came to settle the island fringes of Scotland, where there was land evidently available for the taking – even, if need be, at sword-point – and for the building of home and farm, byre and boat-noust along what would soon be a principal sea-road of the northern world linking Dublin, by way of the ship-haven in Scapa Flow, with the trade-port of Kaupang at the entrance to Oslofjord. So too, should he and his sons think of going again a-viking between seed-time and harvest, the Hebridean seaboard offered ease of access to lucrative raiding, an abundance of lairs for viking longships, and it had, after all, been recog-nised by Irish tradition as a pirate coast since prehistory.

It would be no less than realistic to suggest the first conquest of the north-men in Alba having been their unchallenged command of the western sea, with their longships – oak-built, fast-driven by sail or oar, and incomparably seaworthy in the most testing conditions of the north Atlantic – representing so revolutionary an advance on the hide-hulled curragh which had equipped the formerly formidable Dalriadic war-fleet. The first impact of such a con-quest on the Celts of the west was thus the severance beyond repair of the 'bridge of curraghs' which had been, for at least four hundred years, the great thoroughfare of the 'sea-divided Gael' and to drive a wedge of oak bound with iron between the Irish of Erin and of Alba.

The second impact was an inevitable consequence of settlement so far from the Scandinavian homeland, to which some would have brought wom-enfolk and others not. Sufficient numbers of ninth-century Norse graves in the Outer Hebrides have been found to contain female burials as to indicate the northmen of apparently high social stature having brought with them wives and daughters. Others would doubtless have found wives among women of native Celtic stock, and even the fragmentary evidence of the annals confirms intermarriage between Norse and Gael to have occurred at a very early stage of Scandinavian settlement, thus even earlier in the Hebrides than in Ireland. The offspring of such unions are called by the Irish sources *gall-gaedhil*, literally 'foreign Gaels', and reputed by them to have been still more violent and rapacious than those of pure Scandinavian stock.

The occurrence in the sources of a Gaelic–Norse personal name-form is really the only means by which history can identify an individual as having been of these *gall-gaedhil*, and the earliest dated such reference marks also the first appearance in the annal record of a man who has been shown to cast a long shadow over the subsequent history of Gaelic Scotland. His name appears twice in the, admittedly very late, *Annals of the Four Masters* as *Godfraidh mac Feorghus* – or Guthfrith, son of Fergus – which combines a Gaelic patronymic with a Norse given name, indicating a son born to an Irish or Scots father by a Norse mother, and thus suggesting beyond reasonable doubt a first generation *gall-gaedhil*.

This Guthfrith was evidently born to a father of noble rank, because he is styled *toiseach* ('chieftain') by both of his entries in the annals, of which the first recognises him as *toiseach Oirgiall* or 'chieftain of the Airgialla' at the remarkably early date of 836. The Airgialla have been already mentioned here as kindreds descended from vassal allies of the sons of Niall of the Nine Hostages and endowed by them with lands in the north of Ireland, but some of them would seem also to have been settled around Lorn in Dalriada, on the evidence of the survey of the hosting strengths in the *Senchus fer nAlban* which numbers a sizeable contingent of 'Airgialla' in the host of the Cenel Loairn. It would seem then that Guthfrith's father was a noble of these Airgialla in Alba where he would have been most likely to have found a Norse wife at such an early date. A father of such rank and kindred would, no less reasonably, have conferred upon Guthfrith the similar stature of a *toiseach* – best translated in this instance as 'a noble-man' – among the Airgialla in Ireland no less than in Scotland. His later area of activity and authority, however, can only have been in the west of Scotland, and specifically in the isles, in the light of his obituary entered by the annalist at 853 which styles him *toiseach Innsigall*, or 'chieftain of the Hebrides'.

This Guthfrith has been shown to have been a direct ancestor of the Clan Donald Lords of the Isles,[7] but his importance here is as a warlord of the *gall-gaedhil*, because it is no accident that Kenneth mac Alpin should make his earliest dated appearance in the sources as an ally of the Hebridean Norse just four years before his succession to the kingship of the Scots of Dalriada:

> Guthfrith mac Fergus, chieftain of the Airgialla, went to Alba to strengthen Dalriada at the request of Kenneth mac Alpin.

'SON OF THE CLAN OF AEDAN'S SON'

The man whose name appears in the Irish annals in its original Gaelic form of *Cináed mac Alpín* – Kenneth, son of Alpin[8] – has been recognised for very nearly a thousand years as the king who brought the Picts under Scottish domination at the point of entry of the kingdom of the Scots into the Middle Ages and can thus take the credit for the newly emergent nation in north Britain being since called 'Scotland' and not 'Pictland'. If such was his achievement – and no historian has yet been able to deprive him of it – then he stands at the strategic centre of the history of the kingdom of the Scots, but his origins and lineage are very much more obscure than the medieval king-lists would have history believe and when the famous story of his slaughtering Pictish rivals trapped between feasting-benches is traced to source it would seem to be only a story after all. When the historical Kenneth mac Alpin, who commands a position of such crucial importance for the Celtic kingdom of the Scots on the threshold of the Middle Ages, remains also its greatest enigma, then the blame can be laid nowhere else but upon the sources of history.

The great weight of what is known of Kenneth, as of his dynastic successors, derives from two principal sources, both of them having been already mentioned here. The more intriguing is the cryptic *Prophecy of Berchan*,[9] a text of the late eleventh century deriving from more ancient Gaelic historical tradition, while the more informative is the *Chronicle of the Kings*, surviving in variant forms of text in different manuscripts none of them older than the twelfth century, but of which one especially – that preserved in the Poppleton manuscript[10] – is generally thought to derive, at least in part, from an original closely contemporary with Kenneth himself.

While the evidence of these two sources, taken together, provides almost all that is known of Kenneth, neither of them can offer any year date for him and, consequently, a starting point for his chronology must be sought elsewhere. There is, in fact, only one reliably accurate date for Kenneth to be found in the early sources and it is the year of his death – from the obituary entered by the *Annals of Ulster* at 858:

> Kenneth, son of Alpin, king of Picts, died.[11]

When that date, supplied by the most authoritative Irish annal source for the period,[12] is set against the reign-lengths accorded him by the *Chronicle of the Kings*, it is possible to construct an outline chronology of Kenneth's kingship. He 'ruled Pictland prosperously for sixteen years', which must place his date of accession to the kingship of Picts sixteen years before his death and, thus, at 842 or 843. To which the *Chronicle* adds that 'two years before he came to Pictland, he had received the kingdom of Dalriada', which would, by the same process, place his succession as king of Dalriada to a date no later than 841, if not even as early as 840.

Kenneth can be said, then, to have first achieved historical prominence as king of Dalriada, and the legitimacy of his claim on such a kingship can only have been founded upon descent from its royal house, inevitably through his father who is everywhere identified as Alpin. It is at just this point that first shadows begin to gather around Kenneth, because there are very real doubts as to the historical authenticity of this 'Alpin, son of Eochaid' and, for Professor Duncan, 'Alpin remains a wraith whose very descent from the royal line of Dalriada may be suspect'.[13]

His name is nowhere to be found in the *Annals of Ulster*, which represents the principal annal record of kings of Scots immediately before and after him, and neither is he named in the *Duan Albanach*, so the earliest source to claim him as having been king of Dalriada is just one version of the *Synchronisms* compiled in the eleventh century by Flann of Monasterboice. It would thus seem to have been from this text of Flann's *Synchronisms* that the *Chronicle of the Kings* derived its entry of Alpin as Kenneth's predecessor and added to it the note of his three-year reign. Such a reign-length for Alpin cannot be realistically accommodated by the chronology of kings reigning through the first half of the ninth century,[14] but it is of exactly the same duration as the reign-length reliably accorded an earlier Alpin, son of Eochaid and great-grandson of Domnall Brecc, who is thought to have been killed in the Pictish 'devastation of Dalriada' entered by the annalist at 736. This Alpin had defeated a king of Picts in 726 and 'reigned in his stead', according to the Pictish king-list, until he himself was defeated by two Pictish rivals in two battles entered in the annals at the year 728. Thereafter he fled to the west where he was able to hold some form of kingship in Dalriada for three years during the period of regnal anarchy which preceded the onslaught on the kingdom by Oengus mac Fergus and his Pictish host.

The presence in the king-list of two Alpins in two centuries – both of them accorded the same length of reign and both, also, sons of fathers called Eochaid – must be immediately highly suspect, and all the more so when it is recognised that the compilers of king-lists were at least as anxious to legitimate the descent of their currently reigning dynasty as were the synchronists to present as seamless as possible a succession of kings. Such suspicion leads inexorably on to the suggestion that the *Chronicle* compounded a confusion of two Alpins which had been first introduced, accidentally or otherwise, by an Irish synchronist more than a hundred years earlier – and to the conclusion that the entry of Alpin, father of Kenneth, into the king-list might be at best an error and at worst a spurious contrivance.

To cast such doubt upon the historicality of Alpin's kingship must similarly call into question the authenticity of his lineage as it is presented by the genealogies from the same *Chronicle* source, where Kenneth is the son of Alpin, son of Eochaid, son of Aed Find, son of Eochaid, son of another Eochaid (who is omitted by some versions), son of Domangart, son of Domnall Brecc. The occurrence of so many 'Eochaids' – three of that name within six generations – itself arouses suspicion of a name occurring so commonly as to offer itself as the most plausible stopgap for a genealogist irked by a generation missing from his own original source.

None of which, it must be said, need necessarily point to Kenneth as a usurper entirely devoid of royal lineage. Indeed, such a proposal would be less than realistic when he would have had neither a claim on the kingship nor the status essential to attract a sufficient warband in its support had he not been of some genuine descent from the royal house of the Cenel Gabrain. It is possible, however, that he was of other than its principal line of direct descent, and just such a possibility might well be the implication of Gaelic tradition preserved in the *Prophecy of Berchan*, where the passage concerning Kenneth follows immediately on from that describing Aedan mac Gabran and begins by recognising Kenneth as a 'son of the clan of his [i.e. Aedan's] son'. While Aedan is known from the *Senchus fer nAlban* to have sired seven sons, the one intended here can be reasonably taken to be his successor, Eochaid Buide, who was himself the father of eight sons named in the *Senchus*.

From such a starting point, the task of identifying Kenneth's line of descent from so many possible 'clans of Aedan's sons' would become quite hopeless were it not for the remarkable rarity of his father's name of Alpin. There can be no room for doubt as to the authenticity of Kenneth's patronymic when it is accorded him by the very earliest sources, but the name *Alpín* – apparently the Gaelic form of the Pictish *Elpin* – is entered just twice in the Dalriadic royal genealogies, the first occurring Alpin having been a great-grandson of Domnall Brecc who won the kingship of Picts before being driven out of Pictland to reign for three years in Dalriada. The initial appearance of a Gaelic form of a Pictish name in the genealogy of a Dalriadic royal kindred can only be explained by Alpin having been the son of a Pictish mother – through whom, perhaps, he was able to support his claim on Pictish kingship – but, when a name once introduced usually recurs in later generations along the same direct line of descent, there must be every good reason to suggest the second Alpin having been the direct descendant, in all probability the great-grandson, of the first.[15]

When the lineage and kingship of Alpin, the father of Kenneth, can be called into such serious doubt and even dismissed as contrivance by the compilers of king-lists, it is unlikely that history would have remembered him at all had it not been for the genuinely greater celebrity of his son, but the nature of that celebrity must itself be called immediately into question on the terms in which it is fanfared by the sources. The *Synchronisms* call Kenneth mac Alpin 'the first king from among the Gael who assumed the kingdom of Scone', which may well be not far short of the truth, but the *Prophecy of Berchan* hails him as 'the first king who will reign in the east from among the men of Erin in Alba', which he assuredly was not.

The thirteenth-century *Chronicle of Huntingdon* goes a stage further still in its claim for Kenneth having been 'the first of the Scots to obtain the kingship of the whole of Alba', when he was certainly not the first of the Gael to rule in Pictland and neither was he the first to hold kingship over both the Picts and the Scots. If he 'led the Scots from Argyll into the land of the Picts with marvellous cunning', as one variant text of the *Chronicle of the Kings* claims he did, then he was following along a path which had been beaten out by his forebears through all of three centuries past.

KINGS OF SCOTS EAST OF THE SPINE

If it is true that Gabran, son of Domangart, son of Fergus Mor mac Erc, had established himself as king in the district of Gowrie in Atholl by gift of his father-in-law, then it can be said that the royal house of Dalriada had already begun to expand to the east of the Spine of Britain within fifty years of its migration from Antrim to Argyll in Alba.

If the annal entry at the year 559 of the 'flight of the men of Alba from Bruide mac Maelchon' represents the expulsion of the Scots from Gowrie by the newly ascendant high-king of Picts, then Gabran's initiative did not survive his death in the same year, and it was not to be renewed until the time of his son Aedan, styled by the annalist 'king of Alba'. Whatever the truth of the claim made by the *Prophecy of Berchan* for Aedan's having made war for 'thirteen years against the Pictish host', there is the best of historical evidence from Adamnan for his having defeated the Maeatae Picts at the 'battle of the Miathi' and from the annals for his having suffered defeat by another Pictish enemy at the 'battle of Chirchind' in the Mearns. Such military adventuring east of the Spine is not necessarily to be interpreted as evidence for kingship, or even a claim on kingship, in Pictland, but Aedan's son and successor, Eochaid Buide, is styled 'king of the Picts' in his obituary entered in the *Annals of Ulster* at 629 and it would seem most probable that, whatever its real nature and extent, Eochaid's 'kingship of Picts' derived, by right of the apparent custom among the Picts of succession through the female line, from his mother having been of Pictish noble lineage. While there is no reference by the sources to Eochaid's son and successor, the ill-fated Domnall Brecc, having held or claimed any kingship of Picts, the 'battle of Glen Mairison in which the people of Domnall Brecc were put to flight' entered in the annals at 638 can only be interpreted as another expulsion of the Scots from Pictland. It would have been fully characteristic of Domnall's disastrous reign to have included the loss, with so much else, of Dalriada's last foothold east of the Spine, and there is no further indication by the sources of any renewed Scots expansion into Pictish territory for another hundred and thirty years.

The decades following Domnall's death were the period when, according to Bede, Oswy of Northumbria 'made tributary most of the Picts and Scots in the north of Britain', and the period also when the names of apparently client rulers on behalf of Northumbrian overlordship appear in the Pictish king-list. 'The expulsion of Drust from his kingdom' entered in the *Annals of Tigernach* at the year 672 signals the dismissal of the last of these Northumbrian client kings of Picts and coincides with a Pictish revolt against Oswy's son Egfrith, who had succeeded to the kingship of Northumbria on the death of his father in the previous year. While Egfrith was able swiftly and savagely to put down the insurgents on that occasion – 'filling two rivers with their corpses' according to one closely contemporary English source[16] – the subsequent rise of Bruide mac Beli to the high-kingship of Picts was to spell the end of Northumbrian imperium beyond the Forth when he destroyed Egfrith and most of his war-host with him on Dunnichen Moss beside Nechtansmere in the year 685.

Bruide's victory restored to the Picts, as to the Scots of Dalriada, their independence from Northumbrian overlordship and his kingship can be justly considered as a new Pictish ascendancy, but it has also another significance – and one, ultimately, for the Scots no less than the Picts – by reason of

Bruide mac Beli being the first king of Picts who is entered in the annals as 'king of Fortriu'.[17] This new form of title is the first formal indication by the sources of the transfer of the power centre of Pictland from the Moray Firth – where Columba made his celebrated visit in 564 to the capital fortress of the high-king of Picts at Craig Phadrig close by Inverness – to the south of the Grampians in what is now southern Perthshire. There, between the Rivers Tay and Earn, lay the heartland of the ancient Pictish province of Fortriu and the principal territory of kings of Picts, who were thus to be known as 'kings of Fortriu', from the time of Bruide mac Beli in the last quarter of the seventh century until the extinction of independent Pictish kingship at the mid-point of the ninth.

The decline into chaos of the kingdom of the Scots through the first decades of the eighth century was paralleled by a similar regnal anarchy in Pictland following the death of Bruide in 693, at least until the emergence of the formidable Oengus mac Fergus as king of Fortriu, and effectively high-king of Picts, around the year 729. His military conquest and subsequent subjection of Dalriada through fifteen years after his onslaught of 736 can be said to represent the last ascendancy of Pict over Scot, because in its wake came the most vigorous, and ultimately decisive, eastward expansion by kings of Dalriada. It began in the last decade of the thirty-year reign of Aed Find, who had arrested the long decline of the kingship of Dalriada, restored it to the Cenel Gabrain in 748 and presumably consolidated his kingship through the twenty years thereafter before striking east into Pictland. The 'battle in Fortriu between Aed and Ciniod' (Oengus' successor king of Picts) entered in the *Annals of Ulster* at 768 represents the first recorded thrust to the east of the Spine by a king of Scots for at least four generations.

In the light of what is known of subsequent events, the battle can be taken to have been a victory for Aed Find, even though the annalist does not say as much and it is clear that the annal record of Picto–Scottish relations through the later eighth century is so greatly impoverished as to obscure very much more evidence than it preserves. Indeed, other than the entry of the obituary of Aed Find at 778 and that of his brother and successor Fergus at 781, the annalist offers no further notice of events in Scotland until 789, at which year the *Annals of Ulster* enter 'a battle between the Picts and there Conall mac Tadg was conquered and Constantine was the conqueror'. When that evidence from the annals is set against the corresponding evidence of the king-lists, it becomes clear that the kingship of Picts and Scots had undergone some dramatic rearrangement, because 'the conqueror' in that 'battle between the Picts' was a Gael of the royal lineage of the Cenel Gabrain. His name appears among those of the kings of Dalriada listed in Flann's *Synchronisms* and, in its Pictish form of *Caustantín*, in the list of kings of Fortriu where its entry follows that of the defeated Conall mac Tadg.

This Constantine was the son of Fergus, the brother of Aed Find and his successor in the kingship of Dalriada, who had evidently taken a Pictish bride of the royal house of Fortriu. Their son would thus have inherited equally legitimate claim on the kingships of Dalriada, as successor to his father, and of Fortriu, through his mother by right of matriliny, and Constantine was, in fact, the first to hold both kingships at the same time. He is thought to have been raised among his mother's people and, whether or not he considered himself Pictish rather than Scots, he was evidently recognised as a Pict by the annalist when the context in which he overcame his rival to win for himself the kingship is entered as 'a battle between the Picts' and when his obituary in the *Annals of Ulster* at 820 styles Constantine mac Fergus 'king of Fortriu'.

The evidence of the king-lists for the fifty years after 789 is complex in the extreme and more usefully summarised in outline here than examined in detail,[18] but it can be taken, without any risk of oversimplification, to confirm Constantine as the first of what might be called the mac Fergus dynasty of kings of Picts and Scots. Their kingship was centred upon the formerly Pictish kingdom of Fortriu and their royal palace was at Forteviot in Strathearn, but they themselves were Gaelic Scots and while their kingship may have been initially legitimated by their Pictish matrilinear descent, their form of succession appears indistinguishable from the kingship custom of Celtic Ireland, whereby succession passed from the king to his brother, then to his son and on to his brother's son.

Thus Constantine, son of Fergus, was succeeded by his brother Oengus – whose name appears as *Unuist* in the Pictish king-list – who was succeeded on his death in 834 by Constantine's son bearing the very Pictish name of Drust. Drust would appear to have been the least distinguished of the mac Fergus kings, when some texts of the king-list indicate his having shared the kingship of Fortriu with an otherwise unknown, but evidently Pictish, Talorg, son of Unthoil, through at least some of his three-year reign, and when there is also no certainty as to his over-kingship of Dalriada. The king-list preserved in variant forms by different manuscripts of Flann's *Synchronisms* shows the kingship of Dalriada to have continued in parallel with the kingship of Fortriu – until the entry of Alpin, the father of the Kenneth whose name heads a new king-list as the founding king of a new dynasty – and the names of two kings of Fortriu, Constantine mac Fergus and his nephew Eoganan mac Oengus, appear in both lists. Other than those two, all the names listed as kings of Dalriada through that period are those of more obscure figures, which would suggest that they were, in fact, under-kings subject to the overlordship of kings of Fortriu. It is further possible – at least in some, if not all, cases – that they might not even have been resident in the west and that kingship of Dalriada might have come to represent little more than a tribute-bearing title at the court of the over-king at Forteviot, a possibility which becomes all the more credible in view of the first appearance of the northmen in the western sea being entered in the annals just five years after the accession of Constantine mac Fergus to the kingship of Fortriu.

The descent of the sea-raiders upon the Outer Hebrides in 794 and their subsequent attacks on island monasteries need not have been recognised, at least at first, as any great threat to the kingdom of the Scots and neither would the Norse settlement which followed swiftly in its wake have greatly impinged upon the central territory of Dalriada. Professor Leslie Alcock's study of the principal hillforts of Dalriada known to have been occupied into the later ninth century points to the two principal indices of early Scandinavian settlement – Norse graves containing male or female burials and place names deriving from the Norse *bolstadr* or 'farm' – being concentrated in the islands of the Hebridean seaboard and almost entirely absent from mid-Argyll and Lorn: 'It is evident that Norse settlers were effectively repulsed from the heartland of Dalriada; and it is a reasonable speculation that a major role in the defence was played by the two strongholds of Dunadd and Dunollie.'[19]

While the initial relocation of the principal royal line of the Cenel Gabrain in the east cannot have been as a response to the advent of the northmen in the west, the progressively greater impact of the Norse through the later reign of Constantine and that of his successor Oengus must have brought its pressures to bear on the new Picto-Scottish kingdom of Fortriu. While the capital fortresses in the west might very well have deterred viking raiders and sheltered their surrounding districts from the land-seekers who came after them, the Dalriadic nobility would have been increasingly attracted to the wealth and security offered by the new kingdom in the east as they felt themselves and their future prosperity ever more vulnerable on what was becoming a dangerous frontier in the west.

The kingdom of Fortriu was, of course, secure for only as long as the Norse were contained in the west and it was not until forty-five years after the first recorded appearance of a viking war-fleet in the Hebrides that the fury of the northmen was unleashed on the land of the Picts, but the impact of that first onslaught east of the Spine could hardly have been more dramatic, bringing death in battle to the last of the mac Fergus dynasty and opening the way for the ascendancy of Kenneth, Alpin's son.

While there is no question as to the reliability of the *Annals of Ulster* as a source of the greatest authority for the period, there is something distinctly unusual about the character of the entry at the year 839:

> A battle of the heathens over the men of Fortriu;
> in which fell Eoganan mac Oengus, and Bran mac Oengus,
> and Aed mac Boant; and others beyond counting were slain.

Had the annalist, or his original source, chosen to describe the same event in some such form as 'the devastation of Fortriu by the heathens', then his entry at 839 would have been typical of the numerous notices of Norse incursions which dominate the Irish annals through the first half of the ninth century. It could have been taken, had that been the case, to indicate just one of many viking raids, unusual only in the geographical location of its target area but otherwise an event of a kind with which the annalist had become grimly familiar.

It is clear that the entry of the 'battle of the heathens over the men of Fortriu' does not follow such a formula, bearing instead a much closer resemblance to the style of entry into the annal record of Irish tribal and dynastic conflict through the centuries before the arrival of the northmen, and for good reason, because this was no opportunistic foray by a viking warband. The list of fatal casualties set down in such detail by the annalist at 839 – Eoganan, son of Oengus and over-king of Picts and Scots; Bran, his brother and expected successor; Aed, son of Boant and under-king of Dalriada, and with them their Picto-Scottish nobility in numbers 'beyond counting' – points to nothing less than the effective extinction of the royal house of Fortriu at the hands of the northmen. It is hardly possible to interpret such a death-toll as anything other than the intended outcome of a strategic military operation driven by political purpose, which must raise the question of precisely who might have been the enemy so vaguely identified by the annalist as 'heathens'.

They were assuredly of Scandinavian origin, when the term 'heathens' was applied by the annals to no other people, but they were most unlikely to have been the Norse operating at such great distance from the Irish interior where their war-fleets were heavily engaged in plundering great and wealthy monasteries. They were still less likely to have been the Danes who had only just begun raiding the coast of southern England and whose longships would not be into the Irish Sea for another decade. Such a process of elimination points inexorably to the 'heathens' more likely and much better placed than any other to deliver such a death-blow to the mac Fergus dynasty of Fortriu having been the Hebridean Norse, who had been settled for more than a generation along the greater extent of Scotland's western seaboard by 839, and one of whose warlords was the same Guthfrith mac Fergus who just three years earlier – according to the *Annals of the Four Masters* – 'went to Alba to strengthen Dalriada at the request of Kenneth mac Alpin'.

Some twelve months after the 'battle of the heathens over the men of Fortriu', the *Chronicle of the Kings* recognises Kenneth mac Alpin as king in Dalriada and some two years after that as king in Pictland. It must appear, then, that this Kenneth 'foretold' by the *Prophecy of Berchan* as 'the first king who will reign in the east from among the men of Erin in Alba' was greatly indebted to the death-dealing intervention of the northmen for his dramatic rise to kingship – and it will be interesting to investigate the context in which such a debt might have been incurred.

While Kenneth was quite evidently not the first Scot to hold kingship over the Picts, all the evidence seems to be aware of a qualitative difference between him and those of the mac Fergus dynasty who had been over-kings in Fortriu before him, a contrast in character which has been most recently crystallised in the historian Michael Lynch's recognition of Kenneth as 'a latecomer from the Gaelic west'.[20] From which region of the Gaelic west he came is unknown – because his native territory may have lain to the south on Kintyre or, just as possibly, much further to the north in Lorn – but any man whose family home was anywhere along 'the seaboard of the Gael' and who had grown to maturity by the mid-point of the ninth century had done so through the years of Scandinavian expansion in Scotland when the sea-raiding viking had been overtaken by the land-seeking settler. The northmen would have assuredly been his and his father's neighbours in the borderland of the Norse with the Gael and, as is invariably the way with neighbours, some of them would have been more amenable than others.

If there is any genuine historical substance to the claim made by some versions of the *Chronicle of the Kings* for Kenneth's father Alpin having been killed in Galloway, then it is most probable that he was slain there in contention with the Norse,[21] but a fragment of evidence from Gaelic tradition and at least as ancient indicates Alpin having fathered at least one of his sons on a Norse woman. It has been suggested that Kenneth might have been the son of

a Pictish mother, an idea which would lend convenient legitimacy to his kingship of Picts were it supported by any stronger evidence than the possibility
that his given name *Cináed* might represent a Gaelicised form of the Pictish
Ciniod. While there is no good reason why Kenneth's mother should not have
been of Pictish royal descent, the *Prophecy of Berchan* describes another son
of Alpin, the *Domnall mac Alpin* who was Kenneth's successor in the kingship, as 'the wanton son of the *Gaillsigthe*' or 'foreign wife', which would
indicate his having been born to a Norse mother, and probably outwith
formal wedlock.[22] It is, of course, fully possible that Alpin might have
fathered sons on two women of different stock and that his two sons might
thus have been half-brothers, so while the *Prophecy of Berchan* cannot be
taken as evidence for Kenneth having also been born to a Scandinavian
mother, it does offer evidence for Alpin having entered into at least one close
relationship with the Hebridean Norse.

It was, thus, hardly possible for Kenneth to have grown to manhood other
than fully familiar with the northmen, still more so with the *gall-gaedhil*, and
consequently holding more in common with Guthfrith mac Fergus and his
kind than with his own distant kindred of the mac Fergus dynasty in the east.
Kenneth's reputation as a warrior is recognised by every one of the sources
for his life and times, but nowhere so vividly as in the *Prophecy of Berchan*
where he is called 'a man who will feed ravens, who will conquer in battle;
Ferbasach [perhaps, "Slayer"] shall be his name'. In pursuit of his greater
ambition, such a warlord would eventually have need of the most formidable
ally available to him and, when alliances between Celtic kings of Scots were
so often linked with kinship by marriage, the claim made by a genealogy
from late Clan Donald tradition for the daughter of Guthfrith mac Fergus
having been 'the wife of Kenneth mac Alpin'[23] might assume a real historical
significance.

Alliance with the Hebridean Norse would have provided Kenneth with the
strongest possible opening gambit for his rise to power in the west and marriage to a daughter of their chieftain would assuredly have enabled him to
summon Guthfrith with his kindred of the Airgialla to 'strengthen Dalriada'
in the year 836. Such a construction hinges on evidence from admittedly very
late, and thus always more suspect, sources, but it does supply a plausible
political purpose for the onslaught launched just three years afterwards by
'heathens' – assuredly of Guthfrith's kind, if not of his own warband – on the
'men of Fortriu' and the infliction of such casualties upon the kingships of
Picts and Scots as to provide Kenneth with the broadest scope for his ambition.

The sudden death in battle of the over-king at Fortriu, his under-king of

Dalriada, and most of their potential successors left Kenneth strategically placed to seize kingship in the west. He would have needed thereafter to consolidate his kingship, to render tributary the chieftains of the west, to eliminate such others as were inclined to resist him, and ensure his ability to raise a sufficiently impressive war-host with which to 'lead the Scots from Argyll into the land of the Picts' and there establish himself, just three years after the 'battle of the heathens over the men of Fortriu', as the new power in the land east of the Spine.

Such an account as can be distilled from the evidence of the sources for Kenneth's achievement of his kingship of the Picts is barely cogent and still less chronological. There is no entry in the *Annals of Ulster* with any bearing on Kenneth or his kingdom after the year 839 until the notice of his obituary as 'king of Picts' at 858. The references to his achieving overlordship of the Picts found in the various manuscripts of the *Chronicle of the Kings* may well derive from closely contemporary original sources but they represent very short measure as historical narrative, and the relevant passage in the *Prophecy of Berchan* is at least as cryptic as anything else in that most tantalising text. The later medieval accounts are either transparently derivative or folklore-inspired fiction, with the possible exception of one curious story which is worth investigation, less for its popular currency than for the relative antiquity of its association with Kenneth.

The core of the story is centred on his deceit, entrapment and slaughter of the Pictish nobility and its setting is located, in those versions where it is identified at all, at Scone in the lower Tay valley some fifteen miles south of Dunkeld. The story had evidently gained sufficient currency before the end of the eleventh century to allow allusion to it in the passage bearing on Kenneth in the *Prophecy of Berchan*:

> The fierce men in the east are deceived by him.
> He shall dig in the earth, mighty the art, a deadly pit,
> death by wounding, in the midst of Scone of the high shields.

The story to which those lines allude must be the same one of which the title alone – *Braflang Scóine* or 'The Treachery of Scone' – is included in the list of 'prime stories' of Irish tradition contained in the *Book of Leinster*. It would seem similarly certain that this same story came to the notice of the churchman, scholar and travel writer, Gerald of Wales, on one of his two visits to Ireland in the 1180s and provided him with the original source of the anecdote included in his book *On the Instruction of Princes* written some thirty years later. Gerald makes no mention of Kenneth or of Scone, but he does tell how the Scots invited the entire Pictish nobility to a banquet where they were encouraged to excessive indulgence in food and drink.

> They [the Scots] seized their opportunity and pulled out the bolts which held up the boards so that the Picts collapsed into the hollows of the benches on which they were sitting and into a trap up to the knees from which it was impossible to get up; and immediately slaughtered them all ... taken suddenly and unexpectedly and fearing nothing of this kind from allies bound to them by benefits and companions in their wars.

Another, more prosaic and probably earlier, version of the same story is included in the Scottish king-list from the fourteenth-century *Scalachronica* manuscript, but here the Picts are invited to a conference where they are set upon and slaughtered immediately upon arrival.

'It can hardly be doubted' – in the view of the eminent historian of early Scots kingship, Dr Marjorie Anderson – 'that the story of the *Treachery* was to some extent fictitious', and she points to the formula of treacherous attack at an assembly under truce occurring in Nennius' *Historia Brittonum* and the Russian *Primary Chronicle*.[24] It occurs also in Irish tradition, as does the device of the banquet as a focus for political confrontation or conspiracy, so the *Treachery of Scone* cannot really be taken any more seriously as historical evidence for Kenneth's relations with the Picts than *The Banquet of Dun na nGedh* can be accepted as a realistic account of the contention between Congal Caech and Domnall mac Aed. What can be said of all versions of the *Treachery* story is that they are in full agreement with all the other sources when they associate Kenneth's seizure of power in the east with extremes of violence.

All the different versions of the *Chronicle of the Kings* insist on Kenneth's 'destroying' the Picts – by which is meant the ruling aristocracy of Fortriu and not the populations of north Britain who had latterly been their subjects, because Kenneth's 'conquest of the Picts' was the outcome of an essentially dynastic contest rather than anything akin to what has recently become known as 'ethnic cleansing'. The sources are, none the less, at one in their recognition of the violent nature of that contest. The *Chronicle of Huntingdon*, consciously or not, echoes the Irish heroic tradition in its claim that 'he fought seven times in one day with the Picts, destroying many, and confirming the kingdom to himself', while the *Prophecy of Berchan* summons up all the resonance of bardic battle-song to herald 'the first king who will reign in the east from among the men of Erin in Alba; after use of the strength of spears and of swords, after violent deaths, after violent slaughter'.

It is generally accepted by historians that such unanimous testimony to Kenneth's ascendancy having been prefaced by extreme violence preserves genuine recollection of his kingship in the east having been won ultimately by the iron sword. If it was so, then the most authoritative annal record, which preserves a battle-by-battle record of the eighth-century ascendancy of Oengus mac Fergus, maintains total silence on Kenneth's way of the warrior, a silence which can be quite reasonably explained by the loss to the annalist of the Iona chronicle for the ninth century. It might otherwise have been that the unspecific claims made elsewhere in the sources endorsing the 'violent deaths . . . violent slaughter' tradition preserve recollections of the massacre of 839, which had by earlier sources been associated in some way – even implicitly and, perhaps, not unjustly – with Kenneth's invasion of the east.

It might, thus, have been that the annal record preserves a substantially accurate record of major events and that the characteristic savagery of the northmen had been transferred, in the way of guilt by association, to lesser conflicts by which Kenneth confirmed his kingship of Picts after 842. That there were, indeed, such conflicts can be inferred from the evidence found in the king-lists, where all Pictish lists enter the names of five kings of Picts who reigned after the death of Eoganan in 839, beginning with Eoganan's immediate successor named as *Uurad* (or *Ferat* in the Gaelic form), son of *Bargoit*. His reign would appear to have ended in the same year of 842 when Kenneth's kingship of Picts began, and yet Ferat is followed in the variant lists by as many as four successors, the last of them named as his son, Drust, said to have been killed in 848.

The most realistic explanation of this evidence from the king-lists is in terms of at least one rival dynasty having asserted a claim to kingship when the mac Fergus dynasty was extinguished in 839, being supported by factions of the Pictish warrior aristocracy in their own territorial power base – most probably in Atholl – and there holding out against Kenneth's ambition as their overlord. They were eventually eliminated, apparently one after the other and seemingly by force, especially when the king-lists are able to link the death of the last of them with the story of the *Treachery of Scone*. The Latin lists add to their entry of the name of Drust mac Ferat a note that he 'was killed at Forteviot, or some say at Scone' and the list in the *Scalachronica* manuscript has him 'killed at Scone by treachery'.

When resistance by rival Pictish claimants evidently persisted through the first six years of his reign in the east, Kenneth cannot be considered as having been secure in his over-kingship until the year 848. Set into the context of that chronology, the evidence for his having brought the relics of Columba to Dunkeld in the following year of 849 – 'in the seventh year of his reign' according to the *Chronicle of the Kings* – would indicate it as having been an act of especially political significance for his new kingdom of the Scots.

'THE KINGDOM OF SCONE'

The sources are unanimous in their recognition of Kenneth mac Alpin's succession to the kingship in Fortriu marking a new ascendancy for the Celtic kingdom of the Scots. The king-lists of Picts and of Dalriada, having run parallel for centuries, stop short at Kenneth's point of entry and it is his name which stands at the head of the new list of kings of a unified kingdom wherein was contained the kernel of the medieval Scottish nation.

Kenneth apparently chose Dunkeld to be the principal religious centre of that kingdom and to that end conferred upon it the spiritual and political stature accorded Iona in the old kingdom of Dalriada in the west. In so doing, however, he would seem to have been only restoring to Dunkeld a pre-eminence originally intended for it some thirty years earlier, because the 'church that he had built' there was not of his original foundation, on the evidence of a note accompanying the entry of Constantine mac Fergus in three texts of the Pictish king-lists which claims that 'he built Dunkeld'. If the building meant by that note can be taken, as it surely can, to have been a monastery and not a fortress, then the original monastery at Dunkeld must be credited to the first king of the mac Fergus dynasty and its date of foundation placed prior to that of Constantine's death entered in the annals at 820.

Dunkeld was founded, then, within little more than a decade of the evacuation of Iona following the viking raids, and Constantine's purpose in its foundation would undoubtedly have been to establish a new royal church in the east to serve in place of that recently abandoned in the west. Kenneth's purpose at Dunkeld would seem to have been very much the same, and the building of the church attributed to him by the *Chronicle* was, in all probability, the rebuilding of an earlier monastic church on the same site. The greater significance of Kenneth's patronage of Dunkeld over that of Constantine before him rests upon his bringing to it relics of Columba, a deliberate and decisive political statement reflecting Columba's genuinely historical role as patron saint of the royal house of the Cenel Gabrain from which the genealogies claim Kenneth to have been descended.

No less deliberate a part of Kenneth's intention for Dunkeld would seem also to have been the establishment of a shrine of the great saint of the Gael as a 'Celtic counter-weight' to the then flourishing cult centre of Saint Andrew at *Kilrimont* (later re-named St Andrews) in Fife.[25] There is good reason to believe the mac Alpin dynasty having long maintained an especial reverence for Columba's Iona, and a strange irony too in the evidence for Kenneth, who removed the saint's relics from his holy island, having himself been the first king of Scots to be buried on Iona. Some, but not all, versions of the *Chronicle of the Kings* record Kenneth's having been 'buried in the island of Iona, where the three sons of Erc were buried'. There is, of course, nowhere any reliable evidence for the burial of the 'three sons of Erc' on Iona, and the statement cannot be considered any more historical than the 'three sons of Erc' tradition itself, but the texts of the *Chronicle* claiming Kenneth having been buried on Iona make the same claim for almost all his successor kings of Scots until the last few years of the eleventh century. While there is evidence for kings having been buried on Iona before Kenneth, they were usually ones who had died there in monastic retirement, and so the formal tradition of ritual royal burial in this most sacred earth of Alba can be said to have been one first introduced by the mac Alpin dynasty.

There is another, and most curious, association between church and state in Kenneth's kingdom suggested by a passage in the *Chronicle of the Kings* when it claims that Kenneth 'destroyed the Picts' in retribution for their having 'spurned the Lord's mass and precept'. What was meant by that accusation is quite uncertain, but can most probably be interpreted as a reference to the Pictish king Nechtan mac Derile, whose expulsion of monks of Iona from his kingdom is entered in the annals at the year 717. It was an event which needs to be explained against the background of Iona's isolation resulting from its part in the seventh-century dispute between Celtic and Roman orthodoxies as to the correct calculation of the date of Easter.[26] The prestige and influence of Iona at the head of the Columban *paruchia* suffered greatly through that period on account of its tenacious adherence to the old Celtic custom, and not least in its loss of authority over the Northumbrian church following the decision in favour of the Roman custom reached by Oswy of Northumbria at the Synod of Whitby in 664. By the eve of the eighth century, the Roman orthodoxy was so widely adopted as to leave Iona, and with it its outlying foundations in Pictland, quite isolated among the churches of Ireland and Britain.

Despite the claim made first by Bede and repeated since by many who should know better, there is no evidence for the conversion of the Picts to Christianity having been the personal achievement of Columba himself. It was, in fact, accomplished by the very many monks from Iona who found their way east of the Spine through the century after his death. Christianity was evidently established among the Picts by the last quarter of the seventh century, when the Pictish king Bruide mac Beli, who had defeated the Northumbrians at Nechtansmere, was brought to Iona for burial – according to a fragment preserved in the Irish *Life* of Adamnan, who himself administered the funeral rites. Within a quarter of a century of Bruide's famous battle victory, one of his successor kings of Picts, Nechtan mac Derile, had established a peace treaty with Northumbria and was writing to Bede's monastery at Jarrow for guidance on the correct calculation of the date of Easter. Five years later, and presumably acting on the advice he had received from Jarrow regarding the theological shortcomings of the Columban church, the same Pictish king ordered the monks of Iona out of his kingdom.

It was an act which can be seen in retrospect, and in the light of the Pictish ascendancy which came twenty years later, to have been driven at least as much by political purpose – to prevent the infiltration of his kingdom by men of influence out of the Gaelic west – as by ecclesiastical correctitude, and it can be argued that the enduring achievement of Kenneth mac Alpin was his decisive reversal of what Nechtan had tried to accomplish in 717. Within fifteen years of Kenneth bringing Columba's relics to Dunkeld, its abbot is recognised by the annalist as '*prim-episcop* [principal bishop] of Fortriu' and his name-form of *Tuathal mac Artgus* entered in the annal confirms him to have been a Gaelic Scot.

Whether – as is sometimes claimed – the Pictish tongue was rendered extinct in Kenneth's kingdom cannot be proved, but it is true that the Picts seem to disappear without trace from the historical record at the point when Kenneth achieved kingship over them, a phenomenon which can only be explained by the mac Alpin dynasty of kings having achieved dominance in the land of the Picts for the language, custom and culture of the Gael. If there is any historical substance to the Irish tradition of the Munster prince Conall Corc having established himself as a king in Angus – and there is supporting evidence in Irish oghams and place-name components from that region – then Gaelic must have been introduced into Pictland before the end of the fourth century AD.

Its extensive introduction east of the Spine is rather more historically attributable to at least a hundred years of cultural influence by monks of Iona and other Irish monastic communities in Scotland. So too, the Gaelic tongue and way of life would have assuredly infiltrated the upper echelons of Pictish society as a result of the evidently frequent intermarriage between noble and royal kindreds of Pict and Scot. In fact, so extensive was the contact, peaceful and otherwise, across the Spine of Britain through the seventh and eighth centuries that the language, and with it the culture and customs, of the Gael cannot have been remotely unfamiliar to the Picts by the time that the Gaelic-speaking mac Fergus dynasty established itself in the kingship of Fortriu on the eve of the ninth century. Before the death of the last of the mac Fergus kings of Picts in 839 – suggests Thomas O'Rahilly in his wide-ranging study of Irish history and tradition – 'the kings of *Fortrenn* [Fortriu] had probably become more Scotic than the Scots themselves [and] the accession of *Cináed* [Kenneth] merely gave political sanction to a cultural transformation that had begun long before.'[27]

Dunkeld, then, can be said to represent the sacred centre of that 'cultural transformation', and so too 'Scone of the high shields' would appear – at least from the viewpoint of the Irish sources – to have been its secular counterpart in Kenneth's kingdom. Scone looms into sudden prominence in the orbit of Kenneth and is the place most closely associated with him in Irish tradition, even though the Scottish sources locate his palace – like those of kings in Fortriu before him – at Forteviot on the Earn. It may have been that the Irish recognised Scone as the Scots equivalent of their own traditional centre of king-making at Tara, a possibility suggested by the reference in the *Prophecy of Berchan* to 'Scone of the high shields' when ritual clashing of shields is thought to have accompanied the proclamation of kings in Celtic antiquity. Some recollection of Scone as a focus of king-ship for the Picts of antiquity must have also underlain Flann's claim for Kenneth having been 'the first of the Gael to assume the kingdom of Scone', which must be interpreted as his succession to an already existing kingship rather than his initiation of a new one. Whether or not Scone had been a place of kingmaking in the Pictish period – one akin, perhaps, to Dunadd in the west – it was confirmed as such in the time of the mac Alpin kings and remained so for their successor kings of Scots throughout the Middle Ages.

It was also the place long remembered in tradition – on the evidence of the *Book of Leinster*, the *Prophecy of Berchan*, and more than one Scottish king-list – as the location of the 'black dinner' at which Kenneth is said to have slaughtered his Pictish rivals. Even though John of Fordun makes no mention of treachery at Scone, the account of Kenneth's 'victories against the Picts' contained in his fourteenth-century *Chronicle* still owes more to folklore and fiction than to any historical authority, but it might be possible to extricate just a germ of truth from its claim for Kenneth's motive having been 'to revenge himself for the cruel murder of his father, and of his kinsmen who had lately been slain . . . by the Picts'. A similar claim for Alpin having been slain by the Picts is found in other sources, none of them very much earlier than Fordun, and is thought to derive from a confusion of Kenneth's father with his eighth-century namesake.

The first Alpin, a prince of the Cenel Gabrain who seized the kingship of Picts for two years in the 720s, was defeated in battle twice in the same year by two Pictish contenders, driven out of his kingdom and back to Dalriada, where he is thought to have met his death at the hands of the Picts in 736. I have earlier suggested the possibility of Kenneth having been descended from this Alpin, and, if such had been the case, his alleged motive of vengeance against the Picts might still hold good had he been seeking revenge on behalf of his great-grandfather Alpin instead of his father with the same name. When it is read with that possibility in mind, the entry in the *Annals of Tigernach* at 728 of the last battle fought and lost by the first Alpin in defence of his kingship of Picts might be found to have elements of unexpected bearing on Kenneth, son of a later Alpin.

> A lamentable battle between the Picts at Caislen Credi, and Alpin was routed and deprived of all his territories and people; and Nechtan mac Derile took the kingship of the Picts.

It is at least curious to discover – on no less impeccable authority than the learned Tigernach – that the king who drove the monks of Iona back across the Spine of Britain and the warlord who inflicted the last decisive defeat driving Alpin out of Pictland twenty years later were one and the same Nechtan, son of Derile.[28] Perhaps still more intriguing – and first suggested in the last century by the pioneering historian of Celtic Scotland, W. F. Skene – is the very plausible identification of the place of battle called by the annalist *Caislen Credi* with the 'Hill of Credulity' located by the *Chronicle of the Kings* as having been 'near the royal city of Scone'.[29]

'AND HE INVADED SAXONLAND'

Sheltered in the north by the Grampians and in the west by the Spine of Britain, the relatively secure location of the heartland of Fortriu in the political geography of the early ninth century played no small part in its transformation into the Picto-Scottish kingdom of the mac Fergus kings. If Kenneth mac Alpin had formed his own special relationship with the Hebridean Norse, as he would seem to have done, then his reign in the east might be expected to have brought still greater security to his new kingdom. In the event, however, nowhere was safe from viking attack when the tide of

Scandinavian expansion reached its flood at the mid-point of the ninth century, as is confirmed by the *Chronicle of the Kings* when it records 'the Danes wasted Pictland as far as Cluny and Dunkeld'.

The *Chronicle* offers no year date and no further detail, but the reference by the *Prophecy of Berchan* to Kenneth's having 'harassed the *gaill*' (Scandinavians) almost certainly alludes to the same event and suggests the raiders met with some resistance. If the *Chronicle* is precisely accurate in identifying the raiders as Danes – and it is just possible, though unlikely, that they might have been Norse out of the northern isles – then their viking onslaught can be realistically dated to within a few years before or after 851. There is evidence from both saga tradition and the medieval Danish historian Saxo Grammaticus for the Baltic sea-king Ragnar Lothbrok raiding the Scottish mainland at much the same time as Kenneth became fully established in the kingship of Picts, but it was not until the year 851 that Danish pirate fleets made their first appearance in the Irish Sea and the *dubh gaill* – as the Danes are called in the Irish sources[30] – make their first entry into the *Annals of Ulster*:

> The coming of the *dubh gaill* to *Ath Cliath* [Dublin], who made a great slaughter of the *finn gaill* [Norse], and they plundered the fortress, both people and property.

Having ravaged the capital fortress of the northmen in Ireland, the Danes appear to have sailed north against the Norse settlements in the Hebrides and it is quite possible that some of their warbands might have penetrated the Scottish mainland, even 'as far as Cluny and Dunkeld', in that same raiding season.

The Danes returned to Ireland in greater numbers the following year, bringing their war-fleet into the great sea lough of Carlingford and there facing a ferocious attack by a hundred and sixty Norse longships. The Irish sources describe a savage blood-fray fought out through three days and nights, until the Danes emerged victorious as the new lords of the *gaill* in Ireland with Dublin in their possession and the western sea at their mercy. It was, in the event, to be a short-lived ascendancy of no more than twelve months, because in the year after the battle of the dragonships on Carlingford Lough, there came west over sea a new and formidable overlord whose arrival is entered in the *Annals of Ulster* at 853:

> Olaf, son of the king of the Norse, came to Ireland, and the northmen of Ireland submitted to him and tribute was paid to him by the Gael.

'Olaf, son of the king of the Norse', has been convincingly identified by Professor Alfred Smyth[31] as Olaf Guthfrithsson, son of the reigning king of the royal house of *Vestfold* in Norway, and his task was the subjection to his father's overlordship of the viking chieftains in the west, be they Norse or Dane, from Orkney down to Dublin.

Through almost two decades as Norse king of Dublin, this Olaf was very evidently a remarkable man of power in Ireland and the Isles, facing up to Irish kings and high-kings as confidently as he swept aside any Norse chieftain with pretensions to viking independence. Unless it is entirely accidental that the obituary of Guthfrith mac Fergus, 'chieftain of the Hebridean Norse', is entered in the *Annals of the Four Masters* at the same year as Olaf's arrival in the west is entered in the *Annals of Ulster*, then Kenneth's old ally of seventeen years before would seem to have been one of the first casualties of the new Norse overlord.

The death of Guthfrith would also seem to have left Kenneth in need of a new ally in the west, which situation might well have lain behind a fragment of evidence found in Duald MacFirbis' *Fragmentary Annals of Ireland* for Olaf of Dublin having taken to wife a daughter of *Cináed*. Compiled in the seventeenth century, MacFirbis' *Annals* do represent a late source of sometimes doubtful authority and neither does their reference firmly identify 'Cinaed' as king of Scots, but if Kenneth did indeed secure a new alliance by attaching a daughter to the man hailed by the saga-maker as 'the greatest warrior king of the western sea', it would have been a stratagem fully typical of all else that is known of his diplomacy. There is good evidence from the twelfth-century Irish *Bansenchus* ('History of the Women') for one of Kenneth's daughters having been the wife of the Irish high-king Aed Findliath of the Ui Neill, as there is from the *Chronicle of the Kings* for another of his daughters having been given in marriage to Rhun, heir apparent and later king of the Strathclyde Britons.

While there is little historical evidence for Kenneth's relations with the north Britons, the entry of his obituary in the *Annales Cambriae* indicates him having been a figure of significance to his neighbours on the Clyde and the *Chronicle of the Kings* records one instance of hostility between them with its note that 'the Britons burned Dunblane'. Once again, the *Chronicle* offers no date and no more detail, but Dunblane commanded a principal route linking Fortriu with the old Dalriadic territories in Argyll and would thus have represented a strategic fortress for the kingdom of the Scots. The most plausible recent explanation[32] of an attack on Dunblane by the Strathclyde Britons suggests their having feared finding themselves surrounded by potential enemies when Kenneth launched a policy of expansion south of the Forth, so it would seem likely that the marriage of his daughter into the royal house of Strathclyde was arranged subsequent to hostilities and probably as part of a non-aggression pact between Briton and Scot.

The evidence of the *Chronicle* leaves no doubt of Kenneth's aggressive expansion having been principally directed to the southward, even as far as the Tweed, into what was still the northern extent of Northumbria.

> And he invaded Saxonland six times;
> and he seized Dunbar and burned Melrose.

Some two hundred and fifty years separate Kenneth's ascendancy from the last Scots incursion into Northumbria so decisively repulsed at Degsastan and those years were to see the fortunes of the northern English reach their high peak in the third quarter of the seventh century, before entering upon a long decline thereafter. The Northumbrian ascendancy in north Britain was never to recover from the great reverse at Nechtansmere, while its supremacy among the English kingdoms had been long since overtaken by the rise of Mercia in the eighth century and of Wessex in the ninth, but the ninth-century extent of the Northumbrian kingdom still represented a vast territory extending from the north bank of the Humber to the southern shore of the Firth of Forth.

That northern frontier had been maintained throughout the eighth century by an hereditary dynasty of Northumbrian warlords, effectively sub-kings of the Pictish march and veterans of many bloody contests with the Picts around the Forth, whose capital fortress had long been *Dynbaer*, the Old English name-form from which derives the modern place name of Dunbar. Kenneth's attack on Dunbar thus represented a strike of great strategic importance against a major power base of the northern English and signalled his further aggressive designs on Northumbria leading to his raid on Melrose.

The Melrose intended by the *Chronicle* was not the modern town of that name with its twelfth-century abbey ruins, but the earlier monastery of *Mailros* (now Old Melrose) on a site some few miles downriver formed by a loop in the course of the Tweed. This original monastery of Melrose had been founded as a daughter house of Lindisfarne during the founding abbacy of Saint Aidan and is known, from Bede's *Life of Saint Cuthbert*, to have been already well established by the time of Aidan's death in 651. Bede tells how Cuthbert had been a young man minding sheep on the Lammermuir hills when he saw a vision of Aidan's soul ascending to heaven on the night of the saint's death. Thus inspired to make his own entry into religion, Cuthbert found his way to the monastery at Melrose and there began the monastic career which led to his becoming bishop of Lindisfarne and, following his death in 687, to his recognition as the great saint of the northern English.

On the evidence of just two of his target sites identified by the *Chronicle*, Kenneth's invasions of Northumbria were driven by a political purpose far beyond mere raiding for plunder. They can be seen now to have set a pattern of foreign policy for his successor kings of the mac Alpin dynasty which was eventually to carry the southern frontier of their kingdom down to the north bank of the Tweed. Kenneth's incursions into 'Saxonland' can serve also to indicate something more of the nature and extent of the kingdom of the Scots in his own time, when commitment of so much attention to ambitions south of the Forth would have demanded his full confidence in the security of all other borders of his kingdom, and not least that of his northern frontier.

The greatest extent of the core territory of Kenneth's kingdom of Scone would, in fact, have been much the same as that of Picto-Scottish kings of Fortriu before him and comprised the former Pictish provinces of Fortriu itself, *Fib* (Fife), *Fotla* (Atholl/Angus), and *Circin* (the Mearns). His kingdom would thus have extended from the north bank of the Forth to the Grampians – known as the Mounth in medieval times and thought to have earlier represented the boundary between the northern and southern Picts. To which can be added his dominions in the west, because there is every probability that Kenneth retained some measure of overlordship for Kintyre, mid-Argyll and Lorn as the mainland territories of his original kingdom of Dalriada.

The biggest question mark, then, is left over those territories north of the Mounth, which might be taken to represent his kingdom's most vulnerable frontier. Whether the Norse out of Orkney were established in the far north of the mainland before the later ninth century is uncertain, but there is good evidence for a son of Olaf of Dublin having established himself in Caithness less than twenty years after Kenneth's death. South of Caithness and north of the Mounth lies the territory which had been the power centre of Bruide mac Maelchon, high-king of Picts in the sixth century and was to re-emerge four hundred years later as the Scots province of Moray, but really very little is known of its political status in the interregnum. There is, however, enough evidence (which will bear closer consideration here later) from the genealogies of eleventh-century kings of Scots to confirm there having been a migration of the Cenel Loairn out of their old territory around Oban and up the Great Glen to establish themselves in the region between the Dornoch Firth and the Grampians which is later called Moray. Place-name evidence shows this migration to have been accomplished in the ninth century when the old

Cenel Loairn territory was under increasing pressure from the Norse and at much the same time as the Cenel Gabrain were moving east into the kingdom of Fortriu. It would, then, be no less than reasonable to suggest the new lords north of the Mounth having been an immigrant nobility out of Lorn in Argyll, formerly subject to the over-kings of Dalriada and probably still acknowledging Kenneth mac Alpin as the successor, in some measure, to that same overlordship.

Even so tentative an outline of the political geography of this kingdom of Scone can leave the very least doubt of the medieval Scottish nation having been the legacy left to history by this son of Alpin come late from the Gaelic west.

'He will die', according to the *Prophecy of Berchan*, 'on the banks of the Earn', a statement with which the *Chronicle of the Kings* is in full agreement and to which it can add its own further detail:

> He died of a tumour, on the Ides of February [13 February], the third day of the week,[33] in the palace of Forteviot.

Kenneth's obituary in the *Annals of Ulster* at the year 858 styles him 'king of Picts'. The same title is accorded his three immediate successors – Domnall, his brother, and Constantine and Aed, his sons – by their obituaries entered in the annals, but all their successors through the tenth century were to be styled by the sources 'kings of Alba'. It was not until the succession of the last in the direct male line of descent from Kenneth mac Alpin that a 'king of Scotland' was to be accorded that title in the sources, but not by the Gaelic tradition preserved in the *Prophecy of Berchan* where 'his name is *Forranach*' ... 'The Aggressor'.

5

'His name is The Aggressor'

MALCOLM

THE RIVER TWEED has been recognised, at least in popular currency, for many hundreds of years as the natural frontier between England and Scotland and the use of the phrase 'both sides the Tweed' most often indicates the two nations who for so long faced each other across its waters with varying degrees of suspicious hostility.

Yet the Border line runs today, as it has for the most part of a thousand years, along an approximate diagonal drawn from the Solway Firth to the lower Tweed valley, so the river can, in fact, only be said to mark out the Anglo-Scottish frontier for less than a quarter of its course of some ninety-seven miles from its source in the hills north of Moffat to its outflow into the North Sea at Berwick. The Border lies midstream along the Tweed for just eighteen miles upriver from Berwick before turning suddenly southward from the point where the river is joined by the Redden Burn just beyond the village of Carham, and thereafter the Tweed valley lies entirely within the bounds of what has long been Scotland.

The modern place name of Carham derives from the more ancient *Carrum*, the name of an Anglo-Saxon *vill* or estate which extended some miles outwith the confines of modern Carham village and was gifted by the Northumbrian king Egfrith in the year 672 to Saint Cuthbert, who was at that time prior of the monastery on Lindisfarne. The entry of that land-grant in the tenth-century *Historia de Sancto Cuthberto* – less a history, in fact, than an inventory of the vast landholdings of the community of Cuthbert at that time – marks the first appearance of Carham in the early sources. By the time of Carham's reappearance in the historical record of the twelfth century, where it is mentioned in Richard of Hexham's closely contemporary account of the invasion launched upon Northumbria in 1136 by the Scots king David I, it is numbered among five Northumbrian strong-points targeted by the invader and identified as 'Carrum, by the English called Wark'.

Richard's reference to that change of name attests the significant new development which had overtaken the former monastic estate by the fourth decade of the twelfth century, whereby the northern English baron Walter Espec of Helmsley had been endowed with the 'honour of Carham' by Henry I and raised a castle there on the *kaim*, a ridge formed in Ice Age antiquity of a jumble of rock deposits left by the retreating glaciers. The Old English *Carrum* has been translated by one foremost authority on place names as 'at the rocks',[1] but the local labour recruited to build the defences of Walter's fortress – evidently in the Norman 'motte and bailey' style characteristic of the period – called it by their own name of *Werke*, literally 'the work', from which derives the modern name-form of Wark-upon-Tweed.

Virtually nothing, other than a green mound embedded with a few lower courses of the stone-built walls of its keep, remains to be seen of the original Norman castle or its successive rebuildings. Wark, like its neighbouring village of Carham little more than a mile to its westward, appears now in the guise of an unexceptional north Northumberland village, but its layout follows closely on the ground-plan of the medieval fortress which commanded a strategic ford-crossing of the Tweed and, for some four and a half centuries, represented a Border stronghold of crucial significance. 'Auld Wark upon the Tweed', recalls an old dialect rhyme, 'has been many a man's deid [death]', and that observation from local tradition is well borne out by the nineteenth-century antiquary John Cadwallader Bates, whose thorough-going survey of Northumberland's border holds found 'no castle along the whole line of the Border plays so active a part in the last four centuries of that bloody roll of open wars and treacherous raids as does Wark-upon-Tweed'.[2]

'Auld Wark' was suffering a Scots onslaught at its very first point of entry into the historical record and was to endure another dozen sieges before 1603 when the Union of the Crowns transformed the Border overnight from a long-embattled frontier into an effective formality. Having struck at Wark in his invasion of 1136, David of Scotland returned just two years later to lay it siege twice more, first on his advance to the battle of the Standard at Northallerton and again, following his defeat there by an English army led by Walter Espec, on his return into Scotland some weeks later. It is probable that the Scots maintained a blockade of Wark while their king led the greater part of his forces south into Yorkshire, but he himself resumed command of the siege on his northward retreat, bringing up his war engines against its defences but still failing to take the castle until its garrison, having been reduced to the point of starvation, negotiated its surrender and marched out with full honours of war before the Scots razed their stronghold to the ground.

The fortress was subsequently rebuilt and its defences greatly extended by the year 1174 when David's son and successor king of Scots, William the Lion, attacked Wark's outer bailey with some hundreds of Flemish mercenaries, stone-hurling siege engines, and finally with fire-raising torch and brushwood, but still failed to penetrate beyond its first line of fortification. It was at Wark that Edward II mustered his battle-host before marching to defeat at Bannockburn and just four years later the castle was besieged by Robert the Bruce's army. That assault of 1318 was more successful than had been William the Lion's and secured the surrender of the garrison, but the siege laid in 1342 by the Bruce's son, David II, was abandoned on the approach of an English relief force. The Scots achieved rather greater success in the reign of Robert II, David's nephew and the first king of Scots of the house of Stewart, when Wark was captured and dismantled in 1375 and fifteen years later a deputation of English and Scottish esquires appointed to assess compensation due from the Scots for damage inflicted to the castle reported it 'ruined and worthless'.

There seems to be no record of any Scots reparations, still less English repairs, having been made as a result, but there were evidently sufficient surviving defences to be 'despoiled and thrown down' when the castle was captured again by the Scots in 1398. The capture was blamed in that instance on an insufficient garrison, which would seem still not to have been adequately reinforced in view of an attack twenty years later when the English garrison was put to the sword, a fate inflicted in turn on the occupying Scots soon afterwards when the castle was retaken. The Scots came again to Wark in 1460 to seize and dismantle its castle, very shortly after the accidental death of James II caused by a misfiring of one of his own cannon laying siege to Roxburgh castle a few miles upriver.

The *State Papers of Henry VIII* preserve a detailed account of the rebuilding of Wark by royal command just a few years after the devastating defeat of the Scots invasion of 1513 at Flodden Field, a restoration of defences which were to be seriously tested ten years later when the Scots regent the Duke of Albany brought some three dozen artillery pieces to hammer the castle walls from positions on the north bank of the Tweed. By virtue of a first-hand account set down by the sixteenth-century Scots historian George Buchanan who served with the besieging host while a young man, Albany's siege by cannon fire is probably the best-documented of the assaults on Wark and, although unsuccessful in taking the castle, it did manage to destroy most of the outer walls before the approach of an English relief force compelled withdrawal. There is evidence of just one last siege of Wark, apparently successfully accomplished by the Scots with French allies in 1549, which is poorly recorded but would seem to have still further dismantled the castle and to have been followed by its evacuation.

The English persistence in repairing and restoring the fortress through so many beleaguered centuries bears impressive testimony to its immense strategic importance and even as late as 1551, two full years after its last besieging, a government survey of border defences reported the 'Castle of Warke . . . standeth to very good purpose for the defence of the frontier and the country'.[3]

Through the last half-century of the Border as a hostile frontier, Wark retained a garrison and captain in command, but its function was the policing of the widespread practice of 'Border reiving', criminal and semi-criminal raiding and retaliation unofficially encouraged by the same authorities who officially condemned it and considered to be the 'custom of the country' in a lawless land which had been a war zone for most of five hundred years. When the Union of the Crowns spelled the end of the old Border in 1603 and consigned the Border fortress to history, the 'Castle of Warke' was left to face its last and most relentless assailants. They were time, neglect and decay and it had no defences with which to withstand them.

The military history of Wark, were it to be set down in full and meticulous detail, would represent something little short of a comprehensive history of Anglo–Scottish warfare on the East March and, yet the first and most decisive conflict in that long history was fought in the fields beside the Tweed very close by Wark, but more than a hundred years before the place was called by that name and is thus known to historians as the battle of Carham.

The Border line which lies midstream of the Tweed between Berwick and Redden Burn is shown by the modern Ordnance Survey map to swing south of the river for less than half a mile about one mile east of Wark and the map must therefore be taken to indicate that half-mile stretch of arable land south of the Tweed as a part of Scotland. I have never been able to discover any genuine explanation of how that deviation of the frontier came into being, unless it might have been in some wise connected with the fact that this stretch of riverbank is thought to have been the field upon which the battle of Carham was fought out in the year 1018. It was a momentous blood-fray as well remembered by the medieval Durham chroniclers for its 'miserable slaughter of the people of Saint Cuthbert', as by modern historians for having finally confirmed the Tweed as the southern frontier of the kingdom of the Scots, and its victor was Malcolm, Kenneth's son and second of that name in the high-kingship of Alba.

THE WAY TO THE MOOR OF THE BARDS

Malcolm (from the Gaelic *Máel coluim* or 'follower of Columba') makes his first entry into the historical record at 1005, in which year he emerged from a blood-fray fought out at Monzievaird, 'the moor of the bards' above Crieff in Strathearn, to begin his reign of three decades in the kingship of Scots.

That much is assured by agreement of all the sources, but any more detailed account of events at Monzievaird and those involved in them will have to be constructed from the conflicting evidences preserved by the annalists and compilers of king-lists. It will amount, in fact, to an inevitably incomplete jigsaw of fragments from the sources, but one in which the first key piece must be the reliably dated entry in the *Annals of Ulster* at the year 1005:

> A battle between the men of Alba on either side;
> and in it fell the king of Alba, Kenneth, son of Dubh.

While the annalist's original source appears not to have identified the victor in that 'battle between the men of Alba', the annalist himself seems to have known full well who he was – on the evidence of a line drawn on the manuscript page to link the entry at 1005 with the next appearance of Malcolm's name in the entry of his obituary at the year 1034. This battle, then, can only have been the same conflict described in the *Prophecy of Berchan* where Kenneth, son of Dubh, is called *An Donn* ('The Brown One'), who 'will have eight and a half years in the kingship; a short time, alas, until the Gaels turn upon him . . .'

> The Gaels gather, on the day when they shall be the survivors,
> about him on his bloody bed, between two valleys, not far from
> the banks of the Earn.

Kenneth, son of Dubh, (or, perhaps more conveniently, Kenneth III[4]) is attributed a reign of eight years by all texts of the *Chronicle of the Kings*, a reign-length of precisely the same duration as that accorded his son Giric by some later versions of the *Chronicle*:

> Giric, son of Kenneth, son of Dubh, reigned for eight years. He was killed by Kenneth's son [i.e. Malcolm] in Monzievaird and was buried in Iona.

The 'Verse Chronicle of the Kings', preserved in the thirteenth-century *Chronicle of Melrose*, calls Giric by the later corrupt name-form of 'Grim', but otherwise tells much the same story.

> For the space of eight years, king Grim reigned,
> the son of Kenneth, who was son of Dubh.
> The place where he was slain,
> by Kenneth's son called Malcolm,
> Is said to be the Field of the Bards.

With the king-lists obviously in the throes of one of their more aberrant phases, there would seem to be no obvious explanation of these contradictions, unless one might be discerned in the notable absence of Giric's name from the earlier – and, thus, more trustworthy – versions of the *Chronicle of the Kings*. Eminent scholarly opinion has recently suggested that there was, in fact, no such king as 'Giric, son of Kenneth', and that his appearance in the later *Chronicle* texts can be attributed to a scribal error picking up the name of an earlier Giric from the ninth century and 'inserting a non-existent son for Kenneth III'.[5] Such an interpretation does, at least, offer a convincing alternative to the earlier reading of the evidence which suggested Giric, son of Kenneth, having ruled jointly with his father or as sub-king under him until both were slain by Malcolm at Monzievaird.

The violent death of a king at the hands of his successor or a faction in support of his successor was never entirely unknown even in the earliest generations of the mac Alpin dynasty – on the evidence of Aed, son and third in succession to Kenneth mac Alpin, having been slain in 878 by an alliance of Giric, 'son of Dungal', and Eochaid, son of Rhun, who succeeded him to rule as joint kings[6] – but it had become so regular an occurrence by the end of the tenth century as to represent the almost customary form of succession to the kingship of Scots. Donald, son of Alpin, had succeeded his brother Kenneth in 858 and was succeeded into the kingship by Kenneth's two sons, first Constantine and then Aed. Through the next two generations of the mac Alpin dynasty, the kingship passed alternately – as had been the way of the old Irish custom – between candidates from those two lines of descent.

By the third generation, however, an element of acrimony had grown up between the two branches of the dynasty and Dubh, son of Constantine's grandson Malcolm I, was slain by the men of Moray, seemingly in support of Culen, son of Aed's grandson Indulf, who followed Dubh into the kingship in 966. Several versions of the *Chronicle of the Kings* tell the same strange story of events following Dubh's assassination.

He was killed in Forres, and [his body] hidden away under the bridge of Kinloss. But the sun did not appear so long as he was hidden there, until he was found and buried in the island of Iona.

It is quite possible that one curious memento of that story survives today in the form of the famous carved stone – known, for no good historical reason, as 'Sueno's Stone' – which stands beside the Kinloss to Burghead road just east of Forres. Its marvellously detailed carving, reliably dated to the tenth century and acknowledged as a masterpiece of Picto-Scottish monumental art, shows decapitated bodies lying beneath a bridge with a battle raging all around them and has led, with obvious good reason, to the suggestion that this 'Sueno's Stone' was carved to commemorate the dramatic events surrounding the death of Dubh or, at least, to illustrate a legend which had soon grown up around them.

Dubh's successor Culen met with a similarly violent death in 971, being slain in the course of a personal feud with a Strathclyde faction and succeeded by Dubh's brother, Kenneth II. Kenneth was arguably the most impressive king of Scots of the tenth century and reigned for some twenty-four years until the old feud with the rival line of Aed resurfaced to bring about his death – at the hands of conspirators, according to Fordun's *Chronicle* – at Fettercairn in 995. His successor was Culen's son, Constantine the Bald, who was slain in his turn, just two years later, by Dubh's son, the third Kenneth in the kingship of Scots and it might be said that this Kenneth, son of Dubh, claimed the final victory in the long-running contention between the descendants of the sons of Kenneth mac Alpin when he slew that last of the line of Aed in 997. Within a decade, however, he himself had become the first victim in a new dynastic feud when he was slain on the Moor of the Bards by his cousin, the second Malcolm, king of Scots.[7]

Other than its provenance of his lineage in the direct male line from Kenneth mac Alpin, the formal historical record can offer no account of Malcolm before his sudden and dramatic appearance as 'the Aggressor' at Monzievaird, but there are elements to be found in the passages bearing upon him in the *Prophecy of Berchan* which suggest themselves as allusions to his whereabouts and activities before 1005.

Quite the most significant of these is the description of Malcolm as *loingseach Ile ocus Aran*, a phrase usually translated as 'voyager of Islay and Arran' but recently, and very convincingly, interpreted as 'voyager' in the sense of 'exile' by the American historian Benjamin Hudson who suggests Malcolm having fled – either on the death of his father at the hands of Constantine's conspirators or when his cousin Kenneth mac Dubh seized the kingship two years later – to 'the ancestral lands of Dalriada' and having passed as much as a decade of his young manhood in the Isles.[8]

If 'voyager of Islay and Arran' can be taken as evidence for Malcolm's seeking sanctuary in the Isles during the reign of a rival in the kingship of Scots, it would follow that other references to him in the *Prophecy of Berchan* probably refer to that same period of his life, most especially the one describing him as 'destroyer of *gaill*', because his long exile in the Gaelic west would have assuredly brought him into his first contact with the Norse. The precise nature of that contact is, of course, unknown, but it cannot have been so relentlessly hostile as is suggested by *Berchan* in view of the strong saga evidence for a daughter of Malcolm having become the bride of Sigurd Hlodvisson – called 'Sigurd the Stout' – Norse *jarl* of Orkney.

The term *jarl* – from which derives the later English title of 'earl' – is best translated as 'sub-king' and the *jarldom* of Orkney, formally established in the second half of the ninth century, had come to represent the principal Norse centre of power west over sea before the year AD 1000. Sigurd's influence and ambition was more far-reaching than that of any Orkney jarl before him and the thirteenth-century *Njal's Saga* claims his dominions on the mainland to have included Ross, Moray, Sutherland and *Dalar* or 'the Dales'. It is uncertain whether the saga-maker intended the Norse term *Dalar* to mean the Dales of Caithness or some part of the islands and mainland of Argyll – *Dalar* having derived, perhaps, from the Gaelic *Dalriada* – but there is good evidence for Sigurd having exercised some measure of sovereignty over the Hebridean Norse. Their chieftain through the last two decades of the tenth century had been Rognvald Guthfrithsson, whose obituary entered in the Irish annals at 1005 records him having died in Limerick. It has been taken to imply his having been driven out of his 'kingdom of the Isles' before that date, and, by inference, as a result of the expansionist activities of Sigurd of Orkney. The *Eyrbyggja Saga* – another thirteenth-century source, but one especially well informed on Hebridean affairs – tells of Sigurd's authority extending as far south as Man, while the Irish *Cogadh Gaedhel re Gallaibh* calls him 'earl of the Orkneys and other islands also' and tells of his recruiting warriors from Skye, Lewis, Kintyre, and Argyll into the 'levy of fierce, barbarous men' that he brought to Ireland to fight the battle of Clontarf in 1014.

It is more than likely, then, that Sigurd represented a very prominent and no less formidable presence on Scotland's western seaboard while Malcolm was the exiled 'voyager of Islay and Arran', and their almost inevitable acquaintance at that time sets the context for the statement by the *Orkneyinga Saga* that 'Jarl Sigurd married the daughter of Malcolm, king of Scots, and their son was Jarl Thorfinn'.[9]

The *Orkneyinga Saga*, set down by an Icelander around the year 1200, represents the principal source for the history of the jarldom of Orkney and it tells of the future Jarl Thorfinn Sigurdsson, then a boy of just five years, being fostered at the Scottish court of his grandfather at the time of his father's death in battle at Clontarf in 1014. Although saga chronology can never be considered thoroughly reliable, there is no good reason to suspect the dating in this instance, so the birth of the future Jarl Thorfinn can be assigned to the year 1009 and the marriage of Sigurd to Malcolm's daughter to the year 1008 or earlier.

Malcolm, then, had given one of his daughters in marriage to the jarl of Orkney within a few years of his succession to the kingship of Scots, and there is also a possibility – admittedly much less secure in its evidence, but ultimately of crucial importance for the future history of the kingship of the Scots – that Malcolm gave another daughter in marriage at much the same time to another man of power in the north, Findlaech mac Ruadri, *mormaer* of Moray. The *mormaers* – a title translating from the Gaelic as 'great steward' and, like the Norse *jarl*, meaning 'sub-king', but of territorial rather than tribal sovereignty – of Moray were a dynasty claiming descent from the royal house of the Cenel Loairn who had migrated from their old heartland in the west and up the Great Glen when the Cenel Gabrain were establishing themselves as kings in Fortriu. By the eleventh century, these mormaers had been long established as lords of the land north of the Mounth and south of Strath Oykel, where they formed the cutting edge of Scots ambitions on Norse-occupied Caithness and from where, on more than one recorded occasion of violent contention, they played a part in struggles for succession to the kingship of Scots.

These marriages of Malcolm's daughters to men of such power in the north are most realistically interpreted as devices to secure strategic allies at a point when he felt his kingship to be very much less than secure. Such, then, would seem to have been his situation within just a few years of his succession, and yet Malcolm had been so greatly confident in the first year of his reign as to be able to direct his military ambition south of the Tweed and deep into the territory of what had once been the powerful Northumbrian kingdom.

'ROYAL PREY' UPON CUTHBERT'S LAND

The political map of the lands between the Humber estuary and the Firth of Forth had been more than once transformed through the hundred and fifty years which separate Kenneth mac Alpin's incursions into 'Saxonland' from the succession of Malcolm II to the kingship of Scots. The old kingdom of Northumbria, which had claimed dominion over so much of north Britain in the seventh century and entered upon its deep decline in the eighth, was not long to survive the invasion of England by the Danish 'great host' which landed in East Anglia in 865.

The Northumbrian kingdom can be said, in fact, to have been the first political casualty of the Scandinavian settlement of England, when the Danes seized York in 866 and slew the last of the Anglo-Saxon kings of Northumbria in the following year. For the greater part of a century thereafter, the city which had been the military capital of Roman Britain as *Eboracum* re-emerged as *Jorvik* of the northmen, a Scandinavian power centre comparable only, and closely linked, to Dublin. The initial extent of Danish settlement around York corresponded approximately to that of the old Northumbrian province of Deira with its northern boundary on the Tees, until its first king – the Ivar called 'the Boneless' and reputedly a son of Ragnar Lothbrok – moved on to join the Dublin Norse in the siege of Strathclyde and afterwards establish himself in the kingdom of Dublin. When Ivar died in Ireland in 873, the kingship of Jorvik passed to his brother Halfdan, who overwintered his war-fleet on the Tyne in 874 to plunder across Bernicia as far west as Carlisle in the following spring.

Symeon's *History of the Church of Durham* tells how 'fire and sword were carried from the eastern sea to the western', posing so great a threat to the monastery on Lindisfarne as to cause its abbot and his community to abandon their island, carrying with them to safety the body of their great saint Cuthbert in a coffin of carved oak. For some seven years this 'community of Cuthbert' wandered the north of England in search of sanctuary from the northmen, until the tide of events turned decisively in their favour following the death of Halfdan, when the kingship of Jorvik passed in 883 to one Guthred Hardcnutsson, a young man of Danish background and evident Christian faith. Guthred not only restored to Cuthbert's community its lands between Tyne and Wear, but allowed its bishop to purchase estates on the Tees and to establish a new principal church at *Cuncacestre* (now Chester-le-Street) from where the vast landholdings which represented the 'patrimony of Cuthbert' were to be administered for more than a hundred years thereafter.

While the *Anglo-Saxon Chronicle* for 876 tells of Halfdan having 'apportioned the lands of the Northumbrians [among his warband] and from that time they [the Danes] continued ploughing and tilling them', the place-name evidence shows this second stage of Scandinavian settlement to have extended north of the Tees but stopped short of the valley of the Tyne. 'Beyond the Tyne,' explains the Manchester historian N. J. Higham, 'Northumberland lay outside the normal control of Halfdan's successors, but not outside the influence of Saint Cuthbert. It was within this area that the monastery [of Lindisfarne] had attracted the earliest grant of estates and the community [of Cuthbert] emerged as the major landowners in the whole Tees–Forth province.'[10]

Secular power in this northern extent of the old Northumbrian kingdom devolved on to an hereditary dynasty of English nobles with their power base at the old royal capital of Bamburgh. These northern magnates – first called *ealdormen* in the sources, but styled 'Earls of Bamburgh' and, on occasion, 'Earls of Northumbria' by the eleventh century – make their first entry into the historical record shortly before 914 when they are found in conflict with the Dublin Norse who invaded Northumbria to seize control of Jorvik following the destruction of the Danes by the West Saxons four years earlier.

The dynasty at Bamburgh, however, was to long outlast the kingdom of Jorvik. On the eve of the eleventh century, when the royal house of Wessex was fully established in the sovereignty of all England and the last Norse king of York had been slain on Stainmoor some forty years past, the formidable Uhtred, son and heir-apparent to Earl Waltheof of Bamburgh, can already be recognised as the northern English warlord charged with the defence of what had once been the Northumbrian kingdom but must now be considered 'Cuthbert's land'. It is especially fitting not only that Uhtred's earliest dated entry in the sources should be found in Symeon's *History of the Church of Durham* but that Symeon's reference should associate him so significantly with the foundation of the last and greatest church of Cuthbert.

Symeon's *History*, set down in the early twelfth century, preserves the most detailed account of the foundation of Durham and the events leading up to it, all of which he takes great pains to place within the year 995. He tells of Aldhun, titular bishop of Lindisfarne at Chester-le-Street, being 'amonished by a revelation from heaven that, carrying with him the uncorrupt body of the most holy father [Cuthbert],[11] he should escape by flight, as swiftly as possible, from the eruption about to be made by some pirates who were close at hand. So he took the body with him, and he and all the people who are styled the people of Saint Cuthbert conveyed it to Ripon.' After 'three or four months, peace being restored', the community set out on the return journey, until the waggon bearing Cuthbert's coffin came to a sudden halt at 'a spot near Durham' and could not be made to go further, a refusal interpreted as indicating the saint's reluctance to return to Chester-le-Street, his post-mortal will having more than once before directed the wanderings of his community. After three days of prayer and fasting, 'a revelation was made' to one of the monks 'that they were required to move the body to Durham, and there to prepare a resting place for it'.

So it was – at least on the evidence of Symeon – that the community of Cuthbert brought the shrine of their saint to Durham, 'a place, though naturally strong, not easily habitable'. The site chosen by the saint, and where his shrine is still contained today within the Norman cathedral, was a rocky prominence almost entirely surrounded by a loop of the Wear, but then 'covered with a very dense wood . . . The bishop, assisted by all the population and by Uhtred, earl of the Northumbrians, cut down the whole of the timber and, in a brief space of time, made the place habitable.' Symeon's account, set down a full century after the event, was informed by the traditions preserved within his church which, inevitably, pressed genuine historical record into the service of the cult of Cuthbert. His reference to 'pirates who were close at hand' can only allude to the viking onslaught of the early 990s by the fleets of Olaf Tryggvasson and Swein Haraldsson (called 'Swein Forkbeard'), which represented the last great wave of the Scandinavian impact and was ultimately to place a Danish king on the English throne. There is good evidence for one of these fleets having plundered Bamburgh in 993 on its way to besiege London where they were bought off by the king Aethelred in the September of the following year.[12] The church at Chester-le-Street would have been vulnerable to longships penetrating the Wear and have assuredly offered a tempting target for viking raiders, but would have been at greater risk in 993–4 than in 995 when most of the raiding fleet is thought to have left the English coast.

It would seem at least likely that Symeon had been led to conflate an evacuation from Chester to the greater inland safety of Ripon early in 994 with the foundation of Durham which is dated by all the sources to the following year. If the precision of his dating can be called into question, then so too must be his account of the supernatural direction to the new and eminently defensible site higher up the Wear. At which point the sudden introduction of Uhtred into the proceedings prompts the Durham historian David Rollason to 'wonder whether the move to Durham was really so unpremeditated as Symeon's narrative implies'.[13] The evidence for Aldhun's daughter becoming Uhtred's first wife indicates the two men having formed a close personal alliance – arguably one between church and state in Northumbria without precedent since the time of Aidan, Oswald and the foundation of Lindisfarne in 635 – and leads on to a realistic historical recognition of the foundation at Durham as a joint political initiative by Bishop Aldhun and the future earl Uhtred, placing the shrine of the great saint of the northern English on a natural fortress site and fusing together the magnetism of the cult of Cuthbert with the martial defence of Cuthbert's land.

As to the identity of the enemy against whom that initiative was directed, it might be said that Sir Walter Scott discerned Aldhun and Uhtred's purpose with an unusual historical accuracy in his lines written in 1816 and describing the 'grey towers of Durham' as 'half church of God, half castle 'gainst the Scot'.[14] Durham was to attract the ambivalent ambitions of no less than three kings of Scots in the eleventh century alone, the first of them being Malcolm II in the year following his succession to the kingship.

The first recorded act of Malcolm's reign – as well befits a king called 'The Aggressor' by the *Prophecy of Berchan* – was one of aggressive warfare and, in an ironic reflection of the same source's description of him as a 'king who will redden red spear-points', it was to result in a defeat so grievous as to attract the notice of the Irish annalist – on the evidence of the entry in the *Annals of Ulster* at 1006:

> A battle between the men of Alba and the Saxons.
> And the rout was upon the men of Alba; and they left behind them a
> slaughter of their good men.

The annalist, as so often, provides no further information and the Scottish sources omit any reference to a conflict which is best known to historians from just one source preserved in just one manuscript.

The historical tract called *De Obsessione Dunelmensis* ('Of the Siege of Durham') is found in a twelfth-century manuscript at Corpus Christi College, Cambridge.[15] Whether or not it is the work of Symeon of Durham, it has been confidently attributed to him in the past and he might well have had at least some part in its authorship. The purpose of the tract was apparently to assert the claim of the church of Durham on half a dozen estates around the Tees, a claim deriving from the marital fortunes of Bishop Aldhun's daughter and Earl Uhtred, whose defence of Durham against Malcolm thus forms the subject of its opening paragraphs:

> During the reign of Aethelred, king of the English, Malcolm, king of the Scots, the son of king Kenneth, collected together the entire military force of Scotland; and having devastated the province of the Northumbrians with sword and fire, he laid siege to Durham. At this time, the bishop Aldhun had the government there; for Waltheof, who was the earl of the Northumbrians, had shut himself up in Bamburgh. He was exceedingly aged and, in consequence, could not undertake any active measures against the enemy. Bishop Aldhun had given his daughter, named Egfrida, in marriage to Uhtred, a young man of great energy and well skilled in military affairs . . .
>
> Now when this young man perceived that the land was devastated by the enemy, and that Durham was in a state of blockade and siege, he collected together into one body a considerable number of the men of Northumbria and Yorkshire, and cut to pieces nearly the entire multitude of the Scots; the king [Malcolm] himself and a few others escaping with difficulty. He [Uhtred] caused to be carried to Durham the best-looking heads of the slain, ornamented with braided locks as was the fashion of the time, and after they had been washed by four women – to each of whom he gave a cow for their trouble – he caused these heads to be fixed upon stakes and placed around the walls.
>
> When king Aethelred heard of this, he summoned this young man to his presence during the lifetime of his father Waltheof and as a reward for his courage, and for the battle which he had fought so gallantly, he gave him the earldom [of Bamburgh] which had been his father's, adding thereto the earldom of the men of York.

If this defeat of the Scots following their 'siege of Durham' was the same 'rout . . . upon the men of Alba' entered in the *Annals of Ulster* at 1006 – as it is generally thought to have been – then Malcolm's devastation of 'the province of the Northumbrians with sword and fire' was inflicted in the year following his succession to the kingship.[16] His campaign might be said, then, to bear a striking similarity to the ancient Irish custom known as *cregh rígh*, or 'royal prey', whereby the new king carried the most impressive display of military force he could muster through all the territories over which he claimed dominion, thereby taunting out any who were minded to resist or to challenge him as their overlord.

Malcolm stands at just that point in history where the old Celtic way of kingship had crossed the threshold of the millennium into the medieval world and, when placed into that context, his campaign of 1006 has every aspect of an inaugural 'royal prey'. If such was the intended purpose of Malcolm's invasion of Northumbria and siege of Durham, then the implications are far-reaching indeed if they signal Malcolm's claim to sovereignty as far south as the Wear and, by inference, as far as the Tees on the southernmost frontier of what had once been the territory of Bernicia. Neither would such a Scots claim be without precedent, when his grandfather and namesake Malcolm I is said by the *Chronicle of the Kings* to have 'plundered the English as far as the river Tees . . . in the seventh year of his reign' and the same source claims Kenneth II, son of Malcolm I and father of Malcolm II, to have 'plundered Saxonland to Stanemore [in what is now North Yorkshire], and to Cluaim [possibly the Cleveland Hills to the south of the Tees]'. At least two twelfth-century English sources – the *Historia Regum* attributed to Symeon of Durham and the *Chronica* of Roger de Hoveden – confirm one territory ceded to Kenneth when they record his submission in 973 to the English king Edgar who, apparently in exchange, 'gave him Lothian', by which is meant the lands between Forth and Tweed.[17]

The precise nature and extent of Scots dominion over these lands of Lothian is nowhere recorded, but cannot have amounted to full sovereignty when the *Historia de Sancto Cuthberto* confirms Cuthbert's land to have included extensive tracts north of the Lammermuir hills and most especially the lands of the monastery of Tyningham extending across what is now the county of East Lothian. In the light of which, it is possible that the purpose of Malcolm's siege of Durham bore specifically upon these monastic landholdings in Lothian and – as Professor Hudson has suggested – 'he was attempting to force the community to release to him their claims over lands north of the Haddington Tyne'.[18]

Whatever the true extent of its ambitions, the consequences of Malcolm's war of 1006 were quite disastrous. Not only had he left the greater part of his war-host dead in Cuthbert's land and the heads of his warrior nobility to serve as grisly decoration on the walls of Durham, but he had forfeited also any claim on territory between Forth and Tweed in a year which quite certainly represented the lowest point in his kingship. Even in the eleventh century, a less fortunate king could not have expected long to survive with his prestige so greatly diminished – on the evidence of Malcolm's grandson and successor who was slain by a rival within a twelvemonth of having sustained a very similar defeat in battle – but Malcolm was able not only to survive in the kingship of Scots for more than a quarter-century after Durham but to reclaim, within a dozen years, all and, very probably, more than he had lost by the failure of his 'royal prey' of 1006.

'SON OF THE WOMAN OF LEINSTER'

The marriage of Malcolm's daughter to the jarl of Orkney – which must be dated, on the evidence of the *Orkneyinga Saga*, to a year no later than 1008 – was clearly intended to secure a powerful ally for a kingship under threat, and a closely similar purpose would have underlain the marriage of another daughter to the mormaer of Moray at around the same time. Such strategic alliances by marriage must have played their own part in enabling Malcolm's recovery from so inauspicious a first year in the kingship, but so too did the course of events outwith the bounds of his kingdom through the second decade of the eleventh century, not least among them the outcome of a battle fought near Dublin on Good Friday in the year 1014.

The traditional recognition of Clontarf as the battle which marked the end of Ireland's 'Viking Age' can be traced back to the *Cogadh Gaedhel re Gallaibh* where it is presented as a grand finale to the wars of the Irish with the *gaill*. The *Cogadh* – set down within a century of the event, but recognised now as history recycled into propaganda on behalf of the Munster kings – portrays Clontarf as the decisive defeat of the massed host of the northmen by the men of Erin under their almost saintly high-king Brian Boru, who could not himself take any active part in warfare on a Good Friday but was slain anyway as he knelt in prayer behind the lines. While the most prosaic evidence of the reliable annal record confirms that the battle of *Cluaintairbh* (in its Irish name-form) was fought on Good Friday – which fell on 23 April in the year 1014 – and places Brian Boru at the head of a list of its notable casualties, it can also show that Irish and Norse fought on both sides, because the political reality of Clontarf was much more complex than the *Cogadh* would have history believe.

The term 'viking', first of all, is one barely meaningful in eleventh-century Ireland where the *gaill* had long been 'aliens' in name only. Through the two centuries since they had seized Dublin as their principal power base in Ireland, every form of social and cultural interchange – not least the inevitable, and often political, intermarriage – had rendered the Hiberno-Norse effectively indistinguishable from any other Irish dynasty. The northmen had, in fact, become so integral a component of the Irish polity, economy and society that their expulsion, still less destruction, by Brian in 1014 would have been no more plausible than would have been the extermination of the Picts by Kenneth mac Alpin on the other side of the Irish Sea in 842.

Neither, despite all the claims of his propagandists, was Brian Boru ever king of all Ireland, but most realistically recognised as high-king of Munster with his dominion in the south, while the centre of Ireland represented the territory of his powerful ally Maelsechlainn, southern Ui Neill king of Tara. Whatever the true extent of Brian's ambitions – and his cognomen of 'Boru', the anglicised form of the Irish *Boruimhe*, hailing him as 'Brian of the Tributes' must carry some weight – they were to meet with a determined resistance from the men of Leinster before 1014. The Leinstermen had been the first of the Irish to ally themselves with the northmen, having joined with them in their viking raids quite early in the ninth century, so when the Leinster king Maelmordha found himself threated by the formidable axis of Brian and Maelsechlainn, he turned for military support to Sigtrygg Olafsson, called 'Silkenbeard', Norse king of Dublin.

At which point the northmen entered into what had been initially a contention between Irish factions, when Sigtrygg could call upon the sword-service of fighting men from Iceland and Normandy, York and Man, and, most importantly, from Orkney whence came Jarl Sigurd who recruited Hebridean warbands to join his Orkneymen and Shetlanders as he sailed south to Ireland. Scandinavian involvement in such great numbers led to Clontarf being well remembered in the saga literature set down in Iceland at least two centuries after the battle, lavishly encrusted there with elements recycled from the ancient mythos of the northlands, and yet still preserving some genuine traditions of real historical value.

It is from these saga sources – and principally from *Njal's Saga* – that history has derived its most detailed account of Jarl Sigurd's death at the crucial point when the tide of battle turned in Brian's favour. Sigurd's mother was an Irish princess, the daughter of a king of Ossory, and – at least according to the saga – a sorceress, who had woven for her son a battle-flag bearing a raven motif and endowed with magical powers. Whenever this raven banner accompanied him to war he was assured of victory, but the price of that assurance was the death in battle of the man who actually carried the banner. So it was at Clontarf, say the sagas, that one standard-bearer after another fell in the fray until no more were willing to take up the raven and it was seized by Sigurd himself, who thrust the banner into his tunic and was soon afterwards struck dead by a spear. He would seem to have been in principal command of the northmen and when their line of battle collapsed into rout around him as he fell, the death of Sigurd can be taken to have marked the turning point at which the victory passed to the Munstermen.[19]

There is, of course, no such wealth of detail in the Irish annals where Sigurd is just one of the names entered in a long list of eminent dead. There is, however, one other of those names which, while admittedly obscure in the company, is of especial significance here when it confirms 'Domnall, mormaer of Mar in Alba' to have been slain while fighting as an ally of Brian Boru. There is no other evidence of Scots involvement at Clontarf and so, when it is at least unlikely that the presence on the battlefield of Malcolm and the host of Alba would have entirely escaped the notice of the sources, the participation of this 'mormaer of Mar', presumably attended by his warband, is worth further investigation – and all the more so when it can be shown to reflect a curious sidelight on Malcolm and his lineage.

Reference has already been made here to the story claiming Aedan mac Gabran to have been one of two sons born to the wife of a king of Leinster and exchanged at birth for one of two daughters born to the wife of Gabran, king of Dalriada.[20] While a tradition which does not make its first appearance until some five hundred years after Aedan's death cannot be taken to have any genuinely historical bearing on him and still less upon his true descent, the story is known to have gained currency in the eleventh century and probably in the time of Aedan's descendant, Malcolm II. There is at Glamis a carved cross slab of red sandstone which is traditionally associated with Malcolm and it includes in one corner an inscribed figure – half-human, half-horse, and carrying a pair of axes – which has been interpreted as an allusion to the changeling story. A recent investigation suggests that this figure 'may represent his [Malcolm's] lineage: The two axes turned in opposite directions might refer to the twin boys born to Eochaid of Leinster and his wife during their exile in Dalriada', and adds that the meaning of the Celtic root of the name *Eochaid* is, in fact, 'horse'.[21] Any real historical significance which can be ascribed to the story must bear, then, upon Malcolm, supposedly in the direct line of descent from Aedan mac Gabran but connected also by descent, through his mother, to Leinster.

All the Scottish genealogies confirm Malcolm to have been a son of Kenneth II and thus descended from the Cenel Gabrain kings of Dalriada through the male line of the mac Alpin kings of Scots, but history would know nothing of his maternal lineage were it not for two fragments of testimony from Gaelic tradition preserved in the *Prophecy of Berchan*. There Malcolm is called 'son of the woman of Leinster, strong through battle' and later – if rather less diplomatically – 'the son of the cow that grazed on the banks of the Liffey', but both can be taken to confirm his mother's people having been one of the noble, even royal, kindreds of Leinster which would infer Malcolm's involvement, by obligation of kinship, in the politics of Leinster where, of course, lay also the root of contention leading to Clontarf.

When placed into that context, the story claiming Aedan to have been the changeling twin of the historical sixth-century king of Leinster, Brandub mac Eochaid, begins to look like a politically inspired 'tradition' intended to enhance the prospect of an alliance of Malcolm with a Leinster faction, presumably Brandub's (and Eochaid's) kindred of the *Ui Chennselaigh*. These Ui Chennselaigh were a rival kindred to that of the Leinster king Maelmordha and refused him their support at the time when he was drawing Sigtrygg and the Norse into battle with Brian at Clontarf. The Aedan–Brandub story must inevitably suggest that they were also Malcolm's mother's people and had such been the case, Malcolm would have been faced with a conflict of loyalty on the eve of Clontarf, when the obligation of kinship inherited from his mother would have called him to support the Ui Chennselaigh, who would naturally gravitate to alliance with Brian Boru, while his daughter's marriage to Sigurd of Orkney should have inclined him to the opposing side or, at least, towards a position of neutrality.

When the presence of the Scots mormaer of Mar on the Clontarf battlefield is placed into that context, it begins to look very much like Malcolm's resolution of just such a political dilemma. Mar lay between the province of Moray and the heartland of Malcolm's kingdom of Scots, and its mormaer, while assuredly subject to Malcolm's overlordship, would still be seen from an Irish perspective as a king in his own independent right. Had the victory at Clontarf passed not to Munster but to the Leinster–Norse coalition, Malcolm would have had no great difficulty in disowning the involvement of the mormaer of Mar in the losing side and yet would have still discharged, at least by proxy, whatever obligation to his mother's people. In the event, Domnall of Mar so distinguished himself on the field as to merit a whole chapter of the *Cogadh* being taken up with an account of his prominent part in the fighting and his brave death in single combat with a Norman warrior.[22]

If the testimony of the *Cogadh* is evidence of a similar appreciation on the part of Brian's successor high-kings, then their esteem would have doubtlessly reflected on to Malcolm as Domnall's overlord and, perhaps also, in some measure inspired the extraordinarily high honour with which his obituary was to be entered in the Irish annals twenty years later. It was, however, the death in battle of Jarl Sigurd which was to prove for Malcolm the most fortuitous outcome of Clontarf, when a single spear-throw extinguished the most formidable and ambitious of the northmen in Alba and caused the power of the Orkney Norse to suffer an eclipse through most of the following two decades when the jarldom was apportioned among the three eldest of Sigurd's sons. Their younger brother, the future jarl Thorfinn the Mighty, was just five years old at the time of his father's death and a fosterling at the court of his maternal grandfather, the king of Scots, who was now without rival as the foremost man of power north of the Forth.

The battle of Clontarf can be taken, then, to mark the point at which Malcolm entered upon his ascendancy and, in the few years following, the tide of the times was to run not just in his favour, but at full flood. The one possible threat to his kingship lay in Moray, where the semi-independent mormaers might have been expected to rise in prominence with the Orkney Norse in a period of decline, but the fragmentary evidence of the sources shows the ruling dynasty north of the Mounth becoming entangled in effective civil war before the end of the decade.

Events very much further south were moving still faster into their own turmoil, setting a Danish king over the English by 1016 and presenting Malcolm with the opportunity, just two years later, to reassert with full force of arms the claim of his kingdom on lands to the south of the Forth.

'THE MISERABLE SLAUGHTER OF THE PEOPLE OF SAINT CUTHBERT'

The Scandinavian raiding of England through the early 990s had been renewed in the next decade. The Dane Swein Forkbeard returned year on year after 1002, evidently determined on the conquest he was eventually to achieve in 1013 when the English king Aethelred fled the country to the sanctuary of his wife's homeland in Normandy. When Swein died in the following year, the English nobles refused the kingship to Cnut, Swein's son and intended successor, and Aethelred returned to reclaim his kingdom. Cnut, however, was a man not to be so easily deterred and he was back within the twelvemonth to confront the formidable English resistance led by Aethelred's son Edmund 'Ironside' and his ally Uhtred of Bamburgh.

Uhtred's fortunes had moved into the ascendant through the decade since his defeat of Malcolm at Durham in 1006. When Aethelred rewarded that victory by placing him as earl over his father's dominion north of the Tees and also over the former kingdom of Jorvik, Uhtred sought to better establish himself in Yorkshire by putting aside his marriage to the bishop of Durham's daughter and taking to wife the daughter of an Anglo-Danish magnate of York. He married again and for the third time in 1014 when Aethelred returned to England and sought to secure his military support by offering Uhtred his daughter Aelfgifu as bride.

Thus it was that Uhtred, earl of all Northumbria, found himself in the shires of southern England in the year 1016 on campaign, with his brother-in-law Edmund, against a new Danish invasion until Cnut's war-host turned suddenly northwards to cross the Humber. Uhtred followed, apparently in pursuit and at least as far as York, but there he was forced to submit to the Danish king and to give over hostages as guarantee of that submission. He seems then to have been despatched home to Bamburgh charged with defence of the northern frontier, while Cnut appointed one of his own warlords, his brother-in-law Erik of Hlathir, to the earldom of York and to the command of its Anglo-Scandinavian forces recruited to the Danish host for a summer campaign against Edmund Ironside. Edmund had assumed kingship on the death of his father Aethelred in April but was himself to survive only until the following November when he died of wounds sustained in battle at Ashingdon. By the new year of 1017, Cnut was left as sole king in England, but he was still engaged in consolidating his new sovereignty in the following year when, on the death of his brother, he succeeded also to the kingship of Denmark.

Through all of this period of turmoil, the territory between the Forth and the Tees must have taken on the aspect of an ever more debatable land, an ancient English enclave trapped between the kingdom of the Scots in the north and an outpost of a new Scandinavian empire to the south. Just as Aethelred's distraction with renewed Danish raiding in 1006 tempted Malcolm to his attempted siege of Durham, it may well have been the distraction of England's Danish king back across the North Sea to his homeland on the Baltic which provided Malcolm with his long-awaited opportunity. Whatever it was, in fact, that finally decided him to seize the time, it was in the autumn – and most probably in late September[23] – of the year 1018 when Malcolm came at last in arms to the banks of the Tweed.

The Scots host crossed the river at its lowest fordable point to attack the Northumbrian levies assembled by Uhtred for the defence of Cuthbert's land in the fields just east of Wark and there to inflict upon them the crushing defeat which has entered history – for reasons already explained here – as the 'battle of Carham', without doubt a major landmark in the history of the Border and arguably no less a landmark in the passage of the kingdom of Scots into the Middle Ages. The form of entry of this battle of Carham into the historical record is at least curious.

There is no notice of it – or of any event resembling it – in any Irish annal and neither is it recorded in any manuscript of the *Anglo-Saxon Chronicle*. It is, however, the principal subject of the passage referring to Malcolm in the Scottish *Chronicle of the Kings* and of an entry in the *Historia Regum* attributed to Symeon of Durham, but the most substantial account is that set down by Symeon in his *History of the Church of Durham*:[24]

> In the year of our Lord's incarnation ten hundred and eighteen, while Cnut ruled the kingdom of the English, a comet appeared for thirty nights to the people of Northumbria, a terrible presage of the disaster by which that province was about to be desolated.
>
> For shortly afterwards, that is after thirty days, nearly the whole population from the river Tees to the Tweed, with their nobility, were cut off in a conflict in which they engaged a countless multitude of Scots at Carham. When the bishop [Aldhun] heard of the miserable slaughter of the people of Saint Cuthbert, he was smitten to the heart with deep grief and . . . a few days afterwards he was seized with sickness and died after having held the bishopric for twenty-nine years . . .

The entry placed under the same year date in the *Historia Regum* is more succinct and annalistic in character, but it does provide firm identification of the personalities involved.

> A great battle between the Scots and English was fought at Carham between Uhtred, Waltheof's son, earl of the Northumbrians and Malcolm, Kenneth's son, king of Scots, with whom was in the battle Owen the Bald, king of the Clydesmen.

There is a full measure of support here for Symeon's reference to 'a countless multitude of Scots', when the *Historia Regum* can confirm the presence of Owen, king of Strathclyde, as Malcolm's ally and, by inference, of a Strathclyde contingent among Malcolm's forces.

The kings of Strathclyde – whose territory extended over most of what is now Cumbria – had been clients of the kings of Scots since the early tenth century. The power of the old kingdom of the Britons on the Clyde was finally broken when its capital fortress of Dumbarton fell to a siege by the northmen in 871 and its king was murdered in the following year at the instigation of Constantine, king of Scots and Kenneth mac Alpin's son. The son and successor to that king of the Strathclyde Britons married a daughter of Kenneth, and their son – the Eochaid who was also to reign jointly with Giric mac Dungal in the kingship of Scots until both were deposed in 889 – was the last of a long line of native kings on the Clyde. His successor kings of Strathclyde, notwithstanding the Britonic forms in which their names are entered in the sources, were all offspring, in some wise, of the mac Alpin dynasty. A few were heirs apparent to the kingship of Scots, reigning as sub-kings in the west until they succeeded to the high-kingship at Scone, but most were in a line of descent from a younger brother of Malcolm I, and the last of that line was the Owen called *calvus*, 'the bald', who fought at Carham.[25]

Owen the Bald – who was, in fact, the grandson of a great-grandson of Kenneth mac Alpin – makes no further appearance in the historical record after 1018, which suggests the likelihood of his having been killed in the fighting at Carham. The defeated Earl Uhtred did survive what was to be his last battle, but not for very long, because his Danish overlord – suggests Professor Archie Duncan – 'had no use for a defeated English earl . . . [Uhtred] was summoned to Cnut, who may have feared treason with Malcolm II, and was assassinated at court.'[26] Cnut might have had good cause to suspect treason, but he could hardly blame Uhtred for the defeat at Carham. When Uhtred had first brought Malcolm to battle at Durham a dozen years before, he had under his command 'a considerable number of the men of Northumbria and Yorkshire', but Cnut's division of the northern earldoms in 1016 meant that Uhtred had access only to the manpower he could raise from 'the river Tees to the Tweed' when he had to face Malcolm's onslaught of 1018. His forces at Carham would have been apparently greatly outnumbered and, in consequence, massively defeated in the battle of which the most significant historical outcome was to be the Scots reclamation of the lands of Lothian.

The true sequence and substance of the cession of Lothian to the kingdom of the Scots is left very much less than clear by the evidence of the earliest sources. Lothian is thought to have first been passed to Malcolm's father, Kenneth II, when he made formal submission to the English king Edgar in 973 and there is sufficient place-name evidence to suggest it having been under a Gaelic administration at least as early as the later tenth century. That Scots possession would have been forfeited by Malcolm after his defeat at Durham in 1006 and reclaimed by him after his victory on the Tweed twelve years later. Such, at least, is implied by the tract *On the Siege of Durham*, which makes no direct reference to the battle of Carham but clearly alludes to its outcome when it says of Uhtred's brother 'Eadulf, surnamed *Cudel* [or "cuttlefish"], a lazy and cowardly fellow [who] succeeded him in the earldom', that:

> He yielded up to the Scots the whole of Lothian, to soothe them and to procure a peace; and hence it was that Lothian became added to the kingdom of Scotland.

That statement alone poses more questions than answers for historians, and has led to more than one scholarly interpretation of the part played in events by this Eadulf Cudel. It may have been that he succeeded to the earldom, however briefly, following his brother Uhtred's murder and before Cnut assigned the territory north of the Tees to his own man, the Erik of Hlathir whom he had already placed over Yorkshire and appointed as earl over all Northumbria – 'just as Uhtred had been' according to the *Anglo-Saxon Chronicle* – soon after the battle of Carham. It may even have been that Eadulf succeeded his brother but only as Erik's vassal administrator in the north, which would well correspond to his disparagement by the author of the Durham tract. It might otherwise have been that Eadulf went over to the Scots immediately after or even before the battle in the hope of succeeding his brother as Malcolm's 'mormaer' over a resultant Scots province bounded by the Forth and Tees.

Any of these interpretations allow some measure of possibility that Eadulf conceded Lothian rather than have the victorious Malcolm carry his invasion any further south of the Tweed, but it is no less possible that the same concession was made by Uhtred for the same reason after so devastating a defeat on the battlefield – and that the Durham tract, always anxious to protect Uhtred's reputation, chose to blame the forfeiture on to his evidently poorly esteemed brother Eadulf. If, indeed, Uhtred had ceded Lothian to the Scots in his hour of defeat, it would have been a gesture tantamount to the acknowledgement of Malcolm as overlord. It would also have been viewed – and punished – by Cnut as a second act of disloyalty by a man who had, after all, deserted his own king and father-in-law by his submission to the Dane at York just two years before.

All of which carries further implications for the initial extent of Malcolm's southern ambitions at a time when he might have seen no reason why what still remained of the northern English church and state should prefer to acknowledge a Danish king before a Scots overlord. His father, Kenneth II, had asserted – and been acknowledged in – his overlordship as far south as 'the Rere Cross on Stainmoor' more than forty years before and if Malcolm's ambition extended as far as the Tees he would have been claiming dominion no further to the south than had his father. The Scottish *Chronicle of the Kings* has been interpreted as offering its own evidence for just such an ambition when it notes Malcolm having 'fought a great battle at Carham. He distributed also many offerings to the clergy and to the churches on that day.' Professor Alfred Smyth points to the gold placed by Brian Boru on the altar at Armagh and to the West Saxon Athelstan's generosity to the community of Cuthbert at Chester-le-Street as examples of 'the gift made by an aspiring overlord to the chief church of a client territory' and proposes that 'the record of Malcolm's gifts, doled out not as booty to his warriors, but to churchmen, suggests that his gifts were made to Cuthbert's clergy and their new church founded at Durham, and they symbolised the Scottish victor's role as overlord of Bernicia.'[27] If Professor Smyth is correct in his interpretation, then it might well explain the purpose behind Symeon of Durham's apparent distortion of the chronology of Bishop Aldhun's death. Aldhun is known from the meticulously dated episcopal records of Durham to have died in 1019, the year after the battle of Carham, and yet Symeon's account overlooks the time-lapse to give the impression that he died stricken by grief 'a few days' after the 'miserable slaughter of the people of Saint Cuthbert'. It is a contrivance probably best explained as Symeon's attempting to disassociate Bishop Aldhun from whatever generosity was bestowed on the church of Cuthbert by the triumphant king of Scots.

The implication of Symeon's evidence, then, quite clearly dismisses any possibility of conciliation, still less of alliance, between the kingdom of Scots and the church of Durham, an attitude which must have been just as clear to Malcolm in 1018 and have dissuaded him from any ambitions extending south of the Tweed. The risk of contention with the greatly powerful Cnut must also have played its part in Malcolm's decision to accept the reclamation of Lothian as the most legitimate, and easily held, prize of victory at Carham, and especially when it gave him command of the eastern coastal route to bring within his gift all permitted access by the church of Durham to its Lothian landholdings.

The *Anglo-Saxon Chronicle* for 1031 enters Cnut's return from pilgrimage to Rome. 'In the same year he went into Scotland and Malcolm, king of Scots, submitted to him with two other kings, Maelbeth [of Moray] and Iehmarc [of the Isles].'

What might have been seen as a 'submission' by a West Saxon chronicler would have been recognised by the Celtic Scots, on this as on earlier occasions, as something more closely akin to the Irish custom of *ríg dail* or 'conference of kings', such as had brought Aedan mac Gabran to Druim Ceatt in 575, and of which the real significance was the confirmation of the territorial bounds of its royal participants. Viewed from that perspective, the signal importance of Cnut's Scottish excursion of 1031 lies in his implicit acknowledgement of the boundary on the Tweed which had been won by the sword at Carham some dozen years before. It must be said also that Cnut's northern progress of that year similarly confirmed north Britain south of the

Tweed in English possession. The Scots claim to territory as far south as Stainmoor in the west was not to outlast the eleventh century, but the eastern extent of the Border has been fixed along the Tweed, despite occasional efforts by later kings of both realms to move it in one direction or the other, through all the nine centuries since 1018. It lies there still, even if only for eighteen miles of the river's course, where it can be said to represent the one enduring memorial, at least in popular recognition, to the achievement of Malcolm, king of Scots.

'THE GLORY OF THE WHOLE WEST OF EUROPE'

The reference in the *Prophecy of Berchan* to Malcolm's 'swift morning leap of Moin' and his styling by the *Duan Albanach* 'king of Moin' have both been interpreted – on the grounds of *Dunmonaidh* being thought at one time to have meant Edinburgh – as allusions to Malcolm's seizure of Lothian, but it is just as possible that 'Moin' was the Mounth, in which case the same references would allude to Malcolm's sovereignty north of the Grampians.[28] Therein, of course, lies the central problem with the *Prophecy of Berchan* as a source of history, when the cryptic character of its information must usually be interpreted on the basis of corroborative evidence from the more explicit historical record.

The *Prophecy* has, none the less, ensured the survival of evidence for Malcolm, as for his forebears, which otherwise would have been lost to history. His mother's Leinster connection is one example and its description of him as 'the florid one' might be another – especially when Celtic tradition sustains such a prominent interest in physical appearance – if it preserves a genuine recollection of his unusually red complexion. The sheer profusion of its warlike references – 'a warrior, fortunate, wrathful-hearted', 'a heavy battler of a strong people', 'leap through battle, the florid one' and more – leave no doubt of Malcolm's reputation as an outstanding warlord and it tells, for example, of 'ten battles ... gained by him', when the formal historical record knows of no more than four conflicts involving Malcolm, of which one was assuredly a battle lost rather than 'gained'.

The passage from the *Prophecy* bearing on Malcolm is of exceptional length and its allusion to events apparently unnoticed elsewhere can only be taken to show how very little history really knows of his long reign. There are no more than half a dozen events noticed by the formal historical record which mention him by name and yet he had achieved such high esteem at the time of his death for the entry of his obituary in the *Annals of Tigernach* at

1034 to hail 'Malcolm, son of Kenneth, king of Alba' as 'the glory of the whole west of Europe'.[29] That testimony of Tigernach has been interpreted by Benjamin Hudson as an immediately contemporary acknowledgement of Malcolm as 'overlord of all the Scots . . . recognised as one of the premier kings of the northern Atlantic littoral'[30] and he may very well be right.

Such a stature, and however great might have been its debt to the generosity of fortune, cannot be denied Malcolm any more than it could have been accorded any king of Scots before him. When the contemporary chronicler Marianus Scotus, an Irish monk resident in what is now Germany, entered Malcolm's obituary in his *Chronicon* he chose to style him *rex Scotiae*, 'king of Scotland', and placed that title on the historical record for the very first time. In so doing, though, Marianus might be said to have been marking an occasion of still greater import than the passing of the last king of Scots in the direct male line of the mac Alpin dynasty, if his choice of regal title can be taken to signal the passage of the kingdom of the Scots out of the Dark Ages and into the European Middle Ages.

Seen from a somewhat different perspective, however, Malcolm assumes another significance, and one of more immediate importance here, because it is in the reign of this last of the mac Alpin kings that the history of that extraordinary dynasty seems to come full circle when almost all the known acts of Malcolm seem to present their own distinct reflection, if not a mirror image, of those of the dynastic founder, Kenneth.

Both men, for example, are remembered in the sources as warriors of more outstanding repute than any others of their royal house. The best recorded military activity of Kenneth's reign was his raiding of Northumbria, where the *Chronicle of the Kings* records his burning of Melrose, the monastery where Saint Cuthbert had first entered into the church, and his seizure of Dunbar, the stronghold of the Anglo-Saxon lords of the northern march whose political heirs were the Northumbrian earls of the tenth and eleventh centuries. Some hundred and fifty years on from those invasions 'of Saxonland', the first recorded act of Malcolm's reign was his siege of Durham, which represented an attack on the last and greatest church of Cuthbert and which brought him into contention with the last great English earl of all Northumbria. So too, it was his victory at Carham a dozen years later which finally broke the power of the northern English dynasty at Bamburgh and achieved all that was to be achieved of the ambitions for southward expansion which had found first expression in Kenneth's foreign policy.

Malcolm might be said also to have brought to fulfilment Kenneth's ambitions on the western sector of that same frontier. If the marriage of a daughter of Kenneth to a prince of the Strathclyde Britons can be recognised as the first indication of Scots designs on the kingdom of Stratchclyde, then it was Malcolm who was to accomplish that ambition when, following the death of Owen the Bald, he finally brought Strathclyde within the kingdom of the Scots and reduced the last bulwark of the once-powerful north Britons to the purely nominal status of a 'tanist' princedom (from the Gaelic *tanaise*, 'the next man' or 'the expected one') by placing over it his own chosen successor to the kingship of Scots.

It was Kenneth also who would seem to have built a complete foreign policy upon the old custom of alliance secured by inter-dynastic marriage by the clearly strategic marrying-off of his daughters – one of them into the royal house of the Strathclyde Britons, another to a high-king of the Ui Neill and, perhaps, a third to the Norse king of Dublin. It was a policy pursued still more thoroughly by Malcolm who had sired no male issue, so the future succession to the kingship of Scots would pass to the sons of his daughters whose marriages well reflected the new distribution of power in the land.

SUCCESSION, OF NECESSITY, BY MOTHER-RIGHT

The custom of royal succession through the female line, which had long enabled princes of Scots, north British, and northern English lineage to claim kingship of the Picts, was also to endow legitimacy upon the entry of the mac Fergus dynasty into the kingship of Fortriu in the first decades of the ninth century, but it was to be reduced thereafter to a mere formality and effectively abandoned in favour of the Irish custom.

The sons of Fergus mac Eochaid, brother of the Cenel Gabrain king Aed Find, were able to claim their kingship of Picts by right of their Pictish mother's lineage, and it is more than likely that each of them would have taken Pictish wives of similar royal descent to legitimate the succession of their two sons, but the reality of that succession was already indistinguish-able from the Irish custom whereby the kingship passed to the brother before the son and after him to the brother's son, alternating between those two lines of the same kindred thereafter. The same Irish custom was to govern succession to the kingship of Scots through four generations of the mac Alpin dynasty and would seem to have been underwritten, at least on occa-sion in the second half of the tenth century, with the placement of intended successors into the sub-kingship of Strathclyde and Cumbria.

This custom of tanistry, already mentioned here, is most realistically recognised as a device to distract an impatient successor-in-waiting from any premature, and inevitably violent, bid for the kingship and thereby defuse the risk of contention between potentially rival lines of the ruling kindred. Thus Indulf, son of Constantine II, was placed as tanist king over Strathclyde during some part of the reign of Malcolm I as king of Scots, before he followed Malcolm into the kingship. Similarly Malcolm's son Dubh held the kingship of Strathclyde under Indulf until he himself succeeded to the over-kingship in 962.[31]

It would appear to have been Dubh's brother, the formidable Kenneth mac Malcolm, who tried to subvert this custom of succession – at least according to Fordun and there is no reason to doubt him on this occasion – when he sought to install his son, the future Malcolm II, into the kingship of Strathclyde. Kenneth's reign had been a period of greater contact with the English – and contact of a diplomatic as well as military character – than had that of any king of Scots before him, which might very well have encouraged him to emulate the custom of succession long established in the south whereby the eldest son followed his father into the kingship. Such must have been the implied purpose of his placing his own son into the tanist kingship and also of his assassination of a son of Indulf in 977, clearly with the object of eliminating the most prominent rival claimant and thereby excluding the line of Aed from the kingship.

It was a scheme doomed, none the less, to failure when Kenneth was slain at Fettercairn in 995 – 'by trickery and craft' according to the *Chronicle of the Kings* – and succeeded not by his son Malcolm but by a grandson of Indulf who himself fell victim to Kenneth's nephew and namesake who seized the kingship as Kenneth III. All of which might be thought to have left an enduring impression on the young Malcolm, the more especially so if he had been forced to flee for his life to the Isles and there pass as much as a decade in exile before he could reclaim the kingship by the sword at Monzievaird. When the time came for Malcolm to consider his own successor, there is evidence to suggest him acting almost precisely as his father had done before him, the difference being that he himself had sired only daughters and so any successor of his line would, of necessity, come to the kingship by the same mother-right of former Pictish custom. Malcolm's choice of his own successor was to be made, then, from those sons borne by his daughters to husbands of eminent political stature, and there is evidence – albeit from very different sources of admittedly uneven authority – for there having been three such grandsons grown to full maturity by the last years of Malcolm's reign.

Thorfinn Sigurdsson, who had been a five-year-old fosterling at his grandfather's court when his father fell at Clontarf, was a man of twenty-five by the time of Malcolm's death. This future Jarl Thorfinn the Mighty would have to wait another year before the death of his last surviving brother in 1035 enabled him to claim sole dominion over the Orkney jarldom, but he was already a man of power at the northernmost extent of the Scottish mainland where the *Orkneyinga Saga* claims his grandfather had granted him the earldoms of Caithness and Sutherland. It was another grandson, however, on whom Malcolm would seem to have settled his choice of successor to the kingship of Scots. The chronicle compiled in the early twelfth century by Florent of Worcester is especially well informed on northern history and makes a circuitous reference to Malcolm's successor as 'king of the Cumbrians', which can only be taken to mean the future Duncan, king of Scots, having been placed by his grandfather into the kingship of Strathclyde as successor to Owen the Bald at some point after 1018.

Duncan – in the anglicised name-form of the original Gaelic *Dunchad* – was the son of Malcolm's daughter Bethoc and her husband Crinan, abbot of Dunkeld,[32] but it would be misleading to think of him as, in any sense, a churchman's son. Crinan was, in fact, a 'secular abbot', holding the ecclesiastical office purely as a form of title to the abbacy's estates and income, who need not himself have been in holy orders when he could pay some humble priest as little as possible to fulfil whatever religious duties in his place. Duncan mac Crinan was the son of a major landowner in the heartland of the kingdom, whose power would have been comparable to that of a mormaer if it was in proportion to the great wealth he derived from the royal church of the mac Alpin kings. Duncan himself, however, was destined for very much greater power by a royal grandfather who would seem – even on the enigmatic evidence of the entry in the *Annals of Ulster* at 1033 – to have been clearing the path to the kingship for his intended successor in the year before his own death.

> The son of the son of Boite, Kenneth's son, was killed by Malcolm, Kenneth's son.

The annalist offers no indication as to which Kenneth was the father of the Boite whose grandson was killed by Malcolm. It is sometimes suggested that this Boite was the son of the third Kenneth, king of Scots, and that the death inflicted in 1033 was the culmination of the blood feud taken up by Malcolm on the Moor of the Bards twenty-eight years before,[33] but it might be more realistic to propose the Kenneth intended by the annalist having been Malcolm's father, Kenneth II, which would identify Boite as having been Malcolm's own brother. His grandson would thus have been an exact contemporary of Duncan and, had he lived, would have presented a very serious rival for the kingship, being of direct descent in the male line of the house of mac Alpin.

Malcolm's death is entered in the *Annals of Ulster* and in those of Tigernach at the following year, but with greater precision by Marianus Scotus who fixes its date as 'the seventh day before the kalends of December' (25 November). 'And he died at Glamis', according to the *Chronicle of the Kings*, 'and was buried in Iona.'

None of those sources, however, can provide any account of the nature of Malcolm's passing. He would certainly have been advanced in years by 1034 and might be thought to have died a natural death, were it not for the dark allusions contained in the *Prophecy of Berchan*:

> Five years and thirty his time over Alba in the high-kingship,[34]
> until the day he goes to the battle to meet with the parricides,
> to the swift morning leap of Moin.
> Woe to Alba in opposition to them.

When the cryptic references to 'Moin' and 'the parricides' are set beside the evidence for Malcolm having died at Glamis, they raise the distinct possibility of his having been killed north of the Mounth and in contention with the men of Moray. There are sufficient incidents entered in the annals to suggest a vicious feud erupting on occasion into virtual civil war having been continued between rival branches of the ruling kindred of Moray for at least fifteen years. There would have been no reason for Malcolm to become embroiled in it had not another of his daughters been the wife of a mormaer slain by a rival and the third of his grandsons, now grown to manhood, been a principal claimant to the mormaerdom and heir to the feud surrounding it.

If this same grandson was the *Maelbeth* who accompanied Malcolm to his meeting with Cnut in 1031, then he was also the man known to the *Duan Albanach* as '*Macbethad* with fame' – and with remarkable foresight because his name, at least, was destined for an enduring, even universal, celebrity beyond that of any king of Scots before or after him.

6

'Macbethad with fame'

———

MACBETH

THE ISLAND OF INCHCOLM might be said to have the aspect of a medieval time capsule dropped into a landscape of a later industrial age. Lying about a mile off the north shore of the Firth of Forth, it is set against the backdrop of the two great bridges engineered in the two most recent centuries to bear road and rail traffic across the estuary which separates what was once the old Pictish province of *Fib* from the lands of Lothian.

Barely five miles to the north-west, the industrial centre of Dunfermline and beyond it the naval base at Rosyth together dominate the coastline of Fife, while away to the south the modern urban sprawl of Edinburgh extends over an ever-increasing tract of the opposite bank. Inchcolm, by contrast, looks today very much as it must have done through all of seven hundred and fifty years past, its shore fringed by seals and its profile configured by the splendidly preserved and very substantial remains of a monastery first founded on the island in the twelfth century.

The foundation story of the church on Inchcolm tells of Alexander, the first of that name in the kingship of Scots and a grandson of Duncan mac Crinan, being blown off course while crossing the Forth with a courtly company in the year 1123 and given food and shelter by a hermit on the island. There is good evidence for the profusion of such reclusive holy men to be found in the early twelfth-century *Life* of Alexander's mother, the sainted queen Margaret, who is said to have visited and conversed with 'very many in different parts of the kingdom of Scotland who, shut up in separate cells, were living lives of great strictness'. While Margaret 'could not prevail upon them to accept from her any earthly gift [and instead] used to earnestly entreat them to honour her by prescribing some work of almsgiving of mercy', her son was able to express his gratitude for finding so humble a port in a storm by endowing a priory church on Inchcolm and, apparently, dedicating it to Columba.

.The name Inchcolm does incorporate the oldest Irish form of the name Columba, and while it is far from certain that the 'Colm' commemorated in the island name – deriving from 'Colm's Inch' (or isle) – was the same Columba of Iona known to have been held in especial veneration by Alexander I,[1] it was certainly believed to have been so in medieval times. The king's death in the following year very probably interrupted building work in progress, because there is no further record of Inchcolm until the mid-twelfth century when a charter attests Alexander's brother and successor, David I, having entrusted the administration of its abbey and Augustinian community to the bishop of Dunkeld.

The supposed hermit's cell still to be seen on Inchcolm is traditionally held to be that of the solitary who gave shelter to the king and his companions and – if the later medieval repairs and restoration of the little stone-built hut are evidence of particular care lavished on a building of especial significance for the church's original foundation – then it may very well have been so. The octagonal chapter house is of a form very unusual in Scotland and of a thirteenth-century date, as are the greater part of the church buildings surviving so remarkably complete today, but, like the hermit's cell, they too underwent extensive work in the fourteenth and fifteenth centuries. It is very probable that these later medieval restorations were made necessary by the damage inflicted on Inchcolm during the Anglo–Scottish warfare of the fourteenth century, when it was just one among many churches in the Borders and Lothian known to have been the targets of English raiders.

The first recorded such attack came in the year after Bannockburn, when an English raiding party fell upon one of Inchcolm's landholdings just east of Dunfermline where it met with determined resistance and was, in fact, repelled on that occasion. Twenty years later, another raiding party from the south landed on the island itself to plunder its monastery, an attack which must in great measure have inspired the lines of a hymn written on Inchcolm at around that time calling on 'Columba, holiest of saints' to 'save this choir which sings thy praise from all hostile English raids'. This hymn *Pater Columba* is preserved in a choirbook thought to have been set down around the year 1340 and known as the *Inchcolm Antiphoner*, one of the great treasures of Scottish music in manuscript and also one of the most illuminating sources of evidence for the earliest medieval church music of Scotland.

While there is historical evidence to confirm an early fourteenth-century date for some items included in the *Antiphoner*, it also contains a body of plainchant intended for the celebration of Columba's feast day – in which the musical historian John Purser has detected 'signs of being much older' than the foundation of Inchcolm 'which may have inherited material originally sung and perhaps housed in older manuscript form on Iona itself'. 'It is perfectly possible', suggests Dr Purser, 'that these texts originated in some cases from as early as the seventh to the ninth centuries' and if he is correct in his very impressive conclusion that the *Inchcolm Antiphoner* 'contains the only definitive remnants of the music of the Celtic church', then he is more than justified in describing it as 'one of the most important and neglected manuscripts in the history of plainchant'.[2]

While this ancient choirbook can thus claim pride of place among the surviving legacy of the church of Inchcolm, there is another antiquity still to be seen on the island which is older than the *Antiphoner* and has been the subject of rather more attention over at least four centuries. It is a recumbent oblong tombstone of the Anglo-Scandinavian form known as the 'hogback', one and half metres in length and little more than half a metre at its highest point, carved out of sandstone with an attempt to suggest a roof-tiled effect on its upper surface and the still quite distinct forms of bear-like beasts at each terminal. It is thought to be the oldest example of the form in Scotland and of a date as old as the mid-tenth century, but the antiquarian W. G. Collingwood, who made a special study of such carvings earlier this century, was able to identify the Inchcolm hogback as one of the 'Heysham' type and, thus, date it to the first half of the eleventh century.[3] Such a date would well correspond to the reference to the same stone made by the early sixteenth-century Scots historian, Hector Boece, in his account of events he places in the year 1040.

Boece's *History* tells of a battle fought in the seventh year of the reign of Duncan at Kinghorn on the coast of Fife, where had landed the Danish king 'Sweno' with his war-host 'against whom were sent Macbeth and Banquo and slew a great part thereof and the remnant chased to their ships . . .'

> The Danes who fled to their ships gave great sums of gold to Macbeth to suffer their nobles who were slain at this last jeopardy to be buried at Saint Columb's Inch. In memory thereof many ancient sepulchres are sited in the said Inch, engraved with the arms of the Danes.

Boece – or *Boethius* in the Latin name-form under which he wrote his seventeen-volume *History and Chronicles of Scotland* – is thought now to be a very much less than reliable authority, but his book was considered in its own time and long after to be the standard work. It was originally written in verse and in Latin when it made its first appearance in 1527, but was soon after rendered into Scots prose by John Bellenden whose translation was published in 1536 and later acknowledged by the English chronicler Raphael Holinshed as having been a principal source for his own *Chronicle of Scotland* of the 1580s.[4]

The chronicles attributed to Holinshed are, of course, well known for their having provided William Shakespeare with the background material for his history plays, and it was Holinshed's *Chronicle of Scotland* which similarly supplied the supposedly historical inspiration for *The Tragedy of Macbeth*. It is fully possible that Shakespeare also made use of Bellenden's rendering of the Boece original as well as the Boece-inspired material he found in Holinshed, but there can be no doubt at all of Hector Boece having been the source of inspiration for Ross' speech placed in the first act of *Macbeth* and telling of the terms imposed by the Scots in the wake of their victory over the northmen.

> Now Sweno, the Norways' king, craves composition;
> Nor would we deign him burial of his men
> Till he disbursed, at Saint Colum's Inch,
> Ten thousand dollars to our general use.

It has been a long time since Boece was last considered a reliable historian and his *History* is almost unanimously regarded by modern scholarship as very largely fiction. There is, for example, no evidence for there ever having been an historical Banquo and the character of that name recruited for Shakespeare's *dramatis personae* was quite surely one of Boece's invention, with the most probable purpose of supplying a legendary ancestor for the Stewart kings of Scotland. If Boece intended a genuinely historical personality for the Danish king he calls 'Sweno', it cannot have been Swein Forkbeard who had been dead for more than a quarter-century by 1040. Neither can it have been that Swein's grandson and namesake who spent almost all his adult life in Norway and Denmark, which might excuse Shakespeare's recasting him as 'the Norways' king' but not the anachronism of Swein's having died in 1036 without ever having set foot in Scotland, at least to the best of the knowledge of the early sources.

Those early sources, of course, can fully confirm the historical Macbeth having been active in 1040 and for seventeen years thereafter, but they can offer no evidence for his serving as a military commander under the Duncan whom he was afterwards to succeed in the kingship. Boece, however, was not the first later medieval historian to claim that he did so, and it is a claim most plausibly explained as a genuine misapprehension resulting from the translation of the title *dux* as 'general' rather than the more accurate 'sub-king', in which sense it was used by at least one earlier source as the Latin equivalent of *mormaer*.

All of which might be taken to dismiss any association of Macbeth with Inchcolm as entirely a creation of Boece's undoubtedly fertile imagination, were it not for two other indisputable items of supporting evidence. The first of these is the presence on Inchcolm of that hogback tombstone, an arguably eleventh-century example of the monument singularly characteristic of the north of England in the Anglo-Scandinavian period, and the second is the fact of a Danish earl of Northumbria being firmly identified by the earliest sources as the historical Macbeth's most determined enemy. His name, known from those sources to have been Siward, is one which might have been reworked into 'Sweno' by Hector Boece had he wished to elevate him from the status of a Northumbrian earl to that of a Danish king, and Boece was fully capable of rearranging the chronology to move a tradition associated with Macbeth into the reign of his predecessor.

There can be no doubt, if only on the evidence of the hogback tombstone, of Inchcolm in the Forth having been considered a holy place for at least a century before Alexander I was brought ashore there by the storm of 1123, and it was always in the nature of monastic communities to nurture traditions bearing upon the history and sanctity of the site of their own foundation.

Unless Hector Boece can be shown to have conjured up an entirely fictional association and done so, moreover, for no apparent purpose, there must still remain the possibility that his account, however distorted by unhistorical embroidery, might preserve within it a core of genuine tradition linking 'Saint Columb's Inch' with the real Macbeth, high-king of Scots.

THE 'SCOTTISH PLAY' AND THE SOURCES

The *Duan Albanach*, which was composed within living memory of the historical Macbeth, calls him by his Gaelic name-form when it acclaims him as '*Macbethad* with fame' and there can be nowhere any doubt that his name has become better and more widely known than that of any other of Scotland's kings, before him or since. The reason for that extraordinary celebrity – or, perhaps, notoriety – is, of course, William Shakespeare's choice of Macbeth as the title-role of one of the best-known of his tragedy plays, and there is no small irony in the fact that the name which forms the title of this most death-haunted of Shakespearean creations derives from the Gaelic *mac beatha*, 'son of life'[5] – but that is just one among many unfortunate disparities between the Macbeth of history and his theatrical namesake.

Since it is now almost obligatory for any writer on the subject of the Macbeth of history to dissociate him from the Shakespearean character, I had better say it too: Shakespeare's portrait of an obsessive killer driven by an ambitious wife to usurp the kingship by means of bloody murder can find no supporting evidence in the earliest and most reliable historical record of the Macbeth mac Findlaech who reigned as high-king of Scots in the mid-eleventh century AD. The Irish annals enter the violent death of his predecessor Duncan in 1040 and that of his predecessor's father, Crinan of Dunkeld, some five years later, but they mention Macbeth by name in neither of those connections and the only occasion when his name does make an appearance in the annals is in the entry of his own obituary at the year 1057.

The Scottish *Chronicle of the Kings* can confirm that it was Macbeth who slew Duncan and followed him into the kingship to reign for seventeen years until he himself was slain and succeeded by Duncan's son Malcolm, but it also records the burial of Macbeth – like almost all the mac Alpin kings before him – on Iona, which can only be taken to acknowledge the legitimacy of his kingship. Of the immediately contemporary English sources for the period, the *Anglo-Saxon Chronicle* mentions him most prominently in its account of the Northumbrian earl Siward's invasion of Scotland to reclaim the kingdom for Duncan's son, to which the closely contemporary evidence of Florent of Worcester can add nothing more damning than examples of Macbeth's generosity and hospitality, one of them being also confirmed by Marianus Scotus, the Irish chronicler working in Germany, to whom history also owes its most precise record of the dates of Macbeth's kingship.

Such then is the sum of the evidence of the formal historical record, but those early sources were not the sources used by Shakespeare who turned, not unreasonably, to the best-respected works of history available to him in English at the time of his researching a play on a Scottish theme. It was, of course, no accident that Shakespeare's *Macbeth* – which is known to have been first performed in 1606 and thought to have been written in that year – appeared just three years after the arrival in London of Scotland's James VI to succeed Elizabeth I as James I of England. If it was only to be expected that a fashionable London playwright should select a 'Scottish' subject for a new work at such a time, there would seem to have been a further significance in Shakespeare's particular choice because there had already been poems and plays on the same subject written and performed over the preceding ten years. At least one of those earlier treatments incurred official censure for its 'scorn of the King and people' of Scotland and, if the others were also in that vein, it would seem very likely that Shakespeare chose to readdress their theme with the conscious purpose of making amends to the king now reigning over both realms. He is known to have been in correspondence with James and to have given the first performance of his *The Tragedy of Macbeth* before the king and his court on the prestigious occasion of a Danish royal visit, so the play was assuredly intended to flatter England's new king of the Scottish house of Stewart by presenting James' own forebear, Malcolm mac Duncan, as triumphant over the murdering usurper Macbeth in its closing scenes. To do so Shakespeare need have looked no further in his historical researches than to the *Chronicles* of Holinshed and, perhaps also, to Bellenden's recension of Boece, so he can hardly be justly accused of inventing an English libel upon the king of a very different Scotland more than five hundred years before, when he drew upon the best available sources of which he knew and which were themselves informed by earlier Scottish histories of acknowledged authority. The historical Macbeth was already being transformed beyond the recognition of the earliest sources at least two hundred years before Shakespeare ever heard of him and the enduringly popular image of an ambitious killer driven in equal parts by dark forces and a demonic queen was, at least initially, entirely the creation of learned Scots historians.

There is, in fact, no suggestion of Macbeth having been a usurper, still less a murderer, by any source set down within three hundred years of his death, and when such suggestions do first occur in the later fourteenth century they are made by historians who – as the Celtic scholar, Peter Berresford Ellis, points out – were 'anglicised Scotsmen . . . almost totally removed, linguistically and culturally, from the eleventh-century Scotland of which they were writing'.[6] Such indeed was John of Fordun whose *Chronicle* written in the later fourteenth century is the first history to disparage the legitimacy of Macbeth's succession and to brand him an oppressor, but even Fordun does not accuse him of murder. That charge is first levelled at Macbeth in the *Orygynale Cronykil of Scotland* composed by Fordun's contemporary Andrew of Wyntoun who also supplies the earliest indication of a supernatural, even occult, aspect to Macbeth's kingship when he introduces the 'weird sisters' with their prophecies of royal destiny which Wyntoun describes as being revealed in a dream. It is Wyntoun also who makes the first known reference to those other prophecies assuring Macbeth that he will be undefeated until Birnam wood comes to Dunsinnen hill and that he will not be slain by any born of woman. He does not, in fact, attribute either of these two foretellings to the 'weird sisters', and neither does Boece, nor his translator Bellenden, but by the time Boece's history appeared in Bellenden's Scots recension, the 'weird sisters' had materialised as physical entities confronting Macbeth in an encounter which was to be reworked by Shakespeare into his famous scenes with the three 'black and midnight hags . . . upon this blasted heath'.

It is this powerful occult element of 'night's black agents' which, perhaps more than any other, has so securely fixed Shakespeare's *Macbeth* in the popular imagination and must also have led to the superstition attached to the work by theatre people who customarily refer to it as 'the Scottish play' rather than tempt bad luck by using its actual title. All of which can be traced back to Andrew of Wyntoun who is, none the less, not to be lightly dismissed as an historical source when he was the prior of the same monastic foundation on Loch Leven which is known to have been generously endowed by Macbeth and his queen some three centuries earlier. His own church would, thus, have had an especial interest of very long standing in the historical Macbeth and Wyntoun's *Cronykil* does imply at least some acquaintance with the more kindly disposed earlier sources when it makes reference to 'many pleasant acts in the beginning of his reign under colour of justice, but at last he showed his cruelty and perverse mind, set to shedding of blood more than to any zeal or justice'.[7]

In view of his eminent appointment to a church of known association with the historical Macbeth, there is every likelihood of Wyntoun having had access to information preserved in its monastic tradition and not necessarily available to other historians, so when he prefaces his account of the prophecy regarding Birnam wood and Dunsinnen with a clear statement of Macbeth's firm belief in *fantoun fretys* – or 'ghostly prophecies' – it is fully possible that he was informed by some genuine recollection of the man himself. An unusually high regard for superstition would, after all, have been just the sort of personality trait which might have been remembered, even with due measure of disapproval, by a monastic community about a king with whom it had once had personal contact. It would seem, though, that any such authentic recollection had become entangled with elements deriving from still more ancient Celtic tradition, which have been shown to indicate Macbeth's significance in terms of the cultural fusions of his own time, and in which context Wyntoun's evidence will later bear some further consideration here. Suffice it then for the moment to point to Andrew of Wyntoun as the first firmly identifiable source of Macbeth's association with dark prophecies and demonic elements which was to be much elaborated by Boece and Bellenden before passing into Shakespeare's hands.

Boece has already been mentioned as the source of the character of Banquo, invented by him to supply a fictional forebear for the royal house of Stewart, and the character of 'Lady Macbeth', which was to be later refined by Shakespeare into his tragedy's 'fiend-like queen', would seem to have been another of Boece's devising. It must be assumed that he did not know the name of Gruoch – by which the wife of the historical Macbeth is called on her one and only entry into the authentic historical record – or that if he did, he chose to omit it for some reason of political discretion, but Boece does, however, have a name for Macbeth's mother, whom he identifies as 'a second daughter of King Malcolm [II] named Doada'.

Whatever might have been his authority for that name is unknown. It occurs nowhere else in the sources and may very well have been one entirely of his own invention, but Hector Boece is certainly not alone in claiming the mother 'on whom was gotten Makbeth' to have been a daughter of Malcolm II and Macbeth and Duncan thus to have been 'sisters' sons'. Andrew of Wyntoun describes Duncan as having been Macbeth's *eme*, a word used sometimes to mean 'uncle' but one which could just as well indicate a 'cousin' and which would perfectly correspond to the evidence of the *Chronicle of Huntingdon* when it uses the term *nepos* to indicate both Macbeth and Duncan having been 'grandsons' of Malcolm II.

The inference must be one of Wyntoun, and perhaps also Boece and Bellenden, having had access to some form of the same source used by the canons of Huntingdon when they compiled their *Chronicle* for Edward I of England in the late thirteenth century, but it is the substance rather than the provenance of the claim which is of first importance here. If Macbeth was indeed the son of a daughter of Malcolm, even of one who was herself born out of holy wedlock, his claim on the kingship would have been no less than that of Duncan when it was equally founded on the former Pictish custom of succession by mother-right. There is, of course, no reason why the king-lists, at least in their surviving form, should indicate such a right of succession, but it may very well have been the allusion intended by the *Prophecy of Berchan* when it hails Macbeth as 'the generous king of *Fortriu* [who] will take Alba'.[8] Indeed, the claim of Macbeth to the high-kingship of Alba might have been stronger than that of Duncan, when his father is known – on the evidence of all the king-lists and genealogies – to have been Findlaech mac Ruadri, one of the hereditary mormaers of Moray who were recognised by the Irish annals as kings in their own right and for whom the genealogists claim ultimately direct descent from the royal kindred of the Cenel Loairn in Dalriada.

THE HOUSE OF MORAY

Among the various contents of the Irish manuscript collection compiled in the eleventh and twelfth centuries and preserved now as 'Rawlinson B502' in the Bodleian Library, there is to be found a genealogical text bearing on the kings of Scots and considered to be of eminently reliable authority. One section of this genealogy is taken up with the descent of Macbeth and traces his lineage back through three and a half centuries to the Ferchar Fota of the Cenel Loairn whose son Ainbcellach seized the over-kingship of Dalriada from the Cenel Gabrain in the last decade of the seventh century.

Ainbcellach, who appears to have slain a grandson of Domnall Brecc to win the kingship, was to reign for only a year until he was deposed, probably as a usurper, and 'carried in chains to Ireland', according to the *Annals of Ulster* at 698. Within some two years his brother Selbach had established himself in the kingship, but Ainbcellach was back in Scotland to reclaim his kingdom by 718, at which year the annalist enters his death in battle with Selbach at Finglen on the Braes of Lorn. Five years later Selbach abdicated to retire into religion and was succeeded in turn by his two sons until 733 when the kingship passed to Ainbcellach's son, Muiredach. Throughout most of this period, the political reality of over-kingship in Dalriada must be considered an increasingly dubious concept, but Muiredach was still established in some semblance of sovereignty when the Scots of Dalriada suffered the massive Pictish onslaught of 736.

From that point onwards, the Cenel Loairn disappear from the annal record and when they – or, at least, those individuals identified by the genealogists as descendants of their royal kindred – reappear in the early sources for the later tenth century, they have come to represent an hereditary dynasty of mormaers of Moray. The sources offer no account of how or when this transformation came about and it can only be explained by their migration out of their ancestral lands of Lorn and up the Great Glen into the region around the Moray Firth.

There is, of course, no indication from the sources as to when this migration took place or of how long it might have taken to accomplish. It might even have begun in the mid-eighth century following the Pictish conquest by Oengus mac Fergus, which seems to have been inflicted most heavily on the Cenel Loairn, but the place-name evidence for Gaelic settlement in the ninth century would indicate the Cenel Loairn nobility having moved up into Moray at the time when Norse land-taking in the wake of viking raids had begun to make a real impact on the west of Scotland. It would seem then that the Cenel Loairn had done much the same thing north of the Mounth, and at

much the same time, as had the Cenel Gabrain on Tayside, establishing themselves over Moray while the mac Fergus dynasty and its mac Alpin successors
established themselves in the kingship of Fortriu. The new political relationship between those two kindreds, however, represented no great departure
from the former arrangement in the west, when the royal house descended
from the Cenel Gabrain translated its ancient claim to over-kingship of
Dalriada into a new sovereignty over Scots and Picts, and thus imposed on
the descendants of the Cenel Loairn the effective status of subject kings who
were later to be styled mormaers.

The first reference in the sources to these sub-kings in Moray occurs in the
Annals of Tigernach at the year 976 where one of three Scots mormaers
involved in an Ui Neill raid into Offaly is named as *Donnchad mac
Morgaind*, or Duncan, and evidently the son of the same man identified by
the Rawlinson genealogy as *Morggán* and a great-great-grandson of
Ainbcellach, son of Ferchar Fota. This Duncan was, in fact, the uncle of the
Ruadri whose son and successor Findlaech is the next mormaer of Moray to
make an appearance in the historical record.[9] Findlaech's obituary is entered
at the year 1020 in the two most authoritative of the Irish annals, but his dramatic entry into history is placed more than twenty-five years before that
date by two saga sources – *Olaf Tryggvasson's Saga* and the *Orkneyinga Saga*
– in their accounts of the battle fought at a place which is called in the Norse
Skidamyre between Sigurd the Stout of Orkney and the 'jarl who was called
Finnleik'.[10]

The dispute between the jarls of Orkney and mormaers of Moray arose
out of their rival claims to dominion over Caithness, where the Norse interest
can be traced back to the time of Thorstein the Red, a son of the Olaf who
had established himself as Norse king of Dublin in the mid-ninth century.
This Thorstein Olafsson is said by one of the most reliable saga-makers to
have set himself up in the north of the Scottish mainland and there he carved
out a territory extending over all of what is now Caithness and the eastern
part of Sutherland. There can be no doubt that Thorstein's conquests on the
mainland were made in alliance with the Orkney Norse and, following his
death around the year 875, the claim he had staked on Caithness passed to
the jarls of Orkney.

It was a claim which has recently been the subject of illuminating
investigation by Barbara Crawford, a foremost modern historian of
Scandinavian Scotland who offers a stunningly simple explanation of the
determination with which the Orkney jarls pursued their interest in the
northern mainland. It is in the nature of island life to be dependent in great
measure on seafaring, and all the more so for the viking-descended jarls of

Orkney whose power and prosperity depended ultimately upon the ocean-going longship which, in its turn, depended for its construction on the essential raw material of good ship-timber. The greater the jarls' sphere of power and influence became, suggests Dr Crawford, 'the greater their need for constant and ready access to timber nearer home. There can never have been, even in prehistoric times, availability of wood sufficient for shipbuilding purposes in the Northern Isles. This may well have been a very good reason why the earls strove so hard to extend their power into the Scottish mainland, and there may have been more woodland in Caithness and Sutherland in the early historic period than there is today. When the earls were looking for good ship-building timber which could be easily brought to the coast . . . they needed to look no further than the Firthlands of easter Ross and south-east Sutherland.'[11]

Long before the arrival of Thorstein the Red all of those lands lay within the territory of the Picts, and the name Caithness represents a Norse-derived form of the old Pictish name for their province of *Cat*. All such Pictish provinces had lain, at one time or another, under the sovereignty of their high-kings who, from the end of the seventh century onwards, were, of course, the kings of Fortriu. Following the Scots infiltration of the kingship of Fortriu in the early ninth century and the effective establishment thereafter of a high-kingship of Picts and Scots by Kenneth and his mac Alpin successors, kings of Scots could consider themselves fully legitimate heirs to the old Pictish claim on Caithness, and the prosecution of that claim fell naturally to the mormaers of Moray as their northernmost client rulers.

So it was that when one of the more formidable Orkney jarls found himself facing such expansive Scots ambitions as those of Kenneth II, contention over Caithness was virtually inevitable. Just such a situation arose – according to the *Orkneyinga Saga* – at some point after 985, in which year Sigurd the Stout, son of Hlodvi, succeeded his father into the jarldom of Orkney.

Sigurd became a powerful jarl and the ruler of widespread lands. He held Caithness by force against the Scots and made a viking cruise over the sea every summer when he plundered the Hebrides and in Scotland and Ireland.

It happened in one summer that the Scots jarl who was called Finnleik came down [into Caithness] from Scotland with an army of overwhelming numbers. Finnleik challenged Sigurd to battle at Skidamyre in Caithness and named a day for the fighting. Sigurd went to consult his mother who was a sorceress and he told her that the odds must be at least seven to his one.

She told him: 'I would have reared you in my wool basket all these years had I known you would want to go on living for ever. A man's life is ruled by fate, not by his own coming and going, so it is better to die with honour than to live in shame. Take you now this banner, which I have worked for you with all the skill I know, for my knowledge tells me that it will bring victory to the one before whom it is borne, for all that it will bring death to the one who bears it.'

This banner was finely made and richly embroidered with the figure of a raven, so that when the banner was caught by the wind it would seem as if the raven was spreading its wings in flight, but Sigurd was angry at his mother's words. He gave the men of Orkney back their land-rights in exchange for their sword-service, and then crossed over to face Jarl Finnleik at Skidamyre, where the two war-hosts were drawn up in full battle array. At the moment the armies clashed, Jarl Sigurd's standard bearer was struck dead and the Jarl told another to take up the banner, but soon he too was killed. Three of his standard-bearers were slain, but it was Jarl Sigurd who won the day.

The battlefield called *Skidamyre* in the Norse, or *Skithmór* in the Icelandic of the saga, is quite certainly the moor beside Skitten farm, just some five miles north-west of Wick in Caithness, and there is a standing stone in that place said by local tradition to mark the site of a significant defeat in battle. While the stone had stood there for some thousands of years before even the first northman saw the land of Caithness and the sagas tell of more than one battle fought on Skidamyre, the tradition attached to the standing stone may very well be a genuine recollection of Sigurd's victory over the man the saga calls *jarl Finnleik*, but who is more properly known by his Gaelic name-form of Findlaech, mormaer of Moray.

Findlaech himself survived the battle and for a full quarter-century follow-ing, during which time – if the evidence of the canons of Huntingdon, Wyntoun and Boece can be relied upon – he must have taken to wife one of the daughters of Malcolm II, as also, and at much the same time, did Sigurd of Orkney. The saga sources admit no doubt as to Sigurd's dominion over Caithness throughout his long reign in the jarldom and neither is there any evidence of further contention between the Scots and the Orkney Norse through some forty years after the fight at Skitten. The death of Sigurd, when he himself took up the raven banner at Clontarf, has an obvious bearing on the situation after 1014, but the absence of any contention through the pre-ceding decade must imply that the succession of Malcolm II as king of Scots in 1005 enabled some form of peace settlement over the question of

Caithness. It is fully probable that the marriage of Malcolm's daughter to Sigurd formed a part of such a settlement and especially in view of the saga claim for Malcolm having promised the 'earldom' of Caithness and Sutherland to the young son of that marriage, namely his grandson the future Jarl Thorfinn.

It is significant that the only contention in the north of Scotland noticed by the sources for the later years of Malcolm's reign arose not between the men of Moray and the Norse of Orkney, but between the men of Moray themselves. If Professor Hudson is correct in recognising a virtual 'civil war' north of the Mounth in the second decade of the new millennium,[12] the entry in the *Annals of Tigernach* at the year 1020 would confirm the mormaer Findlaech, although no longer a young man, to have been its most notable casualty.

Findlaech mac Ruadri, mormaer of Moray, was slain by the sons of his brother Maelbrigte.

Thus it was that sovereignty in Moray passed in 1020 to one of those sons of Maelbrigte accused by the annalist of the slaughter of their uncle Findlaech. The new mormaer was Malcolm mac Maelbrigte, but the annals have no further notice of him until their entry of his obituary, following an apparently peaceful death, in 1029. His successor would seem to have been his brother Gillacomgain, the only other named son of Maelbrigte, who is certainly styled 'mormaer' by the *Annals of Ulster* entry of his obituary three years later, were it not for the implication by the *Anglo-Saxon Chronicle* of a rather more complex situation having emerged by 1031. It was in that year, of course, that Cnut, the Danish king of England, came north to meet with the king of Scots and, at least according to the *Chronicle*, to accept his 'submission'. What might have been the true nature of that meeting has already been discussed, but the item of evidence from the *Anglo-Saxon Chronicle* of most immediate interest here is its identification of those accompanying Malcolm, probably as far south as Cumbria or Strathclyde, to attend this 'conference of kings'.

These two – who are described together with Malcolm as 'famous foreign lords' by lines of older Icelandic verse preserved in *Saint Olaf's Saga* – were undoubtedly Malcolm's sub-kings but their names are known only from the entry in the *Chronicle*. One of them, called by the chronicler *Iehmarc*, has been convincingly identified as Echmarcach Rognvaldsson, successor to his father, the 'Rognvald, king of the Isles' whose obituary is entered in the *Annals of Ulster* at the year 1005.[13] The other is called *Maelbeth*, a name which can only represent the chronicler's Old English form of the Gaelic *Macbethad* and can thus be taken to confirm the presence of Macbeth, son of Findlaech, in company with his grandfather Malcolm in 1031 at what amounts to the eleventh-century equivalent of an international summit conference.

If Echmarcach was in attendance as Malcolm's sub-king of the Isles, then Macbeth must have attended in a very similar capacity for Moray, and yet did so in the year prior to the violent death of his cousin Gillacomgain who is still recognised as 'mormaer of Moray' when his obituary is entered in the *Annals of Ulster* at 1032:

> Gillacomgain, Maelbrigte's son, mormaer of Moray, was burned and fifty of his men with him.

While the annalist makes no mention of Macbeth in connection with the death of Gillacomgain, all the evidence suggests a renewal of violent contention between two branches of Moray's ruling kindred in the generation after Findlaech. The *Anglo-Saxon Chronicle* indicates Macbeth assuming the role of a sub-king while his cousin Gillacomgain, accused by the annalist of killing Macbeth's father, was still mormaer of Moray. Suspicion of responsibility for Gillacomgain's death by burning can only fall, if not on Macbeth himself, then on a faction acting in his support and, if Macbeth was indeed the grandson of Malcolm II, it is no less likely that the king of Scots was also in some way involved.

The probability, then, must be of the young Macbeth having found sanctuary at Malcolm's court after the death of his father in 1020 and, having reached an age of suitable maturity, being appointed mormaer of Moray in opposition to Gillacomgain as an act of deliberate policy on the part of the king of Scots. Malcolm was evidently anxious in the last years of his reign to eliminate potentially rival claimants to the succession, and to that end had killed the 'grandson of Boite' in 1033, so it would have been well in character for him to have similarly disposed of Gillacomgain to install his own candidate as mormaer of Moray.

The evidence of the *Chronicle of the Kings* locating the death of Malcolm at Glamis raises the question as to whether it was his involvement in the vicious politics of Moray which cost him his life, but the precise circumstances of Malcolm's death pale in importance beside the situation which it brought about and the subsequent course of events by which first one, and then another, of his grandsons followed him into the high-kingship of Scots.

'THE RED KING WILL TAKE THE KINGDOM'

If Florent of Worcester's reference to Duncan mac Crinan having been 'king of the Cumbrians' can be taken to confirm his appointment to the tanist kingship of Strathclyde, then this son of Malcolm's daughter Bethoc and the abbot of Dunkeld was the *tanaise*, the 'expected one' chosen to succeed his grandfather in the kingship.

So indeed he did on the evidence of all the sources, none of them more meticulous in their dating than Marianus Scotus who notes Duncan's reign having begun on the feast of 'the mass of Saint Andrew' – or 30 November – in the year 1034. Marianus' precision in matters of calendar detail offers the most reliable evidence for Duncan having been inducted into the kingship at Scone exactly five days after the death of Malcolm at Glamis 'on the seventh day before the kalends of December' (25 November), and the proximity of those two dates might be shown to carry an unexpectedly strategic significance for the circumstances of the succession.

Even if Malcolm had signalled Duncan to be his successor, such an intention would not necessarily have been the deciding factor when there were two other equally legitimate, and perhaps rather more formidable, claimants in the persons of Macbeth mac Findlaech and Thorfinn Sigurdsson. The apparent acceptance without contention of Macbeth as Duncan's successor is arguably the very best evidence for the legitimacy of his claim by mother-right, but Thorfinn's claim would have carried no less legitimacy and there is one remarkable fragment of evidence to indicate his ambition having indeed extended to the high-kingship of Alba. The chapters of the *Orkneyinga Saga* bearing on Thorfinn are illustrated with verses attributed to one Arnor, his *jarlaskald* or 'earl's poet'. If these passages are genuine – and there is no reason to doubt them – they must represent immediately contemporary evidence for his activities and thus when Arnor describes his jarl as 'the man of the sword, seeking Scotland's throne' he must be taken very seriously indeed.

Duncan, then, was not unrivalled in his claim on the kingship, but he was, in all probability, the claimant best placed by his geographical location to assert it. Macbeth would have been doubtless engaged somewhere in Moray at the time of Malcolm's death and Thorfinn, who was then still sharing the jarldom with his brother Brusi, is said by the *Orkneyinga Saga* to have been based in the north of Caithness, but there is no reason to believe Duncan having been elsewhere than in Dunkeld or thereabouts on Tayside. It was just such a likely location of the interested parties which led one of the most trenchant of Scotland's historians, the late Professor Gordon Donaldson, to suggest that 'Duncan became king, possibly because he was the eldest or ablest, but just as likely because, on Malcolm's death, he managed to beat his rivals to the scene of royal inaugurations at Scone, much as in England Henry I beat his brother Robert to Winchester'.[14]

Once the successor had come to the place traditionally appointed for king-making and there undergone whatever inaugural ritual – which would have included, among other ceremonies, the proclamation of his royal lineage before an assembly of subject nobles[15] – his succession would have been, at least formally, secured by respect for the ancient sanctity accorded Celtic kingship. In reality, though, any such security from contention would have been no more than a pure formality by the eleventh century, if indeed it had ever been otherwise, and would have held only for a decent interval during which the successor king would be expected to demonstrate his prowess in the kingship. It must be said that the surviving historical record of the reign of Duncan mac Crinan offers no evidence for his having accomplished any such demonstration.

Whatever Fordun might have meant by his curious statement that 'during the short period of Duncan's reign, nothing was done whereof mention should be made', the combined evidence of the sources for Duncan's six-year reign amounts to a relentless chronicle of defeats in battle leading almost inevitably to the blood-fray in which he himself was slain. The first of these military reverses can be dated to the early years of his reign, if the evidence of the *Orkneyinga Saga* is to be relied upon and if Duncan was the same person as the man it calls 'Karl Hundisson'.[16] The saga refers to the death of 'the king of Scots', presumably meaning the demise of Malcolm II, after which 'Karl Hundi's son succeeded to the realm of Scotland and claimed possession of Caithness also, as had Scottish kings before him. But Jarl Thorfinn had Caithness, thinking it to be his proper inheritance from his grandfather and refusing to pay any *skatt* [tribute] for it.'

A Scots warband despatched to Caithness by the new king soon withdrew when it found itself hopelessly outnumbered by the Norse it had been sent to intimidate and was pursued along its course of retreat by a triumphant Thorfinn who 'subdued Sutherland and Ross and plundered far and wide over Scotland'. In angry response, 'King Karl' himself came north with a fleet of eleven warships which caught up with Thorfinn's fleet moored on the south-east coast of the Orkney mainland, only to suffer an ignominious defeat with the loss of his own flagship in a sea-fight off Deerness. Having managed to escape with his life, 'Karl Hundisson' went about recruiting a new war-host 'from the whole of the south of Scotland, from east and west and south as far as Kintyre' and calling also upon a contingent of Irish allies drawn, in all probability, from his great-grandmother's people in Leinster.

Meanwhile Thorfinn's principal lieutenant surprised the mormaer whom Karl had tried to place over Caithness and slew him in Thurso, before joining the jarl in Moray where, according to the saga, he had assembled his great war-host 'raised in Caithness and throughout Sutherland and Ross'. The saga chapter concludes with an account of Karl's forces being brought to battle at *Torfnes* – a place which has been identified as Burghead on the southern shore of the Moray Firth, but is perhaps more likely to have been Tarbat Ness in the Dornoch Firth. 'Reddened weapons fed well the wolves at Torfnes' sang Arnor the skald, and Thorfinn emerged triumphant from the slaughter to follow up his victory with plunder-raiding 'as far south as Fife', according to the saga, while 'Karl took flight, though some men say that he was killed'. If 'Karl Hundisson' was Duncan mac Crinan – and I cannot believe that they were not one and the same – 'some men' were in error, because the historical Duncan reappears in the sources just a few years later to face defeat in battle once again, but this time much further to the south on a raid into Cuthbert's land.

Duncan had evidently become involved in the treacherous politics of Anglo-Danish Northumbria some few years earlier than his succession to the kingship of Scots, when he took to wife a close kinswoman of the Danish warlord Siward, who was to become earl at York in 1033.[17] Siward emerged thereafter as the inevitable rival to the Eadulf of Bamburgh – a son of Uhtred by his Danish wife – who is said by the *Historia Regum* attributed to Symeon of Durham to have launched an attack on Scots territory with a raid into Cumbria in 1038. In the following year Duncan, king of Scots, laid siege to Durham.

Whether he was seeking revenge for Eadulf's incursion or, perhaps, making a gesture in support of an alliance by marriage with Siward's faction, or even attempting to restore the damage inflicted upon his prestige by Thorfinn's victory is uncertain, because he might have been prompted by any or all of those motives. None of them were, in the event, to be satisfied by his expedition on the evidence of Symeon's *History of the Church of Durham* which shows Duncan to have been no more successful in 1039 than had been Malcolm's siege thirty-three years earlier.

Duncan, king of the Scots, advanced with a countless multitude of troops and laid siege to Durham, and made strenuous but unsuccessful attempts to carry it. For a great proportion of his cavalry was slain by the besieged and he was put to disorderly flight, in which he lost all his foot-soldiery whose heads were collected in the market place and hung up upon posts.

Not long afterwards the same king, upon his return to Scotland, was murdered by his own countrymen . . .

So, indeed, he was. Unlike his more fortunate grandfather, who had suffered a very similar reverse in that same place in the first year of his reign yet been able to survive in the kingship through three more decades and with his reputation more than fully restored, Duncan was not to survive into the autumn of the following year.

The earliest sources preserve a properly comprehensive, if less than fully explanatory, record of the death of Duncan. The *Annals of Tigernach* and the *Annals of Ulster* enter it at the year 1040 and style him *ard ri Albain* ('high-king of Alba'). Marianus Scotus' *Chronicon* fixes the date still more precisely as 'the nineteenth day before the kalends of September' (14 August), while the *Chronicle of the Kings* locates the place of his death at *Bothngouane*, now Pitgaveny near Elgin, and of his burial 'in the island of Iona'. Both those last-named sources are able also to identify the man who brought him down and followed him into the kingship as 'Macbeth, Findlaech's son'.

None of which corresponds to the Shakespearean scenario of Macbeth despatching knife-wielding assassins to stab an aged king to death in his bed. There is no good evidence to indicate Duncan having been much older than Macbeth or Thorfinn and especially when Tigernach describes him being 'slain by his subjects at an unripe age'. The most plausible historical reconstruction of events is prompted by Duncan having been killed near Elgin, a location which suggests the men of Moray having rejected an over-lord whose prestige was damaged beyond repair and Duncan responding with a subsequent royal progress north of the Mounth accompanied by an intimidating show of force. It was not uncommon for a Celtic king to venture in person and in full military array into subject territory for the collection of taxes and tribute. It would usually have been a flourish of sovereign authority presenting a ceremonial challenge to a recalcitrant sub-king, but for Duncan to issue such a challenge, however ceremonially, to a mormaer of Moray with no less a claim on the high-kingship than his own, would have been tempting fate, and Macbeth mac Findlaech, beyond endurance.

The evidence of the early sources confirms the outcome of such a venture for the principals involved having been very much as might have been expected in the prevailing circumstances of the year 1040. The same outcome, however, should perhaps be reviewed in its somewhat wider political context, because Macbeth of Moray was not the only man of power with a claim by mother-right to the kingship of Scots and Thorfinn of Orkney, the 'man of the sword seeking Scotland's throne', had already demonstrated his military ascendancy over Duncan. When the whole sequence of events is seen from that perspective, there is a convincing ring of *realpolitik* to Professor Donaldson's suggestion that 'it would be understandable if Duncan's two cousins, Thorfinn and Macbeth, then ganged up against him . . . and the circumstances suggest that he fell victim to a joint attack by his two cousins, who, after thus disposing of him, partitioned the kingdom between them. Macbeth got the royal title, but Thorfinn, the *Saga* says, held nine Scottish earldoms, which by any reckoning looks like a generous share.'[18]

The peace and prosperity recognised by all the earliest sources as hallmarks of Macbeth's reign would have hardly been possible had he not reached some accommodation with the mighty Thorfinn and such an arrangement would infer a political alliance if not indeed a personal friendship between cousins. It is, then, at least curious that there is no mention of Thorfinn in any Scottish or Irish source and neither is there any appearance of Macbeth, at least under that name, in the *Orkneyinga Saga*, omissions which have led, on at least one recent occasion, to the hypothesis that they were one and the same man.[19] Such a proposal is, of course, immediately disallowed by all the genealogical sources, but the evidence – from the *Orkneyinga Saga* in the case of Thorfinn and from Marianus Scotus in the case of Macbeth – for both of them having been on pilgrimage to Rome at much the same time prompted Professor Donaldson to suggest that 'even if they were not one man under two names, Macbeth and Thorfinn may have been fellow-travellers'.[20]

Macbeth's pilgrimage to Rome, reliably dated by Marianus to the year 1050, is of interest for reasons which will bear later consideration here, but suffice it to say at this point that the fact of his even having considered a journey of such duration over so great a distance offers remarkable evidence for his sheer confidence in the security of the kingdom and his sovereignty over it at the end of his first decade in the high-kingship of Scots.

THE 'FRUITFUL SEASONS'

It is, I would have thought, scarcely possible to recognise any semblance of the Shakespearean character in the passage from the *Prophecy of Berchan* which is thought to hail the advent of *Macbethad* in the kingship.

Afterwards the Red king will take the kingdom . . .
 After slaughter of Gael, after slaughter of *gaill*, the generous king of Fortriu will take Alba.
 The red-faced, yellow-haired, tall one, I will take delight in him.
 Brimful in the west and in the east will be Alba during the reign of the luxuriant Red One.

Those lines, set down no more than fifty years after his death and almost certainly composed within living memory of his reign, are the best surviving evidence of the closely contemporary Gaelic appreciation of Macbeth and thus worthy of some close attention here.

Their placing of his succession 'after slaughter of Gael, after slaughter of *gaill* [or northmen]' can only allude to the disastrous warfaring of Duncan's reign, and even specifically to the blood-fray at *Torfnes*, but their evocation of Macbeth's reign as a time of great abundance in Scotland is of more far-reaching significance. Evidence to the same effect is found also in the 'Verse Chronicle of the Kings' – included in the thirteenth-century *Chronicle of Melrose* but of rather greater antiquity – which may well have been written by Ailred, future abbot of Rievaulx, when he was in Scotland at the court of David I in the 1130s:

> Macbeth became king of Scotland for seventeen years;
> and in his reign there were fruitful seasons . . .

So too in Wyntoun's *Cronykil* which says of Macbeth's 'seventeen winters as king in Scotland' and 'all his time was of great plenty, abounding both on land and sea'.

The achievement and maintenance of general prosperity is attributed in modern times to good government and much the same attribution has been claimed for Macbeth's kingship. It is, of course, true that harvests would have suffered greatly from the death toll and disruption incurred by the warfaring of Duncan's reign, but the description of Scotland as having been 'brimful in the west and in the east' in the time of Duncan's successor has, I suspect, a stronger association with ancient and even magical beliefs than with the government of economics. The inauguration of a king in pre-Christian Celtic Ireland symbolised his ritual 'marriage' to the tribe and, in some wise also, to the land of the tribe, thus inescapably associating kingship with fertility. Such beliefs surviving from prehistoric antiquity were absorbed rather than diminished by the impact of Christianity and were passed on, with so many other customs of kingship, from the parent Irish culture into that of Gaelic Scotland where – even as late as the eleventh century and if only in the collective unconscious of the Gael – a reign of 'fruitful seasons' betokened a rightful king being justly favoured by fortune. All of which amounts to an early medieval equivalent of what is called now the 'feel-good factor' and bears at least as much upon good weather as it does upon quality of kingship, but there is also consistent evidence from a range of sources to indicate the historical Macbeth having been especially remembered for his remarkable personal generosity.

Incorporated into the *Register of St Andrews* is a Latin abstract of the Gaelic chartulary (or 'donations book') from the island monastery on Loch Leven in Fife which was placed under the administration of St Andrews in the mid-twelfth century but was believed to have been founded by Saint Serf (or *Servanus* in his Latin name-form) around the year 540. The texts of three documents preserved in this St Andrews collection bear on Loch Leven between 1037 and 1054 when it was still a community of *céli dé* – or 'culdees', adherents of a movement which sought to restore and preserve the monastic customs of the ancient Irish Celtic church – and the beneficiary of generous endowments by Macbeth and his queen.[21] One of these documents of donation enters Macbeth's grant of the lands of *Bolgyne* to the culdees of Loch Leven 'with the utmost veneration and devotion', while two others preserve a record of the similar endowment of the lands of *Kyrkenes*. These last are, perhaps, of the greater interest because they record the land grants having been made to the culdees 'from motives of piety and for the benefit of their prayers' in the joint names of 'Macbeth son of Findlaech and Gruoch, daughter of Boite, king and queen of Scots'.[22]

The Loch Leven charters are, in fact, the only surviving evidence for the name and lineage of Macbeth's queen and it is fortunate that they tell history as much as they do about her. The location of the 'lands of Kyrkenes' granted on her behalf has been taken to suggest that Gruoch's own estates lay also in that part of Fife, which would have a further significance for the royal kindred from which she was descended. If her father was the same 'Boite, son of Kenneth', whose grandson had been killed by Malcolm II in 1033 – and no historian seems to be in any doubt that he was – then Gruoch was either a niece of Malcolm or a granddaughter of Kenneth III. It is, by reason of the same uncertainty attending Boite, of course not possible to know which, but she was undoubtedly born of a royal kindred which had been at violent odds with Malcolm and was, presumably, also hostile to the house of Dunkeld whereto Malcolm had pledged the succession. Gruoch can thus be identified with a faction sharing some common cause with Macbeth, but she might have also had reason for hostility towards him because it seems more than likely that she had earlier been the wife of Macbeth's cousin, the mormaer Gillacomgain who was burned to death in 1032.

This complex marital sequence rests, at least as far as I have been able to discern, on the genealogical evidence for the Lulach who followed Macbeth into the kingship in 1057 to reign for just some seven months until his own death in the following year. This Lulach is identified by the genealogy from the *Book of Ballymote* as the son of Gillacomgain mac Maelbrigte, but the note of his lineage entered in the *Chronicle of the Kings* calls him a 'nephew of the son of Boite'. Lulach's father was thus of the male line of the house of Moray and claiming descent back to the kings of the Cenel Loairn, but his mother can only have been a daughter of Boite descended from a branch of the mac Alpin dynasty and, presumably, the same daughter of Boite called Gruoch who is known to the Loch Leven charters as Macbeth's queen. It is just this jigsaw of the genealogical evidence which has enabled historians to recognise Gruoch as a granddaughter of either Kenneth II or Kenneth III who became the wife of Gillacomgain, mormaer of Moray, and the mother of his son, Lulach. Following the violent death of Gillacomgain, she had evidently accepted his successor Macbeth mac Findlaech as her second husband in an apparently political marriage, probably made before Macbeth's elevation to the kingship of Scots and intended to seal a peace settlement between the contending kindreds of Moray.[23]

It is not known whether Gruoch accompanied her husband on his pilgrimage to Rome. If she did, the entry at the year 1050 in Marianus Scotus' *Chronicon* makes no mention of her, but it does offer further evidence of Macbeth's generosity when it tells of him having 'scattered silver like seed to the poor at Rome'. Pilgrimage to Rome had become something of a vogue among western magnates even by the second quarter of the eleventh century. Cnut is known to have returned from Rome before coming to Scotland to take Malcolm's 'submission' in 1031 and the pilgrimage made by Thorfinn of Orkney some twenty years later – at much the same time as, if not in company with, Macbeth – may well have been inspired by Cnut's example. Others who came in the wake of Macbeth along the same pilgrim road included a son and successor to Brian Boru in the kingship of Munster and Echmarcach, the king of the Isles who attended Malcolm's meeting with Cnut and who is said by Marianus Scotus to have died in Rome. While Cnut may have introduced the fashion for royal pilgrimage, it would seem likely that these Scots and Irish kings were drawn to Rome less by his example than by the foundation there of the monastery *Sanctae Trinitatis Scottorum* ('Holy Trinity of the Scots and/or Irish') around the time of Macbeth's pilgrimage.

Marianus Scotus – whose Irish name was Moel Brigte and who had been a monk at Moville in Down until he was banished into penitential exile in Germany – was just one of very many Irish monks who had been finding their way to the continent since the end of the sixth century and in still greater numbers by the ninth century as a consequence of the viking onslaught. The monasteries founded by these *peregrinati* of the Irish church eventually came to represent a Gaelic-speaking monastic information network which spanned the greater extent of continental Europe. So it was that Marianus Scotus working on his chronicle in the Rhineland in the mid-eleventh century would have been kept informed by his compatriot clergy in Rome of the arrival there of pilgrim kings from the Celtic west and, in particular, of the generosity shown by the king of Scots. Macbeth's extravagant offerings 'to the poor at Rome' were, in all probability, distributed through the good offices of the brothers of *Sanctae Trinitatis Scottorum* and it may even be – as Benjamin Hudson is unkind enough to suggest – that 'one of the reasons why Macbeth receives a good report in the contemporary ecclesiastical records could be tied to donations to a new Gaelic monastery at Rome.'[24]

There is, though, no aspect of Macbeth's pilgrimage to Rome quite so significant as its implication for his confidence in the security of the kingdom he left so far behind on his pilgrim road. It was a confidence in which he was evidently justified when he left for Rome and on his return to Scotland, but it was to be justified, in the event, for only four more years.

BEFORE AND AFTER 'THE DAY OF THE SEVEN SLEEPERS'

When the determined opposition to Macbeth did eventually materialise in 1054, it came not from within the kingdom of Scots but from south of the Tweed and at its head stood Siward, the Dane from Cnut's following who had become earl of all Northumbria in 1041, and now emerged as the most formidable champion of the house of Dunkeld.

It would not, however, be true to suggest the total absence of evidence for hostility to Macbeth in Scotland at any point in the first fifteen years of his reign. While his succession following the death of Duncan was apparently achieved without contention, it was only to be expected that a kernel of hostility towards him would be nurtured at Dunkeld for as long as Crinan remained alive. In the event, the abbot of Dunkeld was to survive his son by fully five years, sufficient time at least to indicate Macbeth not having entered the kingship hell-bent upon the destruction of every potential opposing faction.

Duncan's two sons, however, did flee the kingdom – according to Fordun and again there is no reason to doubt him – at some point, if not immediately, after their father's death at the hands of Macbeth. The younger of them found his way to the Isles from where he was to emerge half a century on and under his Gaelic name-form of *Domnall Bán* ('Donald the White-haired') as his brother's successor in the kingship, but the son of Duncan who claims first importance at this point is the elder, Malcolm, who is thought to have fled first to Cumbria, the territory Boece claims had been earlier 'presented to him' by his father. Malcolm could have been no older than ten when Duncan was slain, so if Boece is not mistaken in his claim for so young a prince having been 'presented' with Cumbria – meaning presumably his being placed into the tanist kingship of Strathclyde – even such a sub-kingship could have been no more than titular. The real government of Cumbria had probably passed, perhaps even as a formal regency, to Duncan's wife's kinsman the earl Siward and it was certainly into Siward's orbit that Malcolm found himself on his flight from Macbeth's kingdom after 1040.

Malcolm would thus have been approaching the threshold of manhood in Anglo-Danish Northumbria by 1045, at which year the death of his grand-father is entered in the *Annals of Tigernach*:

> A battle between the men of Alba on one road, wherein was killed Crinan, abbot of Dunkeld, and a multitude along with him, that is nine score of his fighting men.

Tigernach's Irish phrase *ar aenrian*, translating as 'on one road', is usually taken to mean a hosting of the men of Alba for a united expedition, the term 'road' being used in the sense of 'warpath' to mean 'raid'. There is a sub-stantially similar entry in the *Annals of Ulster* at the same year and the evi-dence of these most reliable Irish annal sources would confirm some violent contention having broken out between rival factions brought together within a Scots war-host leaving Crinan and so many of his warriors as its fatal casu-alties.

All of which, when placed into the political context of Scotland in the 1040s, would seem to represent a spontaneous revolt against Macbeth's over-lordship having been immediately and forcibly suppressed, unless it can be linked in some wise to the fragment of evidence entered in the *Annals of Durham* – but in no other source – at the year 1046.

> Earl Siward came to Scotland with a great army and expelled its king Macbeth and appointed another, but after his [Siward's] departure Macbeth recovered the kingdom.

It would seem most likely that the Durham chronicler had simply misplaced an item intended for 1054 under the year 1046, were it not for the fact that he does also enter Siward's invasion of 1054 under that year. There is also an anecdote in the twelfth-century history by Henry of Huntingdon which tells of one of Siward's sons having been killed while leading a Northumbrian attack 'to acquire Scotland' prior to 1054 and a reference in yet another twelfth-century source – Geoffroi de Gaimar's *L'Estorie des Engles* (a 'history of the English' composed in Norman French verse) – which mentions Macbeth's breach of an otherwise unknown 'treaty' with Siward having provoked the invasion of 1054.

Despite the virtual certainty that Macbeth's pilgrimage to Rome in 1050 would have been unthinkable if there had been any recent threat from a Northumbrian ally of the house of Dunkeld, it is still tempting to look for some involvement of Siward in Scotland around the time of Crinan's revolt just five years earlier. There are so many intriguing possibilities, not least among them that of Siward having been the enemy against whom the men of Alba were hosted 'on one road' in 1045. There is also the question of who might have been Siward's candidate to replace Macbeth in 1046, when Malcolm was still no older than sixteen and Duncan's brother Maldred would have been the only remotely qualified claimant of sufficient maturity. It is also, perhaps, just possible that Boece's account of tribute paid to Macbeth for the burial of the Danish dead on Inchcolm after the 'battle of Kinghorn' might have formed a part of the 'treaty' mentioned by Geoffroi of Gaimar, but the evidence is really too slender to enable serious speculation.

More substantial, and very much more significant, is the record of events dated to the summer of 1054 by the northern recension of the *Anglo-Saxon Chronicle*:

> At this time the earl Siward went with a great host both by sea and land into Scotland; and fought against the Scots and put to flight their king Macbeth, and slew all that were most noble in the land, carrying away much war-spoil, such as no man had gained before.
>
> And there were slain his son Osbern and his sister's son Siward, and numbers of his house carles [bodyguard], and also of the king's on the Day of the Seven Sleepers [27 July].

The same battle was important enough to be noticed by the Irish annalists, being entered by Tigernach and, in greater detail, by the *Annals of Ulster* at 1054:

> A battle between the men of Alba and of Saxonland; wherein fell three thousand of the men of Alba and one thousand and five hundred of the Saxons, including Dolfin, son of Finntuir.

[197]

A tradition at least as old as the late fourteenth century locates the battle-field from which Macbeth was 'put to flight' around his stronghold of Dunsinnen built, according to Wyntoun, of 'tymber and stane' on the south bank of the Tay some five miles north-east of Scone. The symbolic royal centre at Scone was, in all probability, the real target of Siward's attack on Macbeth's kingdom, which was made not only in the interest of his kinswoman's son now grown to manhood, but also – according to Florent of Worcester – 'by the king's command'. Edward, called 'the Confessor' and the son of Aethelred II, had reclaimed the throne of England for the West Saxon royal house following the death in 1042 of Harthacnut, the last of Cnut's Danish successors in the English kingship. Wyntoun tells of the young Malcolm having been brought, presumably by Siward, to meet Edward soon after his flight from Scotland and it is thought that he spent some part of his later boyhood as a royal protégé at the English court. When set into that context, the clear implication of the evidence of Florent of Worcester and those later medieval English historians deriving from him is of Siward being sent into Scotland by the English king with the intention of driving out Macbeth and installing Malcolm as a client king of Scots indebted to the earl of Northumbria and accepting Edward as his ultimate overlord. For all Siward's military energy and reputation and despite the premature claims of the medieval English sources, such a purpose was not to be so easily accomplished.

Siward's northern progress in 1054 followed much the same form of strategy as that of his viking forebears who had advanced on York almost two hundred years before, as his land-forces – described by Florent as 'an army of horse' – travelled as cavalry and his warships followed the parallel sea-route up the east coast. His army crossed the Forth, probably near Stirling, to advance on Tayside by way of Strathearn and there make contact with his war-fleet which had sailed into the Firth of Tay. Having thus assembled on Tayside what must have been an impressive war-host, the Earl of Northumbria brought Macbeth and the men of Alba to battle on Dunsinnen hill, where the *Anglo-Saxon Chronicle* would imply the victory having gone to Siward, even if at no small cost when both his son and nephew were among the slain. The entry of the battle in the *Annals of Ulster* offers its own independent evidence for the heavy death-toll on both sides, but names just one individual casualty as 'Dolfin, son of Finntuir'. This Dolfin is recognised now by historians as one of Malcolm's allies and, in all likelihood, a great-grandson of Crinan, but his name was probably singled out for mention by the annalist mistaking him for Thorfinn of Orkney.

Much more important, though, is what the Irish sources do not say of the battle, and they do not claim or even imply any outright victory for Siward. What might have been the real outcome of the blood-fray on the Day of the Seven Sleepers hinges then upon interpretation of the claim made by the *Anglo-Saxon Chronicle* for Macbeth having been 'put to flight'. It is clear, first of all, that he was not deprived of either his life or his kingship. He may very well have been forced to concede territory to Malcolm, who would seem thus to have won some measure of sovereignty in southern Scotland, which gain was, according to Florent, 'as the king [Edward] had directed'. The most significant result of the battle would seem, then, to have been a redistribution of territory, which, even if it amounted to an effective partition, is more plausibly recognised as a peace settlement between armies who had fought each other to a bloody stalemate than the outcome of a total defeat of one by the other.

Neither can the sources provide conclusive evidence for the extent of the territory won by Malcolm. Florent most certainly implies Malcolm having won kingship of Cumbria, and probably overlordship of Lothian besides. It is quite possible that he was able to reclaim his father's territory on Tayside, which might have confirmed him as sub-king of Cumbria and mormaer of Atholl, but fell far short of an over-kingship of Scots. It is no less likely that the claim by the *Anglo-Saxon Chronicle* for Macbeth having been 'put to flight' meant nothing more than his strategic withdrawal to the greater security of his own ancestral heartland of Moray where he would still have represented a high-king of Scots to whom Malcolm owed more legitimate submission than to any English overlord.

As for Earl Siward, his fruits of a costly campaign amounted to 'war-spoil such as no man had gained before', which is in itself no little testimony to the 'fruitful seasons' believed to be characteristic of Macbeth's reign. Siward was, in fact, to die – not in battle, as he is said to have wished, but of natural causes and in his own bed – before the end of the following year and the death of his most powerful ally can only have set back any immediate further advancement of Malcolm's ambition. It would, in fact, be three more years before the entry in the *Annals of Tigernach* at 1057 is able to confirm 'Macbeth, son of Findlaech, high-king of Alba slain by Malcolm, son of Duncan'.

'And he was killed', according to the *Chronicle of the Kings*, 'at Lumphanan and was buried in the island of Iona.' The date of the death of Macbeth is placed by Marianus Scotus in the month of August and still more precisely on the fifteenth day of that month, because the festival he means by 'the Nativity of Saint Mary' is the one called now by the church calendar the Feast of the Assumption of the Virgin. There is an especially dark synchronicity in that date for the death of Macbeth because it was, in fact, the seventeenth anniversary of the day on which he had slain Duncan to claim from him the high-kingship of Scots.[25] The precise circumstances in which Malcolm came to slay Macbeth are nowhere elaborated by the sources, but the place of his death – at Lumphanan in the eastern foothills of the Grampians and just a few miles north of the river Dee – at the southern-most extent of Moray must indicate Malcolm having come north to challenge the high-king in his own country.

It would seem, though, that Macbeth's warband was undefeated at Lumphanan even though he himself was slain in what was, presumably, a battle involving some numbers of fighting-men, because Malcolm did not immediately, or even very soon after, succeed to the kingship. Macbeth's name is, in fact, followed in the king-lists by that of his stepson, Lulach mac Gillacomgain, whose claim on the kingship would have been fully legitimate if his mother was the daughter of Boite and thus descended from the mac Alpin royal house. It might seem, and has been more than once suggested, that the succession of Lulach represented an impromptu acclamation of a new chieftain by what remained of Macbeth's warband at a point of crisis, but the formal entry in the king-lists of his name, lineage and reign-length, arguably signifying his inauguration with full ceremony at Scone, would suggest otherwise. The different entries of Lulach's reign-length found in the sources vary from three months, four months, and four and a half months in different texts of the *Chronicle of the Kings* to seven months in the *Duan Albanach*, which last figure would correspond well enough to the period between August 1057 and March 1058 proposed by the meticulous Marianus as the full extent of Lulach's kingship. The best explanation of such discrepancies must surely lie in the few months it might have taken Lulach to reach Scone for inauguration into the kingship amidst the inevitable chaos following the death of Macbeth and would, thus also, indicate his full and formal induction as successor king of Scots. There is, however, quite sufficient evidence from the early sources to indicate the circumstances in which the short reign of Lulach was brought to its end on 'the mass of Saint Patrick in the month of March' according, once again, to Marianus Scotus.

The entry in the *Annals of Tigernach* at 1058 records 'Lulach, king of Alba, slain by Duncan's son, by treachery'. One manuscript of the *Chronicle of the Kings* calls him *Lulach fatuus*, or 'Lulach the Fool', which might represent a disparaging nickname by sources favouring a rival kindred but might also commemorate his folly in falling into a lethal trap sprung upon him by Malcolm. Such would certainly be implied by the evidence of the 'Verse Chronicle of the Kings' from the *Chronicle of Melrose*, which also locates the place where he was slain having been north of the Mounth and well within the lands of Moray.

> The unfortunate Lulach was king for three months
> until he fell into the hands of the same Malcolm.
> The man met his fate at Essie in Strathbogie where,
> alas!, through lack of caution the hapless king perished.

Malcolm had apparently mustered enough support to pursue Lulach deep into his own territory and there to have slain him by some stratagem which was evidently considered 'treachery' by an immediately contemporary source.

Thus it was that the son of Duncan made his entry into the king-lists as the Malcolm III who was to reign for fully three and a half decades and to be remembered as 'Malcolm Canmore',[26] the founder of a dynasty which was to extinguish all that remained of the Celtic character of the kingship of Scots.

CELTIC KINGDOM NO MORE

'It was Malcolm's destiny', in the view of the historian R. L. Graeme Ritchie, 'to be confronted by Normans all his life.'[27] It is certainly true that Malcolm would have been exposed to powerful Norman influence while a prince in exile at the English court of the half-Norman Edward the Confessor and it is true also that he met his death, at Alnwick in 1093, by the treacherous hand of a Norman knight high in the service of a Norman earl of Northumbria. Malcolm's 'confrontations' with the new feudal culture from France were as uneven as they were complex in character, but it was his destiny to be Scotland's king at the time of the Norman conquest of the neighbouring kingdom to the south in 1066 and, in 1072, to acknowledge William the Conqueror at Abernethy where – according to the *Anglo-Saxon Chronicle* – he 'gave hostages and was his man'.

What might be called the 'Norman conquest' of Scotland was quite different from that of England, being achieved rather later and less dramatically – worked by influence, intermarriage and infiltration, rather than armed invasion – but achieved it surely was, and the process best described as Scotland's 'feudalisation' which made its first progress during Malcolm's long reign was to be finally and fully accomplished in the reign of his youngest son, the first David, king of Scots. By the time of David's death in 1153 a formerly Celtic kingdom had been transformed, by obligations to English kings, by intermarriage of the English and Scots royal families, and – perhaps most decisively – by the impact of an Anglo-Norman aristocracy imported from the south and given Scottish estates in return for military service. It was a transformation made most visibly evident by the appearance in Scotland of castles and mail-armoured knights on horseback, of coinage and towns signifying an emergent new economy, and stone-built monasteries for the reformed religious orders who followed in the wake of the new feudal nobility.

By reason of that great sea-change having begun in Malcolm's reign, it is his predecessor Macbeth who has been more than once recognised as Scotland's 'last Celtic king'. Such a description is not strictly accurate, when there is no reason to consider his foster-son and successor Lulach – or, for that matter, Malcolm's Gael-favoured brother and short-lived successor Domnall Ban – to have been any less Celtic than Findlaech's son. In view of his successor mormaers of Moray having been able to hold out against the overlordship of the Canmore dynasty for more than seventy years after his death, Macbeth might be more accurately described as the 'last Celtic *high-king* of Scots', which form of words would still recognise him, with full justice, as the landmark figure in whose wake Scotland was a Celtic kingdom no more.

There is, then, no small irony to be found in the evidence for it having been Macbeth who accepted the first Norman knights into Scotland. The early Norman influence imported by Edward the Confessor on his succession in 1042 provoked a tide of distaste among the English, whose resentment focused especially on the 'castle-men', those knights brought over from Normandy and set up as lords in the land along England's troubled border with Wales. This anti-Norman feeling found its champion in Earl Godwine of Wessex – whose son, of course, is best known as the king Harold brought down by a Norman arrow in 1066 – and it was Godwine who forced upon the Confessor a compromise settlement whereby all but a few of his Norman companions were to be expelled from the court, from the church, and most especially from their castles. Florent of Worcester mentions two of these last by name in his chronicle for the year 1052:

> Osbern, surnamed Pentecost, and his ally Hugue, surrendered their castles
> . . . and went into Scotland, and were there kindly received by Macbeth,
> king of the Scots.

Such an hospitable welcome shown to warriors driven from home into exile was no more than might have been expected under Celtic custom and all the more so on the part of the 'generous king of Fortriu', but neither would the employment of free-range fighting men have been in any way untypical of long-standing kingly practice in Ireland or, indeed, in Scotland. Had such been the arrangement between Macbeth and his Norman guests, then he would wait no more than two years for occasion to call upon their sword-service, on the evidence of Florent of Worcester's reference to 'the Normans whom we mentioned before' having fallen in battle beside the 'many thousands of Scots' slain on the Day of the Seven Sleepers.

It is, perhaps, best to interpret any and all evidence for the historical Macbeth in terms of Celtic custom, because this most famous of all the kings of Scots was assuredly and entirely a creature of the Celtic Scotland of his time. To propose Macbeth as the last great Celtic king of Scots is, by definition, to argue for his historical significance being cultural in character, and from that position it is possible to suggest Shakespeare having preserved, however unknowingly, some genuinely historical insights into the Celtic character and context of the real Macbeth. Those insights hinge upon the elements of occult prophecy used by Shakespeare to such dramatic atmospheric effect, but derive ultimately from Wyntoun's claim for Macbeth's great faith in supernatural foreknowledge, 'in fantoun fretys . . . and sychlike fantassy'. If, as has been already suggested here, Wyntoun was drawing on genuine recollections of the man himself which had been preserved in Loch Leven tradition since the eleventh century, then the monstrous character of Shakespeare's construction can be said to contain at least some trace, however distorted, of the personality of its historical original. Even if Macbeth's superstitious nature was entirely of Wyntoun's devising – and I cannot believe it to have been so – then the examples he chooses for its illustration can still be recognised as survivals from the oldest Celtic tradition.

There is, first of all, the characteristically Celtic tripartite structure of the three prophecies bearing on Macbeth – that he will become king, that he cannot be slain by one born of woman, and that he will be overthrown only when Birnam woods come to Dunsinnen hill – and also, contained within those prophecies, an unmistakable echo of the traditional motif of the three-fold death of kings which is found throughout the full range of early Irish sources. This mythic three-fold death – usually accomplished by various combinations of wounding, drowning and burning but always resulting from a prophesied sequence of three improbable events – can be traced back in time at least as far as the second century BC, when it would appear to be represented in the sacrificial scene shown on the Gundestrup silver bowl found in Denmark but certainly of Celtic and probably of northern Gaulish origin. The same theme had evidently found its way into the culture of Celtic Ireland where it was so well to survive the impact of Christianity as to be still current among the Irish when Adamnan wrote his *Life of Columba* at the end of the seventh century AD.

Adamnan's account of Columba's prophecy of the death of Aed Dubh, the renegade prince and false priest who murdered the high-king Diarmait mac Cerbaill, tells how it was fulfilled when Aed 'was transfixed by a spear, and fell from the prow of a boat into the water of a lake, where he perished', presumably by drowning. So too, the killing of the high-king Diarmait is said by his death-tale to have been foretold by his druids and accomplished by Aed, the man prophesied as 'Diarmait's bane', by 'slaughter, drowning and burning'. Similar prophecies of three-fold death occur throughout the Irish myths and sagas – as also in the historical record of the Irish annals – where kings warned of fatal hazards go to great lengths to avoid them, but are invariably outwitted by destiny and so suffer the death foretold. The same tradition passed from Ireland into Gaelic Scotland, where allusions to it have been found in Hebridean lore even as recently as the nineteenth century and where Macbeth has been recognised by the Irish historian F. J. Byrne as 'but the best-known of Celtic kings lured to their death by the false security of contradictory promises'.[28]

The prophecies associated with Macbeth and deepest rooted in Celtic tradition of prehistoric antiquity were evidently known to Wyntoun, to Boece and to Bellenden, all men of great learning but of a culture so far removed from that of Celtic Scotland that they were unable to recognise the old traditions surrounding its last high-king as other than at best half-pagan and at worst hell-spawned. Such recognition might be best illustrated by another story, found only in Wyntoun, which alleges Macbeth having been conceived in an encounter of his mother with the devil. Here is another theme with its roots deep in the Irish Celtic tradition where tales of supernatural conception are included as one of the categories of 'prime stories' listed in the *Book of Leinster*. Such stories invariably tell of kings and heroes being fathered by a *fer sidhe*, a 'man of the Side' or otherworld, who would be inevitably recognised by Wyntoun – or any other late medieval anglicised-Scots cleric – as some form of demon. Just such an interpretation quite naturally led to Wyntoun's suggestion of Macbeth having been sired by the devil while the same story would, of course, appear quite differently in Celtic tradition where it would endow Macbeth with all the magical associations of an otherworld-aspected hero alike to Cuchulainn and Finn mac Cumaill.

The same line of enquiry proves no less revealing when applied to the female trio who give voice to the prophecies bearing on Macbeth in Shakespeare's play and who are listed in his *dramatis personae* as the 'Three Witches', because they represent a phenomenon which does not have its original in Irish Celtic tradition. It is, however and as Nora Chadwick points out, one 'wholly characteristic of Norse supernatural women, and especially of prophetic women'.[29] On at least one occasion in the play Shakespeare calls his three witches the 'weird sisters', which is the same term applied to them by Wyntoun and by Bellenden in his translation of Boece's Latin word *fata*. The modern usage of 'weird' to mean strange or bizarre is no older than the eighteenth century, before which time it still retained the meaning of the Anglo-Saxon word from which it derived and that word *wyrd* meant fate or destiny.[30] The three 'weird sisters', then – as they were intended by Wyntoun, who has them appear to Macbeth in a dream, and by Boece and Bellenden, who give them physical presence – surely have their origin in the old Norse tradition of the three women who sit beside the well which springs from the roots of *Yggdrasil*, the 'World Ash Tree', and there spin out the destiny of humankind. These were known to the Icelander Snorri Sturlusson, compiling his prose *Edda* in the early thirteenth century from much more ancient skaldic materials, as 'three maidens whose names are Wyrd, Verdandi and Skuld. These maidens shape the fates of men and we call them norns.'

Through the two and a half centuries during which the Norse presence in the northern and western isles had extended to the mainland of Scotland, there had come about an inevitable cultural interaction between traditions inherited from the primeval northlands with those of the Celts of the west. So it must have been, again as Nora Chadwick suggests, that 'the oral history of Macbeth has been influenced by the oral history of his hereditary enemies, the Orkney jarls . . . In particular stories of Norse witchcraft and Norse mythology, themselves in some measure the product of the skalds, appear to have left their imprint on the collection of legends which must have gone to make up the life story of the benefactor of the Culdees of Loch Leven.'[31]

There is, however, a far wider significance to the appearance of Scandinavian norns in the guise of the 'three weird sisters' of the Macbeth tradition if it can be taken to reflect the fusion of Norse and Gael which had emerged in the north, and still more evidently in the west, of Scotland and been already long established there by the eve of the feudal impact on the kingship of Scots. When this most famous of all Scottish kings is placed into that context, his true importance extends far beyond that of Shakespeare's villain recast as a Highland hero, because he can then be said not only to represent the last high peak of the Celtic kingdom of the Scots but also to foreshadow the future history of the Celtic–Scandinavian cultural province which survives today throughout as much of the ancient heartland in the west as can still be called Gaelic Scotland.

AN AFTERWORD

I DON'T KNOW what part 'inspiration' might or should have in historical writing, but I do know that the real starting point of almost all my books has been the moment when I settled on a title for what had thus far been just an idea. Maybe for that reason, the place, time and circumstances of deciding on a title have always fixed themselves firmly in the memory.

Alba of the Ravens suggested itself to me in the south of Islay on the Mull of Oa, a place which is famous for its views across to the coast of Ireland on a clear day. This occasion, however, was not a clear day, but a wet September afternoon when very little of anything could be seen through the heavy blanket of mist rolled out over rough moorland – until that great pair of sable wings lifted up from the heather scrub before dissolving moments later into the dense grey distance. It was that raven in that place on that day who called to mind the lines anciently attributed to Columcille and from which, within the hour, I was to borrow the title of this book.

I have thought of that bird very many times since then, and usually to wonder how greatly his ancestral knowledge might expand upon such fragmentary record of the past as has been preserved by mere human effort. His forebears would have seen the hide-hulled fleet which brought Fergus Mor out of Antrim to become the over-king of Dalriada in Alba, just as later generations of the same raven kindred on the Oa must have watched the curraghs carrying Aedan – and Columba with him – to the momentous conference of kings in Derry. So too, it was one of his own dark kind on the mainland away to the east who was said by the bard of the Strathclyde Britons to have 'gnawed the head of Domnall Brecc...'

If such thoughts read today like wilder imaginings, I think they would not have seemed so in Celtic antiquity, because this largest of the family *corvidae* has been considered a creature of unusually magical significance to humankind since the most distant prehistory, and nowhere more so than among the Celts of the west. Raven lore is found in abundance throughout the mythic literature of the oldest Irish tradition, where it is invariably associated with omens of prophecy and most often with those bearing on death and blood-fray. The raven is, after all, a natural feeder on carrion who would have been a familiar attendant on the battlefield, where his black plumage, mighty beak and pitiless eyes would have assumed the most sinister aspect. Thus the riddle from one of the stories of the Fenian Cycle asks the question 'What is blacker than a raven?' and offers the answer as 'Death'.

The association of ravens with foreknowledge in Celtic Ireland would seem not always to have been so grisly, because the Celticist Miranda Green has found them 'used by Irish Druids in augury, predicting the future by studying the flight of birds', and she goes on to suggest 'the connection between ravens and oracular utterances may have arisen because of the harsh but distinctive "voice" of the raven, which may have been perceived as resembling human speech.'[1] Some similar reputation passed over from Celtic Ireland into Gaelic Scotland, where the people of the Highlands and Isles are reliably reported as believing the raven to be 'the most prophetical' of birds as recently as the 1760s.

As with its oracular reputation, so with its Celtic name, *fiach* in Old Irish, which passed into the Scots Gaelic as *fitheach* substantially phonetically unchanged and still echoing something of the raven's cry. The modern English word 'raven' is also pronounced much as was the Anglo-Saxon *hraefn* from which it is directly descended, but which itself would seem to derive ultimately from the same ancient northern original as does the Old Norse *hrafn*. The literature of the Scandinavian skalds and saga-makers is at least as rich in raven lore as is that of the Celtic tradition and the raven was similarly recognised by the northmen as a bird of omen and creature of the supernatural. It was, if anything, still more emphatically associated by them with death in battle, as is illustrated by the saga evidence for the magical raven banner bringing victory to the Orkney jarl Sigurd, but death to the warrior who carried it into battle.

The Norse seafarer is known to have had a more practical interest in the raven, carrying birds which may have been specially bred for the purpose aboard his longship and releasing them on voyage in the north Atlantic to secure an early indication of approaching landfall beyond the horizon – just as the biblical Noah is said to have done with ravens from his Ark in the

Genesis account of the Flood. The association of ravens with the Deluge mythos is of the greatest antiquity and has been traced back to source in the Babylonian original, but the most potent, even most ancient, association of the raven in the northern world is with the foremost of its gods, the 'All-Father' called Woden by the Anglo-Saxons and Wotan in his Teutonic incarnation, but known to the Norse as Odin.

Odin it was, according to the skaldic tradition, who hung for nine windy nights from the ash tree beside the well at the world's end until he came upon the magical alphabet of the runes – from the Old Norse *rún* whose meaning is best preserved in the modern German *raunen* or 'mystery' – and thus gained mastery of those symbols of power recognised throughout the ancient northlands. The persona of Odin is as complex as the long list of titles – most fully preserved in Snorri Sturlusson's *Prose Edda* – by which he was honoured in skaldic tradition. Just one of those titles, however, is of especial importance here and it is *Hrafnagud* ('Raven-God'), an allusion to his two ravens who flew out each dawn to circle all the world and returned to 'sit on his shoulders and speak into his ear all the news they have seen and heard . . .'

'Their names', continues the *Edda*, 'are *Hugin* and *Munin*.' Thought and Memory.

'Errätst du auch dieser Raben Geraun'? 'Can you read those ravens' runes?' Siegfried is asked by Hagen the Nibelung's son at the darkest moment of Wagner's *Ring* cycle.

When I settled on its title that afternoon on the Oa, I was far from sure whether it would be possible to write the book at all and certainly had no idea that by the time I came to do so I would have made my home on an island in the western sea with ravens as my wild neighbours. There have been very few mornings while I've been at work on these pages when I have not seen them flying from the moor to make a ritual circuit round the house, and usually calling out to me in those voices as hoarse as the north wind they ride. At this very late stage in what has been a long search, I can only hope that I have read their runes aright.

NOTES AND REFERENCES

ABBREVIATIONS

PSAS   *Proceedings of the Society of Antiquaries, Scotland*
RCAHMS   Royal Commission on the Ancient & Historical Monuments of
         Scotland
TGSI   *Transactions of the Gaelic Society of Inverness*

1 FERGUS MOR

1. These carvings on the rock surface beneath the summit at Dunadd have presented a major problem of conservation since they were first uncovered in 1904.
Especially vulnerable to natural erosion and at still greater risk from human
attention, they were first protected with glass plates until, in 1978, the entire
carved surface – other than the rock-basin – was covered with a protective layer
beneath a remarkable facsimile cast in artificial stone. The especially interested
reader will find a fully detailed survey of Dunadd in RCAHMS, *Argyll: Inventory
of the Monuments*, vol. 6 (1988), pp.149–58.
2. The two forms of Celtic language are also known as 'q-Celtic' and 'p-Celtic',
by reason of the consonant sounding 'q' (or 'k') in the Goidelic form occurring as
'p' in the Britonic. The most convenient illustration is found in the respective
terms for 'son of', which occurs as *mac* in the Goidelic (e.g. Scots Gaelic) and as
map in the Britonic, from which is derived the *ap* prefix of many Welsh sur-
names.
3. S. Piggott, *Scotland before History* (1992), p.87.

4. The various systems of dating used by the Irish annals are far too complex for any attempt at explanation here. Suffice it to note that all dates assigned to annal entries here represent what is recognised as the true historical date of the event entered by the annalist.

5. J. Bannerman, *Studies in the History of Dalriada* (1974), p.73.

6. The Poppleton Manuscript, a fourteenth-century codex named for its compiler, the monk Robert of Poppleton, and now in the Bibliothèque Nationale, Paris (Ms Latin 4126). The especially interested reader will find the text and a full explanatory account of its Scottish passages in M. O. Anderson's *Kings and Kingship in Early Scotland* (1980), pp.235–60.

7. A. and B. Rees, *Celtic Heritage* (1961), p.135.

8. The term *Cruithin* occurs elsewhere in the Irish sources, usually in the form of *Cruithnigh*, and applied to the Picts, an occurrence which led some historians until quite recently to identify the *Cruithin* of Ireland as 'Irish Picts'. The term has been shown to be erroneous, if only because the term 'Pict' first occurred and has continued to be used in application to the peoples of northernmost Britain. If, as is now generally believed, the origin of *Cruithin* was as a 'q-Celtic' form of the 'p-Celtic' *Brython* (Briton) then its application can be considered equally valid for the Picts as a people resident in Britain and for the *Cruithin* as a people who had anciently come from Britain to settle in Ireland. To which should be added the fact that there is no evidence for the use of a 'p-Celtic' tongue by any of the peoples of Celtic Ireland.

9. F. J. Byrne, *Irish Kings and High-Kings* (1973), p.48.

10. Genealogies from the *Book of Leinster*, the *Book of Ballymote*, Rawlinson B502, and the *Book of the Uí Máine* (fourteenth–fifteenth century), of which just the last three named claim the descent of Oengus.

11. The *Book of Ballymote* and the *Lebor Brecc* ('The Speckled Book').

12. W. J. Watson, *The History of the Celtic Placenames of Scotland* (1986), p.215.

13. It is thought now that Niall's cognomen *Noígiallach* – literally 'Nine-Hostager', but usually translated as 'of the Nine Hostages' – derived from his overlordship of the Airgialla reflecting the custom whereby a vassal people gave to their overlord a hostage, usually of their royal kindred, to be kept as a guarantee of their loyalty. One hostage from each of the nine peoples of the Airgialla – which name translates as 'hostage-givers' – would have provided Niall with the nine hostages with which he is traditionally credited. The barely plausible claim for Niall having held hostages from all the Irish provinces, kingdoms of mainland Britain, and even Gaul can be dismissed as later legendary aggrandisement. For a full account the interested reader is referred to T. F. O'Rahilly's *Early Irish History and Mythology* (1946), p.233.

2 AEDAN

1.   *Seachd bliadhna romh 'n bhrath,*
            Thig muir thar Eirinn ri aon trath,
            'S thar Ile ghuirm, ghlais,
            Ach snamhaidh I Chaluim chleirich.
                    Carmina Gadelica (ed. A. Carmichael, 1928), vol. ii, p.348.
            (Seven years before the day of doom,
            The sea will come over Erin at one watch,
            And over blue-green Islay,
            But float will I[ona] of Colum[ba] the cleric.)

2. The name-form of 'Iona' originated as a late medieval misspelling of *Ioua*, the seventh-century Latin form of its older Irish name, which occurs variously in the early sources as *Hí*, *Hii*, *Ia*, *Eo*, or simply *Í*, the form preserved in modern Scots Gaelic. For the most authoritative explanation, the interested reader is referred to W. J. Watson's *The History of the Celtic Placenames of Scotland* (1986), pp.87–90.

3. The chronology appended by Bede to his *Historia Ecclesiastica* places the foundation of Columba's monastery on Iona in the year 565. While Bede's date is perfectly plausible and was set down just forty years after Adamnan, there are two reasons why it cannot be accepted as fully historical. The first is that Bede places Columba's arrival in Britain in the same year and thus two years after the true date confirmed by Adamnan. The second reason is that Bede, unusually for him, does not identify the source of his information, which was assuredly of either Irish or Pictish origin.

4. A. A. M. Duncan, *Scotland: The Making of the Kingdom* (1978), p.44.

5. J. Bannerman, 'The Scots of Dalriada' in McNeill and Nicholson (ed.), *An Historical Atlas of Scotland c.400–c.1600* (1975), p.14.

6. The evidence of the early sources for matrilinear royal succession among the Picts is not at all consistent and far from conclusive, so the whole subject has long been one of scholarly dispute and yet Bede, who was in closer contact with Pictish kings than any modern historian, was in no doubt in the early eighth century that 'the custom has been observed among the Picts to the present day'. I am inclined to the view that there was a Pictish custom of royal succession through the female line, and one of prehistoric antiquity, which was already breaking down, even as Bede was writing, by reason of closer contact between the Picts and other cultures – first the Angles but later, and more importantly, the Scots – who followed forms of patrilinear royal succession. All of which will be shown to have its own bearing on Picto-Scottish kingship in the ninth century and later.

7. *De Situ Brecheniauc*, in a thirteenth-century manuscript from an eleventh-century original, and *Cognacio Brychan*, in a fourteenth-century manuscript from an original set down before 1200. As the kingdoms of the north Britons collapsed one after the other through four centuries of pressure from Northumbrians, Norse, Danes and Scots, the record of their history and genealogy was taken by the last of the north British nobility to Wales, where it found its way into the Welsh sources referred to on various occasions in these pages.

8. Adamnan's 'island of Hinba' has been identified as the Isle of Jura and is believed to have been the location of the first of Columba's foundations in Scotland. See J. Marsden, *Sea-Road of the Saints* (1995), pp.98–127.

9. Just one very late medieval Irish genealogy, found in the fifteenth-century *Great Book of Lecan*, claims Aedan as the son of Eochaid and Feidelm and it may well have prompted the very much later note made in the margin of the eleventh-century *Prophecy of Berchan* and asserting that 'Aedan belongs to Leinster according to his genealogy'. Both of which claims can only derive from the tradition invented at least four hundred years after Aedan's death.

10. 'The Convention of Druim Cett' in J. Bannerman, *Studies in the History of Dalriada* (1974), pp.157–70.

11. J. F. Kenney, *The Sources for the Early History of Ireland: Ecclesiastical* (1968), p.427.

12. W. J. Watson, *The History of the Celtic Placenames of Scotland* (1986), p.62.

13. By Professor Bannerman in the thoroughgoing analysis of the *Senchus* contained in his *Studies in the History of Dalriada* (1974), specifically pp.146–52.

14. The *Annales Cambriae* at 584 enter *bellum contra Euboniam* ('war against the Isle of Man') and the use of *Eubonia*, the Latin form of the Britonic name for the Isle of Man, dispels any possible confusion with the Manau on the Forth.

15. A. A. M. Duncan, *Scotland: The Making of the Kingdom* (1978), p.43.

16. The *Prophecy of Berchan*, which survives only in an eighteenth-century copy of seventeenth-century transcription of a text of late eleventh-century origin, is certainly not a genuine 'prophecy' and neither does it have any more than a nominal association with the historical eighth-century Irish abbot Berchan of Clonsast. It is, instead, an assembly of bardic material almost entirely concerned with the kings of Ireland and Scotland of which the passages concerning kings of Scots are those of greater interest here. All but one of those kings is of the ninth century and later – the exception being Aedan mac Gabran, whose inclusion derives from the claim for his being the principal forebear of the mac Alpin dynasty – and only one of them, Domnall Ban (or Donald III), is identified by his proper name, all the others being identified by cryptic cognomens.

17. While Adamnan recognises both Artur and Domangart as 'sons of Aedan', the genealogical material in the *Senchus fer nAlban* identifies them as having

been his grandsons. Because the original of the *Senchus* was set down at least forty years before the Adamnan *Life of Columba*, it has the stronger claim to accuracy when it names Artur and Domangart as sons of Conaing, son of Aedan. It can be said in Adamnan's defence that in another reference to the same prophecy made at the time of Aedan's ordination, he does describe it as 'concerning the future of Aidan's sons, grandsons, and great-grandsons'.

18. I. M. Smith, *Brito-Roman and Anglo-Saxon: The Unification of the Borders* (1983), p.9. My earlier account of Degsastan in *Northanhymbre Saga* (1992), pp.68–9, accepted the location of the battlefield at Dawstone in Liddesdale, and I was persuaded to reconsider that position by a conversation with Dr Smith little more than a year before his untimely death. My reconsidered view is the one expressed here and is greatly indebted to Dr Smith's researches.

19. The twelfth-century *Life* of Saint Lasrian of Leighlin (d. 639) claims the saint's mother to have been a daughter of Aedan and the niece of a king of Britons, which would indicate her mother – and, thus, one of Aedan's queens – having been a British princess.

3 DOMNALL BRECC

1. N. Newton, *Islay* (1995), p.26.

2. RCAHMS, *Argyll: Inventory of the Monuments*, vol. 5 (1984), p.22.

3. A. O. Anderson, *Early Sources of Scottish History* (1990), vol. i, pp.158, 233.

4. J. Bannerman, *Studies in the History of Dalriada* (1974), p.102.

5. Domhnall Maceacharna, for example, locates *Cladrois* in the south of the Rhinns of Islay in his *The Lands of the Lordship* (1976), p.30.

6. Connad Cerr is otherwise identified in the *Senchus fer nAlban* and the *Synchronisms of Fland Mainistrech* as a son of Eochaid Buide. While the original text of the *Senchus* would represent the oldest and, thus, most authoritative source, its existing form is the latest in a long sequence of copies into which have been introduced inevitable confusions of closely similar names. My view expressed here follows the genealogy set down in the *Chronicle of the Kings* descending Connad Cerr and his son Ferchar from the Cenel Comgaill, because it alone is consistent with the annal evidence to make any sense of the shifting alliances of the ruling kindreds of Dalriada with the Cruithin of Ulster.

7. The annalist's *Osric mac Albruit* does bear a distinct resemblance to the name of Osric, son of Aelfric, known to Bede as the 'apostate king' of Northumbria, but they cannot have been the same man, because Osric, son of Aelfric, did not die until 632. The name of the *Osric* slain at Fid Eoin is more probably a corrupt rendering into Irish of Oslac or Oslaf who are named as two of the sons of

Aethelfrith by the Northumbrian genealogy preserved in Nennius' *Historia Brittonum* and Symeon of Durham's *Chronicle of the Angles*.

8. A. O. Anderson, *Early Sources of Scottish History* (1990), vol. i, pp.158–9.

9. Despite the claims of later medieval sources for its having represented the high-kingship of all Ireland, the kingship of Tara was an almost exclusively Ui Neill institution until the end of the tenth century and is most realistically recognised as the overlordship of all the lines of Niall and their vassal peoples. Neither were the prehistoric earthworks at Tara in Meath in use as a royal centre after the mid-sixth century, when hagiographical tradition claims Tara to have been abandoned after being cursed by the saints of Ireland led by St Ruadhan of Lorrha. It is thought now to have been more likely that the site simply fell into decay as Ui Neill power – and with it the nominal kingship 'of Tara' – became centred in the north of Ireland. It must, however, be noted that, while the principal fortress of the historical Domnall mac Aed was at Ard Fothadh near Donegal town, the hill-fort of Dun na nGedh is located near Dowth on the Boyne and within sight of Tara Hill.

10. The *Cenél Conaill* ('clan of Conall') and the *Cenél Eogain* ('clan of Eogan'), were the two principal – and often rival – kindreds of the northern Ui Neill, being descended respectively from Conall Gulban and Eogan, the two sons of Niall of the Nine Hostages who had conquered the greater part of the ancient kingdom of Ulster in the fifth century. Saint Columba was of the Cenel Conaill, whose territory extended over most of what is now Donegal, while the lands of the Cenel Eogain lay on the Inishowen Peninsula.

11. Physical impairment represented an automatic disqualification from king-ship in Celtic Ireland. There is evidence from the annals for the deliberate mutilation, usually in the form of blinding, of a king by his over-king with the purpose of irrevocably depriving him of his kingship as punishment for especially grievous wrongdoing.

12. A. P. Smyth, *Warlords and Holy Men* (1989), p.26.

13. Cummene's work is properly called *Liber de virtutibus sancti Columbae* ('Book of the miraculous powers of Saint Columba'), but is usually and more conveniently referred to as 'the Cummene *Life* of Columba'. The one fully authentic surviving passage from Cummene's book is found in the manuscript of Adamnan's *Life of Columba* copied by the Iona scribe Dorbbene before the year 714. The Cummene text would appear to have been added by Dorbbene to Adamnan's text, but fits so well into its place as to suggest Adamnan's chapter on the ordination of Aedan mac Gabran having followed very closely an original account from the Cummene *Life*.

14. In their modern standard edition of *Adamnan's Life of Columba* (1961), p.48, A. O. and M. O. Anderson suggest Cummene having written his book while

in retreat or retirement on Rathlin Island, off the coast of Antrim and thus within the Irish territory of Dalriada, which would still better correspond to his meaning Irish Dalriada when he refers to 'this kingdom'.

15. A. O. Anderson, *Early Sources of Scottish History* (1990), vol. i, p.164.

16. J. Bannerman, *Studies in the History of Dalriada* (1974), p.106.

17. Fully explored by Hermann Moisl in 'The Bernician Royal Dynasty and the Irish', *Peritia* 2 (1983).

18. J. Marsden, *Northanhymbre Saga* (1992), pp.112–15.

19. Oswy had, in fact, already succeeded his brother Oswald in the kingship of Northumbria by the time of the death of Domnall Brecc. Bede confirms Oswald to have been slain by Penda at the battle of Maserfeld in the August of 642. Domnall Brecc was killed at Strathcarron 'at the end of the year, in December', according to Tigernach.

20. J. Bannerman, *Studies in the History of Dalriada* (1974), pp.155–6.

21. Dunaverty on the Mull of Kintyre and Tarbert on Loch Fyne were the principal fortresses of the Cenel Gabrain by the mid-eighth century, when Dunadd in mid-Argyll and Dunollie at Oban were strongholds of the Cenel Loairn.

4 KENNETH

1. Dunkeld appears as *Dún Callden* in the eleventh–twelfth-century Gaelic notes inscribed in the ninth-century Book of Deer and as *Dúne Chaillden* in the *Annals of Ulster* at 873, both names shown to derive from the name *Caledonii* applied by Ptolemy to the northern tribes of the people later known as Picts.

2. See note 5 to Chapter 2.

3. A *paruchia* was effectively a confederation of monasteries, all of them founded by the same saint or by his successor abbots. The mother church was thus invariably the saint's own principal foundation and if not his original place of burial then assuredly the place of keeping of his shrine.

4. I have found the origin and meaning of the term 'viking' most convincingly elucidated by Krístjan Eldjárn, formerly of the National Museum of Iceland, in his paper 'The Viking Myth', in Farrell (ed.), *The Vikings* (1982), p.266.

5. The Hebridean archipelago south of Skye lay within the territory of Dalriada and would, consequently, have been recognised by the annalist's Iona source as a part of Ireland. The Outer Hebrides north of Skye lay outwith the territory of Dalriada and, thus, would have been still considered 'islands of Britain'.

6. It does seem likely that Columba's relics were brought back from Kells to Iona after 849, in the light of the entry in the *Annals of Ulster* at 878: 'Columcille's shrine, and also his relics, came to Ireland in flight from the *gall*.'

While the annalist does not state that they came from Iona, there is really nowhere else outside Ireland they might have been brought from. The division of the relics in 849 does not appear to have included their shrine, which was on Iona in 825 and would seem not to have been removed until 878 – in which year, incidentally, an especially aggressive Danish warband is known to have been at large in Scotland.

7. By David Sellar, whose paper 'The Origins and Ancestry of Somerled', *Scottish Historical Review* 45 (1966), pp.134–7, demonstrates Somerled mac Gillebride, founding dynast of Clan Donald and forebear of the Lords of the Isles, having been in direct line of descent from this same Guthfrith mac Fergus.

8. It has become fashionable to call Kenneth by his Gaelic name-form of *Cináed*. While I appreciate that some readers find such usage more evocative of a sense of antiquity, I suspect that others might not and when the name appears so variously in the early sources – as both *Kínad* and *Cinad*, for example, within one paragraph of the Poppleton manuscript of the *Chronicle of the Kings* – I have chosen to use its more familiar English form here.

9. See note 16 to Chapter 2.

10. See note 6 to Chapter 1. References made here to the *Chronicle of the Kings* are to the version preserved in the Poppleton manuscript unless otherwise indicated.

11. 'On the Ides [13] of February' according to the *Chronicle of the Kings*.

12. The similarly authoritative *Annals of Tigernach* have not survived for the period between 766 and 975.

13. A. A. M. Duncan, *Scotland: The Making of the Kingdom* (1978), p.58.

14. The *Chronicle of Huntingdon* places the death of Alpin in the year 834. Compiled in the 1290s as a 'digest' of Scottish history for Edward I while he considered which English vassal he should place on Scotland's throne, it represents a late source of no great authority, but it is the only one to offer any specific date for Alpin's death.

15. See also the chart GENEALOGY II on p.230 below for an illustration of the 'official' and alternative lines of Kenneth's descent from the Cenel Gabrain.

16. Eddius Stephanus, *Life of Bishop Wilfrid*, chapter 19. Eddius' *Life*, written just some ten years after St Wilfrid's death in 709, is published in various editions, but most usefully extracted for its significance here in translation by A. O. Anderson, *Scottish Annals from English Chroniclers* (1991), pp.36–7.

17. *Fortriu* is almost invariably presented by the Irish sources in its Irish language form of *Fortrenn*.

18. The especially interested reader will find a detailed examination of the evidence of the king-lists for this period in M. O. Anderson's *Kings and Kingship in Early Scotland* (1980), pp.188–201.

19. L. and E. A. Alcock, 'Excavations at Dunollie Castle, Oban' in *PSAS* 117 (1987), pp. 129–30.

20. M. Lynch, *Scotland: A New History* (1992), p.40.

21. One other manuscript of the *Chronicle of the Kings* claims Alpin died a natural death. Later medieval accounts – principally the *Chronicle of Huntingdon* and Fordun's *Chronicle* – claiming Alpin to have been slain in battle with the Picts very possibly derive from a confusion with his earlier namesake.

22. 'Wanton son' can be taken to imply some measure of matrimonial irregularity, but – as David Sellar has explained – Celtic Irish and Scots custom recognises 'many types of sexual union, some lasting, some temporary, and some merely transient. As well as a first or chief wife, known as a *cétmuinter*, it was recognised that a man could have a second wife, *adaltrach*, literally "adultress", a term which clearly reflects the Church's disapproval of such unions. The usual purpose of such a second marriage was to produce sons. Various types of concubine inferior to an *adaltrach* were also recognised. The children of most of these unions would be regarded as legitimate for the purpose of succession.' 'Marriage, Divorce and Concubinage in Gaelic Scotland' in *TGSI* 51 (1978), pp.469–70.

23. A. and A. Macdonald, *The Clan Donald* (1896–1904), vol. iii, p.178.

24. M. O. Anderson, 'Dalriada and the creation of the Kingdom of Scots' in Whitelock et al (ed.), *Ireland in Early Medieval Europe* (1982), p.116.

25. The foundation legends of the great Scottish churches cannot be considered fully historical and while the Scottish cult of St Andrew is at best highly dubious, there is good evidence to date the foundation of the monastery of *Kilrimont* to the reign of Oengus mac Fergus in the first half of the eighth century. See A. O. Anderson, *Early Sources of Scottish History* (1990), vol. i, pp.238, 266.

26. The history of the 'Paschal Controversy' is almost as complex as its theology, but the especially interested reader will find an eminently cogent summary in J. F. Kenney's *The Sources for the Early History of Ireland: Ecclesiastical* (1968), pp.210–17.

27. T. F. O'Rahilly, *Early Irish History and Mythology* (1946), pp.372–3.

28. Nechtan mac Derile succeeded his brother Bruide as king of Picts in 706 and reigned until 724 when he entered monastic retirement, probably under forcible pressure from his successor, Drust. Drust was slain and succeeded by Alpin, who was defeated first by Oengus mac Fergus and again in the same year by Nechtan, who had evidently emerged from retirement for the purpose and reclaimed his kingship for a brief second reign until defeated by Oengus in 729. Thereafter Nechtan returned to his monastery where he died in 731.

29. W. F. Skene, *Celtic Scotland* (1886), vol. i, p.288. See also A. O. Anderson, *Early Sources of Scottish History* (1990) vol. i, pp.224, 445.

30. The Irish names of *finn gaill* for the Norse and *dubh gaill* for the Danes are most often translated as 'white foreigners' and 'black foreigners', respectively. The more accurate – and more historically intelligible – translation of the same terms as 'old foreigners' and 'new foreigners' is convincingly proposed by A. P. Smyth in his paper 'The Black Foreigners of York and the White Foreigners of Dublin', *Saga Book* 19 (1975–6).

31. Also by Professor Smyth in his *Warlords and Holy Men* (1984), pp.155–60.

32. B. T. Hudson, *Kings of Celtic Scotland* (1994), p.44.

33. 'The third day of the week' should mean a Tuesday, but A. O. Anderson has pointed out that 13 February was not a Tuesday in 858 but a Sunday. When other evidence confirms the year and there is no reason to doubt the date, Anderson concludes that 'it is not unlikely that the day of Kenneth's death is wrongly given' by the *Chronicle* text in the Poppleton manuscript. *Early Sources of Scottish History* (1990), vol. i, p.288.

5 MALCOLM

1. By Eilert Ekwall – see Beckensall, *Northumberland Place-Names* (1992), p.22.

2. J. C. Bates, *The Border Holds of Northumberland* (1891), p.331.

3. From Sir Robert Bowes' *Book of the State of the Marches* (1551) – passages bearing on Wark quoted in J. C. Bates' *The Border Holds of Northumberland* (1891), pp.350–2.

4. The sources invariably identify these early kings of Scots by use of their patronymic name-forms – e.g. Malcolm mac Kenneth, Kenneth mac Dubh – which should really be preferred to the later practice of identification by number – e.g. Malcolm II, Kenneth III. Despite my personal disinclination towards the numerical style of royal name-form in this period, it is none the less used here, as and where appropriate, in the interest of concision.

5. A. A. M. Duncan, *Scotland: The Making of the Kingdom* (1978), p.116. The especially interested reader will find a fully detailed explanation in M. O. Anderson, *Kings and Kingship in Early Scotland* (1980), p.52.

6. Eochaid was the son of Rhun, king of Strathclyde, and his claim on the kingship of Scots derived from his mother having been a daughter of Kenneth mac Alpin. Eochaid was, thus, a nephew of Aed mac Kenneth whom he followed into the kingship, but the origins of the first Giric, king of Scots, are less secure. His father is identified in the king-lists as 'Dungal', a name formerly interpreted as a corrupt form of *Domnall*, thus indicating Giric as the son of Donald mac Alpin, Kenneth's brother and successor. The Norse-aspected name-form of *Giric* (or, in some usages, *Girig*) is at least unusual among the early nomenclature of the mac

Alpin dynasty, but might still be explained by Donald mac Alpin having been the son of a Hebridean Norse mother. Another interpretation is proposed by B. T. Hudson in his *Kings of Celtic Scotland* (1994) where he identifies *Dungal* not as a corrupt form of *Domnall* (Donald mac Alpin) but as the Dungal, son of Selbach, descended from the Cenel Loairn and a forebear of the house of Moray, which would propose Giric, son of Dungal, as a contender for the kingship from a rival kindred north of the Mounth.

7. The summary history of royal succession through the period of the mac Alpin kings contained in these foregoing pages is illustrated by the charts GENEALOGY III and KING-LIST III, pp.232–3 below.

8. B. T. Hudson, *Kings of Celtic Scotland* (1994), p.111.

9. It has been suggested by some historians that the 'Malcolm, king of Scots' whose daughter married Jarl Sigurd was, in fact, the Malcolm mac Maelbrigte, *mormaer* (or sub-king) of Moray, who is styled *rí Albain* ('king of Scots') by the entry of his obituary in the *Annals of Tigernach* at 1029. It is a suggestion with which I cannot agree, not only because the Irish recognition of kingship differed so greatly from that of the Norse, but because the *Orkneyinga Saga* customarily styles *mormaers* of Moray as 'Scots earls' and not as 'kings of Scots'. Thus, where the saga-maker mentions 'Malcolm, king of Scots', I have taken him to mean Malcolm, king of Scots.

10. N. J. Higham, *The Northern Counties to AD 1000* (1986), p.311.

11. When Cuthbert's body was translated into its shrine eleven years after his death in 687, it is said to have been found quite undecayed and thus a conclusive proof of his sanctity. It was reported still uncorrupt at the time of its translation into the elaborate new shrine in the Norman cathedral at Durham in 1104, on which occasion Symeon himself was one of the nine monks trusted to handle the saint's remains, according to the contemporary account appended to Joseph Stevenson's translation of Symeon's *History of the Church of Durham* (1993), pp.779–85.

12. The attack on Bamburgh is entered at 993 in the *Historia Regum* ('History of the Kings') attributed to (but more probably edited by) Symeon of Durham and in Florent of Worcester's *Chronicon*, a chronicle closely contemporary with Symeon and similarly well informed on northern affairs between the tenth and eleventh centuries. Both these sources date Olaf and Swein's siege of London to September 994, as also does the *Anglo-Saxon Chronicle* for that year.

13. D. W. Rollason, 'The Wanderings of St Cuthbert' in Rollason (ed.), *Cuthbert, Saint and Patron* (1987), p.52.

14. Scott's lines and their date are inscribed on the stone wall of a bridge over the Wear with an especially fine view of Durham Cathedral, but I have not yet been able to locate them anywhere in his published works.

15. CCCC MS 139, which manuscript – produced at Hexham or Sawley-in-Craven – also contains the *Historia Regum* attributed to Symeon.

16. The date of Malcolm's siege of Durham is given as 969 in *De Obsessione Dunelmensis* and is obviously in error when Durham was not founded until 995 and Malcolm did not succeed to the kingship until ten years later still. The generally accepted date of 1006 is derived from the year of entry in the *Annals of Ulster*.

17. M. O. Anderson's paper 'Lothian and the Early Scottish Kings' finds the name 'Lothian' in contemporary use towards the end of the eleventh century and defines its meaning as 'the country south of the Firth of Forth that was part of the Scottish king's dominions and yet not a part of Scotland, and that was remembered to have been at one time the most northerly part of the English kingdom of Northumbria'. *Scottish Historical Review* 39 (1960), p.98.

18. B. T. Hudson, *Kings of Celtic Scotland* (1994), p.112. The relevant passage from the *Historia de Sancti Cuthberto* is translated by A. O. Anderson in *Scottish Annals from English Chroniclers* (1991), pp.60–1.

19. Sigtrygg of Dublin appears not to have taken any personal part in the fighting. Neither did Maelsechlainn, king of Tara, who seems to have broken with Brian shortly before the battle. For a useful summary of the Irish political background to Clontarf – which lies largely outwith the scope of these pages – the especially interested reader is referred to Donncha Ó Corráin's *Ireland before the Normans* (1972), pp.128–31.

20. See pp.56–57 above.

21. A. Tyndale, *Pictish Arts Society Journal* 8 (1995), p.44. The stone – known as 'Glamis No. 2' – is described in detail by Allen and Anderson in *The Early Christian Monuments of Scotland* (1993), pp.221–3.

22. The warrior *Plait* who slew Domnall of Mar is said by the *Cogadh* to have been 'from Francia'. He would thus have come from the Norse settlements around Rouen in the Seine valley, brought together under Rollo, son of Rognvald of Moer (in Norway), in 911 and soon to become the dukedom of Normandy, a major centre within the Scandinavian world of the tenth–eleventh centuries and destined for still greater importance in the subsequent history of medieval Europe.

23. Symeon of Durham mentions a comet in the northern skies thirty days before the battle and there is supporting evidence for a comet visible in the polar regions in the August of 1018, which would indicate the battle having been fought a full month after the comet's disappearance and thus in late September.

24. The battle of Carham is, however, entered in the *Annals of Durham*, a twelfth-century compilation deriving its material prior to 1066 from Symeon and, before him, from Bede. Its account of Carham – translated by A. O.

Anderson in his *Scottish Annals from English Chroniclers* (1991), p.82 – is merely an abridgement from Symeon's *History of the Church of Durham*.

25. The obituary of Owen the Bald – who must be considered the last, even semi-independent, king of Strathclyde – is entered at 1015 in the *Annales Cambriae*, a date apparently entered in error in view of the reliable evidence of the *Historia Regum* for his having fought at Carham in 1018.

26. A. A. M. Duncan, 'The Battle of Carham' in *Scottish Historical Review* 55 (1976), p.28 and *Scotland: The Making of the Kingdom* (1978), p.98. The *Anglo-Saxon Chronicle* has been read by some historians as placing the death of Uhtred in the year 1016, which has led them to propose that either the battle of Carham was fought two years earlier than the date given by the Durham sources or, if their date of 1018 is accepted, that the battle was lost not by Uhtred but by his brother Eadulf. Professor Duncan has shown such a reading of the *Chronicle* to be erroneous and argues – in both works cited above – that the battle of Carham was fought and lost by Uhtred who was subsequently murdered in the same year of 1018. The account of those events offered here is indebted to Professor Duncan's illuminating analysis.

27. A. P. Smyth, *Warlords and Holy Men* (1984), p.236.

28. Explained in detail by A. O. Anderson in his *Early Sources of Scottish History* (1990), vol. i, pp.574–5.

29. The *Annals of Tigernach* are extant for the period from 975 to 1088.

30. B. T. Hudson, *Kings of Celtic Scotland* (1994), p.109.

31. As illustrated by the charts GENEALOGY II, KING-LIST II, GENEALOGY III and KING-LIST III, pp.230–3 below.

32. John of Fordun describes Bethoc – whom he calls by her English name-form of 'Beatrice' – as Malcolm's 'only daughter', and this is best explained as the evidently prudish Fordun seeking to preserve the most seemly reputation for a king he holds in high esteem. Fordun was, of course, a clergyman and the church had long disapproved of any conjugal relationship it had not solemnised, so his statement regarding Bethoc can be taken to mean that she was Malcolm's 'only daughter' born in holy wedlock. Had his other daughters been the offspring of other forms of liaison, the claim of their sons to the kingship would have been in no measure reduced. Fordun's styling Crinan *abthane* is of related interest, when the title – meaning 'chief of thanes' – occurs nowhere else and is best explained by his difficulty in admitting even a secular abbot having been other than celibate.

33. The principal objection to Boite having been the son of Kenneth III is that the great-grandson of a king killed in 1005 could have been no more than a child in 1033. It has been suggested that the problem arises from a scribal error, whereby the annalist inserted the term 'son of' twice and accidentally indicated

a grandson rather than the intended 'son of Boite' – but I would still incline towards the alternative explanation of Boite having been a son of Kenneth II.

34. For all its value as a source of genuine tradition, the chronological evidence of the *Prophecy of Berchan* is often unreliable, as it certainly is here.

6 MACBETH

1. St Colme on the Fife coast nearest to Inchcolm would represent a very unusual form of place-name dedication to Columba and may commemorate another more obscure holy man with a similar name. So too, in that case, might Inchcolm, which island is, incidentally, called *Emonia* by Fordun.

2. J. Purser, *Scotland's Music* (1992), pp.39–45.

3. W. G. Collingwood, *Northumbrian Crosses of the pre-Norman Age* (1989), p.170.

4. The passages of Boece used here have been taken from Bellenden's Scots translation but rendered – for accessibility – into modern English.

5. A. O. Anderson suggests the name Macbeth as 'a corrupt form of *macc-bethad* "one of the elect"'. *Early Sources of Scottish History* (1990) vol. ii, p.232. Nora Chadwick's paper, 'The Story of Macbeth: A Study in Gaelic and Norse Tradition', raises the intriguing possibility that the name Macbeth which 'means "Son of Life" is itself a "name in religion" and probably not the only one under which Macbeth was known, though it is naturally the name preserved in historical records – the work of ecclesiastics'. *Scottish Gaelic Studies* 7 (1951), p.8.

6. P. B. Ellis, *MacBeth, High King of Scotland* (1990), p.155.

7. Passages from Wyntoun used here have been rendered from his original medieval Scots into modern English.

8. *Fortriu* was a term effectively obsolete long before the mid-eleventh century and its use by the *Prophecy of Berchan* in connection with a king of that period must carry a special significance, when the same source has made no reference to Fortriu since its passage bearing on Dubh, son of Malcolm I, and Culen, son of Indulf, both of them dead before the last quarter of the tenth century.

9. As illustrated by the chart GENEALOGY IV, p.234 below.

10. Both the *Orkneyinga Saga* and *Saint Olaf's Saga* place the battle of Skidamor after Sigurd's succession to the jarldom in 985 but before his conversion to Christianity enforced by Olaf Tryggvasson in 995. My own feeling is that a date 'c. 990' is as good a guesstimate as any other. It must be said here that the sagas were all composed in Iceland some centuries after the events of which they tell and cannot be considered as sources of impeccable historicality, but they do sometimes preserve fragments of contemporary material in the form of passages

of skaldic verse serving as illustrations within the narrative. The especially interested reader will find a meticulous examination of the saga evidence for the
Skidamor battle tradition in Nora Chadwick's 'The Story of Macbeth: A Study
in Gaelic and Norse Tradition', *Scottish Gaelic Studies* 7 (1951), pp.4–13.

11. B. E. Crawford, *Earl & Mormaer* (1995), p.12.

12. B. T. Hudson, *Kings of Celtic Scotland* (1994), p.134.

13. B. T. Hudson, 'Cnut and the Scottish Kings', *English Historical Review* 107
(1992), pp.350–60.

14. G. Donaldson, *Scotland's History: Approaches and Reflections* (1995),
pp.106–7.

15. Professor Duncan believes the ceremonial inauguration of Scottish kings at
Scone, even in the form in which it survived until the end of the thirteenth
century, involved 'certainly enrobement, obeisance of the leading men, and
recital of the king's genealogy. The last named must have been carried over from
Dalriada' *Scotland: The Making of the Kingdom* (1978), p.116. There is also an
illustration in one manuscript (Corpus Christi College, Cambridge MS.171
f.205) of Walter Bower's fifteenth-century *Scotichronicon* which shows a Gaelic
bard proclaiming the lineage of Alexander III at his inauguration in the year
1249, and it does seem more than likely that such recitations were the sources of
the genealogies and king-lists preserved in the *Chronicle of the Kings* and elsewhere.

16. There is no full consensus among historians as to the true identity of 'Karl
Hundisson'. Barbara Crawford argues that 'the important role of the rulers of
Moray as rivals for the control of Caithness is certainly relevant . . . since one of
those rulers – MacBeth – also became king of Scots then the identification of
Karl Hundison with the famous usurper seems likely' *Scandinavian Scotland*
(1987), pp.71–4. Quite another interpretation is offered by one eminent editor of
the *Orkneyinga Saga*, A. B. Taylor, who believes 'King Karl' to have been not a
'king of Scots', but 'a mormaer of Ross or of Sutherland (or of both) who
annexed Argyll in 1029' (*PSAS* 71, pp.334–42), I myself remain one of those who
have yet to be convinced that 'Karl Hundisson' (possibly translating as 'low-born
son of a dog') was other than the saga-maker's disparaging cognomen for
Duncan mac Crinan.

17. Duncan's queen is said by Fordun to have been 'a cousin' of Siward and her
name is known – from just one text of the Scottish king-lists – to have been
Suthen. Neither was Duncan's marriage the only such liaison between the house
of Dunkeld and the Anglo-Danish nobility of Northumbria, because his brother
Maldred is said by Symeon's tract *On the Siege of Durham* to have married
Aldgitha, a daughter of Uhtred by his Danish wife and thus a sister to the Eadulf
who defeated Duncan at Durham in 1039.

18. G. Donaldson, *A Northern Commonwealth* (1990), p.51.

19. A possibility first noticed by W. F. Skene in his *Celtic Scotland* (1886), vol. i, p.413, it forms the underlying premise of Dorothy Dunnett's historical novel *King Hereafter* (London, 1982).

20. As note 18 above.

21. It is very likely that Macbeth would have visited the culdees of Loch Leven in person and on more than one occasion, thus enabling first-hand recollections of him to enter the monastic tradition of the church, where they would have come to the notice of Andrew of Wyntoun when he was appointed prior of Loch Leven around the end of the fourteenth century. It is, therefore, fully reasonable to consider Wyntoun having had access to traditions of genuine authority and great antiquity bearing on the historical Macbeth.

22. The texts of the Loch Leven endowments by Macbeth and Gruoch are included among the appendices to William Reeves' *The Culdees of the British Islands* (1864), pp.125–6, where *Kyrkenes* is identified as 'the place which retains its name and is situated a little south of Loch Leven', and *Bolgyne* as the Balgonie on the south bank of the Leven or the other Balgonie, with Mickle Balgonie, south of Loch Leven. Dr Reeves, incidentally, would seem to be alone among historians in pointing out that this is 'the only ancient record of the name of Macbeth's queen'.

23. Again as illustrated by the chart GENEALOGY IV, p.234 below.

24. B. T. Hudson, *Kings of Celtic Scotland* (1994), p.142.

25. In medieval times, the feast days of the church calendar began with the later monastic offices of the preceding day, so Marianus' assignment of an event to a feast day entered under, for example, 15 August in the church calendar might in fact indicate an event of the 14th. This would seem, in fact, to have been the case when he dates the death of Duncan to 'the nineteenth day before the kalends of September' or 14 August in one instance and to 'the Nativity [in fact, the Assumption] of St Mary' or 15 August in another.

26. Malcolm's cognomen 'Canmore' apparently derives from the Gaelic *ceann mor*. When Gaelic names invariably describe a physical feature or appearance, *Maelcoluim ceann mor* is usually taken to mean 'Malcolm of the great head', but Michael Lynch has recently suggested – in his *Scotland: A New History* (1992), p.74 – that 'Canmore' is 'better translated from the Gaelic as Chief rather than great head [and] was probably a part of a reconstruction of the image of kingship'. If he is correct, then the surname would represent a propagandistic attempt to devise a pseudo-Gaelic praise-name for a king who was probably not held in the greatest esteem among the Gael.

27. R. L. G. Ritchie, *The Normans in Scotland* (1954), p.5.

28. F. J. Byrne, *Irish Kings and High-Kings* (1973), p.99.

29. N. K. Chadwick, *Scottish Gaelic Studies* 7 (1951), p.2.
30. The 'Scots tongue' of Wyntoun's time was not, of course, any form of Celtic language, but derived instead – like the contemporary Middle English and, ultimately, modern English also – from the Germanic *Englisc* of the Anglo-Saxons, the language now known as 'Old English'.
31. N. K. Chadwick, *Scottish Gaelic Studies* 7 (1951), p.24.

AFTERWORD

1. M. Green, *Animals in Celtic Life and Myth* (1992), p.178.

GENEALOGIES AND KING-LISTS

GENEALOGY I:

Descent of Kings of the Cenela Gabrain and Comgaill c.498–697

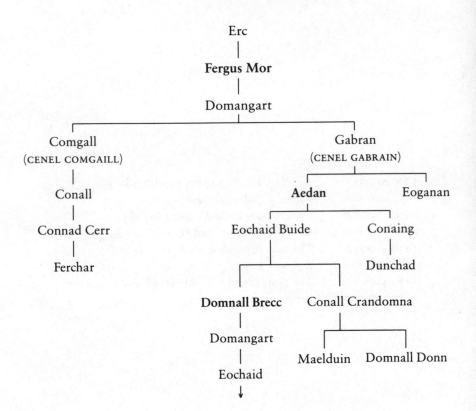

KING-LIST I:
Kings of Dalriada c.498–697

(KINGS OF CENEL COMGAILL DESCENT IN *ITALICS*)

Fergus Mor, son of Erc	d. 501
Domangart, son of Fergus	d. 507
Comgall, son of Domangart	d. 538
Gabran, son of Domangart	d. 558
Conall, son of Comgall	d. 574
Aedan, son of Gabran	d. 608
Eochaid Buide, son of Aedan	d. 629
Connad Cerr, son (?) of Conall	d. 629
Domnall Brecc, son of Eochaid Buide	d. 642
Ferchar, son of Connad Cerr	d. 650
Conall Crandomna, son of Eochaid Buide	d. 660
Domangart, son of Domnall Brecc	d. 673
Maelduin, son of Conall Crandomna	d. 688
Domnall Donn, son of Conall Crandomna	d. 695
Eochaid, son of Domangart	d. 697

GENEALOGY II:

Descent of Kings of the Cenela Gabrain and Loairn 697–842
(SUGGESTED ALTERNATIVE DESCENT OF KENNETH MAC ALPIN IN ITALICS)

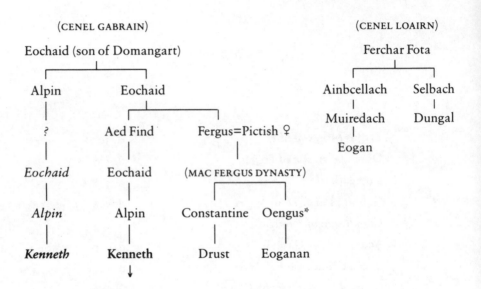

* This Oengus, son of Fergus, (d. 834) is not to be confused with the earlier Oengus mac Fergus, or *Onuist* son of *Urguist*, (king of Picts, 729–61), whose lineage, although obscure, was certainly not of the Cenel Gabrain.

KING-LIST II:
Kings of Dalriada and Fortriu 697–842

(KINGS OF CENEL LOAIRN DESCENT IN ITALICS)

Eochaid, son of Domangart	d. 697
(?) *Ferchar Fota*	d. 697
Ainbcellach, son of Ferchar Fota	d. 719
Selbach, son of Ferchar Fota	d. 730
Dungal, son of Selbach	d. 736?
Eochaid, son of Eochaid*	d. 733
Alpin, son of Eochaid*	d. 736?
Muiredach, son of Ainbcellach	d. 736?
Eogan, son of Muiredach	d. 739?
Aed Find, son of Eochaid*	d. 778
Fergus, son of Eochaid*	d. 781
Constantine, son of Fergus	d. 820
Oengus, son of Fergus	d. 834
Drust,ᶠ son of Constantine	d. 837
Eoganan, son of Oengus	d. 839
Kenneth, son of Alpin	**d. 858**

‡ Dates of obituary cannot be taken to indicate terminal dates of reign through this period of utter confusion in the kingship of Dalriada.
* Reference to GENEALOGY II should obviate any confusion of 'Eochaids'.
ᶠ King of Fortriu, but not entered in the king-list of Dalriada.

GENEALOGY III:

Descent of Kings of Scots of the mac Alpin dynasty 842–1034

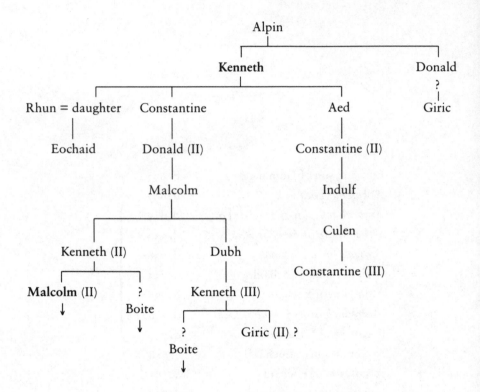

KING-LIST III:
Kings of Scots 842–1034

Kenneth, son of Alpin   **d. 858**

Donald, son of Alpin   d. 862

Constantine, son of Kenneth   d. 877

Aed, son of Kenneth   d. 878

Giric, 'son of Dungal'   ⎰ ruling as joint kings,

Eochaid, son of Rhun   ⎱ both deposed in 889

Donald (II), son of Constantine   d. 900

Constantine (II), son of Aed   d. 952 (abdicated 943)

Malcolm, son of Donald (II)   d. 954

Indulf, son of Constantine (II)   d. 962

Dubh, son of Malcolm   d. 966

Culen, son of Indulf   d. 971

Kenneth (II), son of Malcolm   d. 995

Constantine (III), son of Culen   d. 997

Kenneth (III), son of Dubh   d. 1005 ⎱ possibly ruling

?Giric (II), son of Kenneth (III)   d. 1005 ⎰ as joint kings

Malcolm (II), son of Kenneth (II)   **d. 1034**

GENEALOGY IV:

Descent of Kings of the Houses of Dunkeld and Moray 1034–1153

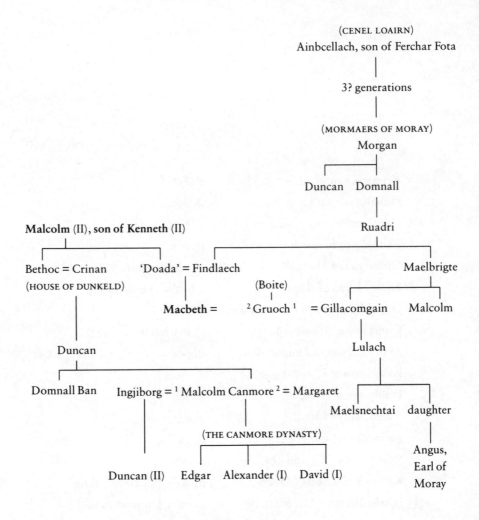

KING-LIST IV:
Kings of Scots 1034–1153

(KINGS OF THE HOUSE OF MORAY IN ITALICS)

Duncan, son of Crinan	d. 1040
Macbeth, son of Findlaech	*d.* 1057
Lulach, son of Gillacomgain	d. 1058
Malcolm Canmore, son of Duncan	d. 1093
Domnall Ban (Donald III), son of Duncan	d. 1107 (deposed 1097)*
Duncan (II), son of Malcolm	d. 1094
Edgar, son of Malcolm	d. 1107
Alexander (I), son of Malcolm	d. 1124
David (I), son of Malcolm	d. 1153

* Domnall's reign as king of Scots was interrupted by that of his nephew, Duncan II, who reigned for six months in 1094. Domnall was restored to the kingship after Duncan's assassination and reigned again until 1097 when he was deposed by Edgar, but is thought to have lived on in captivity until put to death by Edgar's successor Alexander in 1107.

SELECT BIBLIOGRAPHY

ABBREVIATIONS

(ed.) edited by   (trs.) edited & translated by
(rep.) reprint   (rev.) revised edition

PSAS *Proceedings of the Society of Antiquaries, Scotland*
RCAHMS *Royal Commission on the Ancient & Historical Monuments of Scotland*
TGSI *Transactions of the Gaelic Society of Inverness*

Adamnan, see under Anderson & Anderson; Marsden & Gregory; Reeves & Skene
Alcock, L. & E. A., 'Excavations at Dunollie Castle, Oban', PSAS, vol. 117, 1987
Allen, J. R. & Anderson, J., *The Early Christian Monuments of Scotland*, Edinburgh, 1903; rep. Forfar, 1993
Amours, J. (ed.), *Andrew of Wyntoun: The Orygynale Cronykil of Scotland*, Edinburgh, 1914
Anderson, A. O. (trs.), *Scottish Annals from English Chroniclers AD 500 to 1286*, London, 1908; rev. Stamford, 1991
(trs.), *Early Sources of Scottish History AD 500 to 1286*, Edinburgh, 1922; rev. Stamford, 1990
& M. O. (trs.), *Adomnan's Life of Columba*, London & Edinburgh, 1961

Anderson, M. O., 'Lothian and the Early Scottish Kings', *Scottish Historical Review* 39, 1960
> *Kings and Kingship in Early Scotland*, Edinburgh & London, 1973; rev. 1980
> 'Dalriada and the Creation of the Kingdom of the Scots' in Whitelock, D., McKitterick, R., & Dumville, D., (ed.), *Ireland in Early Medieval Europe*, Cambridge, 1982

Anglo-Saxon Chronicle, see under Garmonsway; Thorpe

Annales Cambriae, see under Morris

Annals of the Four Masters, see under O'Donovan

Annals of Tigernach, see under Stokes

Annals of Ulster, see under Hennessy & MacCarthy

Bannerman, J. W. M., *Studies in the History of Dalriada*, Edinburgh, 1974

Bates, J. C., *The Border Holds of Northumberland*, Newcastle, 1891

Batho, E. C. & Husbands, H. W. (ed.), *Hector Boece: The Chronicles of Scotland* (trs. Bellenden), Edinburgh, 1941

Beckensall, S., *Northumberland Place-Names*, 1975; rep. Rothbury, 1992

Bede, see under Colgrave & Mynors; Marsden & Gregory; Sherley-Price

Boece, see under Batho & Husbands

Bromwich, R. (trs.), *Triodd Ynys Prydein: The Welsh Triads*, Cardiff, 1961; rev. 1978

Brooke, N. (ed.), *The Oxford Shakespeare: The Tragedy of Macbeth*, Oxford, 1990

Byrne, F. J., *Irish Kings and High Kings*, London, 1973

Campbell, E., 'A cross-marked quern from Dunadd', PSAS, vol. 117, 1987

Carmichael, A. (trs.), *Carmina Gadelica*, Edinburgh, 1928

Chadwick, N. K., 'The Story of Macbeth: A Study in Gaelic and Norse Tradition', *Scottish Gaelic Studies*, vol. 6, 1949 & vol. 7, 1951

Colgrave, B. (trs.), *Two Lives of Saint Cuthbert*, Cambridge, 1940; rep. 1985
> & Mynors, R. A. B. (trs.), *Bede: Ecclesiastical History of the English People*, Oxford, 1969

Collingwood, W. G., *Northumbrian Crosses of the pre-Norman Age*, London, 1927; rep. Felinfach, 1989

Cormac's Glossary, see under Meyer

Craw, J. H., 'Excavations at Dunadd, etc.', PSAS, vol. 64, 1930

Crawford B. E., *Scandinavian Scotland*, Leicester, 1987
> *Earl & Mormaer: Norse-Pictish Relationships in Northern Scotland*, Rosemarkie, 1995

Donaldson, G., *A Northern Commonwealth: Scotland and Norway*, Edinburgh, 1990
> *Scotland's History: Approaches & Reflections*, Edinburgh, 1995

Duncan, A. A. M., 'Battle of Carham, 1018', *Scottish Historical Review* 55, 1976
  Scotland: The Making of the Kingdom, rev. Edinburgh, 1978
Eldjárn, K., 'The Viking Myth' in Farrell, R. T. (ed.), *The Vikings*, Chichester,
  1982
Ellis, P. B., *MacBeth: High King of Scotland 1040–1057*, Belfast, 1990
Faulkes, A. (trs.), *Snorri Sturluson: Edda*, London, 1987
Fawcett, R., *Dunkeld Cathedral: A Short History and Guide*, Dunkeld, 1990
Florent of Worcester, see under Stevenson
Fordun, John of, see under Skene
Forester, T. (trs.), *The Chronicle of Henry of Huntingdon*, 1853; rep. Felinfach,
  1991
Gaimar, Geoffroi (of), see under Hardy & Martin
Garmonsway, G. N. (trs.), *The Anglo-Saxon Chronicle*, London, 1953; rev.
  1973
Gododdin, The, see under Jackson; Jarman
Green, M., *Animals in Celtic Life and Myth*, London, 1992
Hardy, T. D. & Martin, C. T. (trs.), *L'Estorie des Engles of Geoffroi Gaimar*,
  Rolls Series, 1888–9
Hennessy, W. M. & McCarthy, B. (trs.), *The Annals of Ulster*, Dublin, 1887–91
Henry of Huntingdon, see under Forester
Higham, N. J., *The Northern Counties to AD 1000*, Harlow, 1986
Hudson, B. T., 'Cnut and the Scottish Kings', *English Historical Review* 107,
  1992
  Kings of Celtic Scotland, Westport, Connecticut, 1994
Jackson, K. H. (trs.), *The Gododdin: The Oldest Scottish Poem*, Edinburgh, 1969
Jarman, A. O. H. (trs.), *Aneirin: Y Gododdin*, Llandysul, 1988; rep. 1995
Kenney, J. F., *The Sources for the Early History of Ireland: Ecclesiastical*, rev.
  Dublin, 1968
Lynch, M., *Scotland: A New History*, London, 1991; rev. 1992
Macdonald, A. & A., *The Clan Donald*, Inverness, 1896–1904
Maceacharna, D., *The Lands of the Lordship*, Port Charlotte, Islay, 1976
McNeill, P. & Nicholson, R. (ed.), *An Historical Atlas of Scotland*,
  c.400–c.1600, St Andrews, 1975
Magnusson, M. & Pálsson, H. (trs.), *Njal's Saga*, Harmondsworth, 1960
Marsden, J., *Northanhymbre Saga: The History of the Anglo-Saxon Kings of
  Northumbria*, London, 1992
  Sea-Road of the Saints: Celtic Holy Men in the Hebrides, Edinburgh, 1995
  & Gregory, J. (trs.), *The Illustrated Bede*, London, 1989; rev. Edinburgh, 1996
  (trs.), *The Illustrated Life of Columba*, rev. Edinburgh, 1995
Martin, M., *A Description of the Western Islands of Scotland*, 1716; rep. 1981

Meehan, B., 'The Siege of Durham, Battle of Carham and the cession of Lothian', *Scottish Historical Review* 55, 1976

Metcalfe, W. M. (trs.), *Lives of the Scottish Saints*, Paisley, 1895; rep. Felinfach, 1990

Meyer, K. (trs.), *The Voyage of Bran*, London, 1895; rep. Felinfach, 1994
    (ed.), *Cormac's Glossary*, Dublin, 1913; rep. Felinfach, 1994

Moisl, H., 'The Bernician Royal Dynasty and the Irish', *Peritia* 2, 1983

Morris, J. (trs.), *Nennius: British History and The Welsh Annals*, Chichester, 1980

Newton, N., *Islay*, Newton Abbot, 1995

Ó Corráin, D., *Ireland before the Normans*, Dublin, 1972

O'Donovan, J. (trs.), *The Banquet of Dun Na n-Gedh & The Battle of Magh Rath*, Dublin, 1842; rep. Felinfach, 1996
    (trs.), *Annals of the Kingdom of Ireland by the Four Masters*, Dublin, 1848–51

O'Rahilly, T. F., *Early Irish History and Mythology*, Dublin, 1946

Pálsson, H. & Edwards, P. (trs.), *Orkneyinga Saga: The History of the Earls of Orkney*, London, 1978
    (trs.), *Eyrbyggja Saga*, rev. London, 1989

Paterson, J. W. & McRoberts, D., *Inchcolm Abbey*, Edinburgh, 1984

Piggott, S., *Scotland Before History*, Edinburgh, 1982; rep. 1992

Purser, J., *Scotland's Music*, Edinburgh, 1992

RCAHMS, *Argyll: Inventory of the Monuments*
    Vol. 4: Iona, Edinburgh, 1982
    Vol. 5: Islay, Jura, Colonsay & Oronsay, Edinburgh, 1984
    Vol. 6: Mid-Argyll & Cowal, Edinburgh, 1988

Rees, A. & B., *Celtic Heritage: Ancient tradition in Ireland and Wales*, London, 1961; rep. 1989

Reeves, W., *The Culdees of the British Islands*, Dublin, 1864; rep. Felinfach, 1994
    & Skene, W. F. (trs.), *The Life of Columba, founder of Hy, written by Adamnan*, Edinburgh, 1874

Ritchie, R. L. G., *The Normans in Scotland*, Edinburgh, 1954

Rollason, D. W. (ed.), *Cuthbert, Saint and Patron*, Durham, 1987

Root, M. E., *Dunkeld Cathedral*, Edinburgh, 1950

Sagas, see under Magnusson & Pálsson; Pálsson & Edwards; Taylor; Vigfusson & Dasent

Sellar, W. D. H., 'The Origins and Ancestry of Somerled', *Scottish Historical Review* 45, 1966
    'Marriage, Divorce & Concubinage in Gaelic Scotland', *TGSI* 51, 1978–80

Shakespeare, see under Brooke

Sherley-Price, L. (trs.), *Bede: A History of the English Church & People*, rev. Harmondsworth, 1968

Skene, W. F. (trs.), *John of Fordun's Chronicle of the Scottish Nation*, Edinburgh, 1871–2; rep. Felinfach, 1993

(trs.), *Chronicles of the Picts & Scots*, Edinburgh, 1877

Celtic Scotland: A History of Ancient Alban, Edinburgh, 1886–90

Smith, I. M., 'Brito-Roman and Anglo-Saxon: The Unification of the Borders' in Clack, P. & Ivy, J. (ed.), *The Borders*, Durham, 1983

Smyth, A. P., 'The Black Foreigners of York and the White Foreigners of Dublin', *Saga Book* 19, 1975–6

Warlords and Holy Men: Scotland AD 80–1000, London, 1984; rep. Edinburgh, 1989

Stevenson, J. (trs.), *Florent of Worcester: History of the Kings of England*, London, 1853–8; rep. Felinfach, 1988

(trs.), *Simeon's History of the Church of Durham*, London, 1855; rep. Felinfach, 1993

(trs.), *Simeon of Durham: History of the Kings of England*, London, 1858; rep. Felinfach, 1987

Stokes, W. (trs.), *The Tripartite Life of Saint Patrick*, Rolls Series, 1887

(trs.), *The Annals of Tigernach*, Paris, 1895–6; rep. Felinfach, 1993

Sturlusson, Snorri, see under Faulkes

Symeon of Durham, see under Stevenson

Taylor, A. B., 'Karl Hundason, "King of Scots"', *PSAS*, vol. 71, 1936–7

(trs.), *Orkneyinga Saga*, Edinburgh, 1938

Thomas, F. W. L., 'Dunadd, Glassary: Place of Inauguration of Dalriadic Kings', *PSAS*, vol. 13, 1879

Thorpe, B. (trs.), *The Anglo-Saxon Chronicle*, Rolls Series, 1861

Todd, J. H. (trs.), *Cogadh Gaedhel re Gallaibh* (The War of the Gaedhil with the Gaill), Rolls Series, 1867

Tyndale, A., 'Notes towards a reading of parts of the Glamis stone', *Pictish Arts Society Journal* 8, 1995

Vigfusson, G. & Dasent, G. W. (trs.), *Icelandic Sagas relating to the Northmen in Britain*, Rolls Series, 1887–94

Watson, W. J., *The History of the Celtic Placenames of Scotland*, Edinburgh, 1926; rep. Dublin, 1986

Welsh Annals, The, see under Morris

Welsh Triads, The, see under Bromwich

Williams, A., Smyth, A. P., & Kirby, D. P., *A Biographical Dictionary of Dark Age Britain*, London, 1991

Wyntoun, Andrew of, see under Amours

INDEX